Rose Murray's COMFORTABLE KITCHEN COOKBOOK

EASY, FEEL-GOOD FOOD for FAMILY and FRIENDS

whitecap

Whitecap Books is known for its expertise in the cookbook
market, and has produced some of the most innovative and
familiar titles found in kitchens across North America. Visit
our website at www.whitecap.ca.

EDITORS Patrick Geraghty and Jordie Yow
COVER DESIGN Andrew Bagatella
FOOD PHOTOGRAPHY Leisa Mercer
FOOD STYLING Tara Ballantyne
PROOFREADER Patrick Geraghty

Printed in Canada by Copywell

Library and Archives Canada Cataloguing in Publication

Murray, Rose, 1941-
Rose Murray's comfortable kitchen cookbook.
Includes index.

Originally published: Toronto : McGraw-Hill Ryerson, 1991.

ISBN 978-1-77050-301-4 (softcover)

1. Cooking. 2. Cookbooks. I. Title. II. Title: Comfortable
kitchen cookbook.

TX714.M868 2017   641.5
C2017-903385-9

We acknowledge the financial support of the Government of
Canada and the Province of British Columbia through the Book
Publishing Tax Credit.

Nous reconnaissons l'appui financier du gouvernement du
Canada et la province de la Colombie-Britannique par le Book
Publishing Tax Credit.

17 18 19 20 21 22 6 5 4 3 2 1

For Kent, Allen and Anne.

In memory of my sister, Muriel Barbour.

CONTENTS

....

PHOTO BY Stan Switalski

INTRODUCTION

·····································

"Comfortable" is a word you might normally associate with an old suit that you wear with ease time after time in a number of situations. Or, it might describe a friend with whom you can spend relaxing evenings without worrying about whose turn it is to talk. A comfortable room is one with which you feel completely familiar. It's soothing, calming—one whose contents provide a kind of quiet enjoyment.

I find my kitchen such a room. There's the equipment I use every day—my favourite whisk, those light stainless steel mixing bowls, my mini food processor, the old black-handled fork of my mother's, the conical sieve and tiny ladle from Paris. In the corner, there's the radio that keeps me company on my solitary testing days. On other days, there's plenty of room for someone else to work with me, or for friends to gather while I whip up some appetizers. Often, these appetizers don't even make it out of the kitchen before they're devoured by onlookers. It's like the farm kitchen when I was growing up. Everyone gathered there and frequently didn't even see the parlour. It was my mother's good food that drew them to that room.

In terms of food, "comfort" means many things, too. It means food that tastes good, food that's soothing, like a hearty soup on a cold winter day; food like rice pudding that you remember with some nostalgia from bygone days.

A recipe becomes comfortable when you make it over and over again, knowing it will be good every time. Comfortable recipes are also easy to execute without always including a list of ingredients you don't have in the house.

A cookbook, in turn, becomes comfortable when it is well used and you turn to it time after time for easy recipes that become completely familiar.

I hope this book will be one with which you want to spend some relaxing time and one that you find a good source of reliable recipes, information and inspiration. My wish is that it will become an old friend. It's meant to be well used.

The recipes are all easy, but the emphasis is on good flavours for both family meals and entertaining. Since many of the old classics are simple and good, I've included a few as they have been cooked over the years in my own family. More often, I've updated traditional favourites by either simplifying the method or lightening the ingredients, or both. Sometimes I've created a completely new version along the lines of an old favourite. Most of the recipes call for ingredients you can find in any supermarket, or even things you might have at home (further on I've included a list of items you might like to consider when stocking your pantry, see p. 181). Occasionally, however, I will introduce an ingredient that might not be so familiar—one that I think is worthwhile knowing about for its good flavour contribution.

Some of the recipes are quick as well as easy, and many are quick-to-fix but long-simmering. There's great satisfaction in this type of simple, sturdy cooking. It can be a soothing escape from the pressures of life.

Almost all the entertaining dishes are make-ahead—primarily because it is calming to have everything done before any guests arrive.

And if it isn't? Let everyone gather in your kitchen. My purpose with this book is to make yours as comfortable as mine.

SIMPLE SNACKS AND STARTERS

ONE OF LIFE'S great pleasures is getting together with good friends, and nothing makes a social gathering more enjoyable than good food.

The easy recipes in this chapter make great party food—either as simple starters to pique appetites when people come for dinner, or as nibbles to offer guests who drop in for an evening.

Dips and dippers, nibbles and bites, sit-down first courses—they're all approachable but impressive.

Light Guacamole Dip

MAKES ABOUT 1½ CUPS (375 ML)

Surround this refreshing dip with a colourful selection of crisp seasonal vegetables for a light (but always popular) appetizer or snack. Thinned with plain yogurt, it also makes a delicious sauce for sliced tomatoes, citrus fruit, cold roast beef or chilled seafood.

- 3 large sprigs fresh parsley
- 2 green onions, sliced
- 1 small clove garlic
- 1 ripe medium avocado
- 2 Tbsp (30 mL) fresh lime or lemon juice
- ¼ cup (60 mL) light mayonnaise
- ¼ cup (60 mL) low-fat plain yogurt
- ½ tsp (2 mL) ground coriander (or 1 Tbsp/15 mL chopped fresh coriander)
- Pinch cayenne pepper
- Salt and pepper

IN A FOOD processor or blender, mince the parsley with the onions, dropping the garlic in through the top of the processor with the motor running.

Reserving the pit, peel and quarter the avocado; add to the processor and purée along with the lime (or lemon) juice. Add the mayonnaise, yogurt, coriander and cayenne pepper; season with salt and pepper to taste. Process until smooth.

Transfer to a small serving bowl; push the reserved pit into the mixture to prevent browning. Cover tightly and refrigerate until serving time, or up to 4 hours.

Hot and Classy Crab Dip

MAKES ABOUT 1½ CUPS (375 ML)

Serve this hot appetizer in the centre of a tray of crunchy raw vegetables and crackers.

- ½ lb (250 g) light cream cheese, at room temperature
- One 6-oz (170 g) can crabmeat
- 2 Tbsp (30 mL) finely chopped shallots or onion

IN A MEDIUM bowl, beat the cheese; mash in the crabmeat. Stir in the shallots, lemon juice and hot pepper sauce.

Spoon into a 3-cup (750 mL) baking dish. Sprinkle with the almonds; dot with the butter. (The recipe can be prepared to this point up to 1 hour ahead.)

- 1 Tbsp (15 mL) fresh lemon juice
- Dash hot pepper sauce
- ¼ cup (60 mL) toasted sliced almonds
- 1 Tbsp (15 mL) butter

Bake in a 350°F (180°C) oven for about 30 minutes or until hot and bubbly.

Creamy Potato Garlic Dip

MAKES ABOUT 3 CUPS (750 ML)

Don't be surprised if your guests ask for spoons to finish every bit of this Greek-style garlicky dip. Serve with assorted raw vegetables, grilled bread, pita triangles or fried eggplant sticks.

- 1½ lb (750 g) red or yellow boiling potatoes (about 5)
- 8 cloves garlic, minced
- ½ tsp (2 mL) coarse salt
- ¼ cup (60 mL) olive oil + extra for serving
- 2 Tbsp (30 mL) fresh lemon juice
- Pepper
- ½ cup (125 mL) chicken stock (approx.)

PEEL AND QUARTER the potatoes. In a large saucepan, cover the potatoes with salted water and bring to a boil; reduce heat to medium-low and simmer, covered, for 20 to 30 minutes or until tender. Drain well and mash.

Meanwhile, place the garlic and salt in a medium bowl; mash with the bottom of a teaspoon against the inside of the bowl to release the juices. Beat in the mashed potatoes.

With a fork or hand-held electric mixer, beat in the oil, 1 Tbsp (15 mL) at a time, until completely absorbed. Blend in the lemon juice; season with pepper to taste. Taste and add more salt if desired.

Gradually blend in enough chicken stock to make a smooth creamy mixture (like a soupy purée). Transfer to a serving bowl. (The recipe can be covered and refrigerated for up to 1 day.)

Serve at room temperature or slightly warmed in the

microwave. Just before serving, drizzle with a few drops olive oil.

Caponata Cups

....

MAKES ABOUT 32 HORS D'OEUVRES

These little mouthfuls of crisp toast and tangy, soft vegetable mixture will disappear from your appetizer tray in no time. You can even serve the caponata mixture on crackers or in little purchased crisp tart shells.

TOAST CUPS

- 8 thin slices white bread
- Olive oil

CAPONATA

- 1 cup (250 mL) diced peeled eggplant
- ½ tsp (2 mL) salt
- 2 Tbsp (30 mL) olive oil (approx.), divided + extra for brushing the eggplant
- 1 onion, chopped
- 2 cloves garlic, minced
- ⅓ cup (75 mL) chopped celery
- 1 cup (250 mL) drained canned tomatoes, chopped
- ½ cup (125 mL) chopped sweet red pepper
- 1 tsp (5 mL) granulated sugar
- ¼ tsp (1 mL) pepper
- ¼ tsp (1 mL) dried oregano
- ¼ tsp (1 mL) dried basil
- 1 Tbsp (15 mL) chopped fresh parsley
- ¼ cup (60 mL) chopped pitted black olives
- 2 Tbsp (30 mL) drained capers
- 2 Tbsp (30 mL) red wine vinegar

TOAST CUPS Cut the crusts from the bread. With a rolling pin, roll the bread out flat. Cut into quarters and press into greased miniature muffin cups. (Or, roll out enough bread to cut into rounds with a cookie cutter and fit into muffin or tart cups.) Brush lightly with oil. Bake in a 350°F (180°C) oven for 5 to 7 minutes or until crisp and golden. Let cool. (The cups can be stored in an airtight tin.)

CAPONATA In a colander, sprinkle the eggplant with the salt; let drain for 30 minutes. In a skillet, heat 1 Tbsp (15 mL) oil over medium-high; sauté the onion and garlic for 5 minutes. Add the celery and tomatoes; cook for 5 minutes. Remove from heat.

Rinse the eggplant and pat dry. In a separate large skillet, fry the eggplant in the remaining oil until golden. Remove and place on paper towels. Add the red pepper to the skillet; fry until wilted, adding 1 tsp (5 mL) more oil if necessary.

Add the eggplant, tomato mixture, sugar, pepper, oregano, basil, parsley, olives, capers and vinegar; cook for 15 minutes over low heat, stirring occasionally. (The caponata can be cooled and refrigerated in a covered container for up to 3 days. Serve at room temperature.)

Spoon into toast cups.

Chèvre and Pesto Pâté

....

MAKES ABOUT 1½ CUPS (375 ML)

This pretty appetizer combines the piquancy of goat cheese and the distinctive flavour of pesto. To serve, accompany with slices of French bread for everyone to spread. You can use purchased pesto to make the pâté even faster, but be sure to drain off the oil that is sometimes found on top of the jar.

- ½ lb (250 g) cream-style fresh chèvre (goat cheese)
- ¼ lb (125 g) cream cheese (light if desired)
- Canola oil
- Pesto (recipe follows)
- Basil sprigs
- Walnut halves

IN A FOOD processor fitted with a steel blade, or in a bowl with an electric mixer, blend the chèvre with the cream cheese just until smooth but not liquid.

Brush a 7 × 4–inch (750 mL) loaf pan or terrine with oil; line with waxed paper. Brush the paper lightly with oil.

With a rubber spatula, spread a thin layer of the chèvre mixture right to the edges of the pan, smoothing the surface; cover with a layer of pesto and smooth the surface. Repeat with the remaining mixtures, finishing with the chèvre mixture. Cover and refrigerate for at least 1 hour, or up to 5 days.

To serve, invert onto a serving plate; gently remove the waxed paper. Garnish with basil sprigs and walnut halves.

PESTO

MAKES ABOUT ¾ CUP
(175 ML)

IN A FOOD processor or blender, purée the basil, Parmesan and oil; transfer to a bowl. Stir in the walnuts, butter and pepper.

- 1½ cups (375 mL) lightly packed fresh basil leaves
- ⅓ cup (75 mL) freshly grated Parmesan cheese
- 2 Tbsp (30 mL) olive oil
- 2 Tbsp (30 mL) finely chopped walnuts
- 2 Tbsp (30 mL) unsalted butter, softened
- ¼ tsp (1 mL) pepper

Wild Mushroom Risotto Starter

MAKES 6 TO 8 SERVINGS

On a wonderful trip to the north of Italy with a couple other food writers, I had the chance to visit the oldest mushroom factory in the world in the mountain village of Borgotaro. The woodsy, orange-brown porcini mushrooms in this recipe remind me of the ones we saw that day, and give this simple first course a wonderful flavour (use other dried wild mushrooms if porcini are unavailable). This very comforting dish is really quite easy.

- 1 oz (30 g) dried porcini mushrooms (or other dried wild mushrooms)
- ¾ cup (175 mL) warm water
- ½ cup (125 mL) butter, divided
- 1 onion, chopped
- 2 cups (500 mL) Arborio rice
- ¾ cup (175 mL) dry white wine
- 5 cups (1.25 L) simmering chicken stock (approx.)
- ½ cup (125 mL) freshly grated Parmesan cheese + extra for garnish
- Salt and pepper

SOAK THE MUSHROOMS in the warm water for at least 20 minutes, or until the water turns very dark. Strain through a coffee filter or paper towel–lined sieve and reserve the liquid. Rinse the mushrooms in several changes of water until free of soil; chop and set aside.

In a heavy-bottomed saucepan, melt three-quarters of the butter over medium heat and cook the onion until softened, stirring often. Add the rice and stir until well coated, about 3 minutes. Add the wine and stir until absorbed.

Add the hot stock, ½ cup (125 mL) at a time, stirring constantly and waiting until the stock is absorbed before adding more; cook for 15 to 20 minutes or until the rice is al dente (tender but firm) and very moist, adding more stock if necessary. Add the mushrooms and reserved mushroom liquid halfway through the cooking time.

Remove from heat. Stir in the remaining butter and cheese. Taste and season with salt and pepper, if necessary. Serve immediately in warm shallow soup or pasta bowls. Sprinkle with more cheese.

Quick Cognac Pâté

MAKES 3 CUPS (750 ML)

There are good prepared pâtés readily available these days, but this one is much less expensive, easy to prepare and goes a long way. Pass it around with French bread, crackers and pickled garlic, or cornichons.

- 1 lb (500 g) chicken livers
- ½ tsp (2 mL) celery seeds
- ½ tsp (2 mL) peppercorns
- 1 tsp (5 mL) salt, divided
- 1 cup (250 mL) unsalted butter, cut into bits
- 1 Tbsp (15 mL) dry mustard
- ¼ tsp (1 mL) nutmeg
- ¼ tsp (1 mL) cayenne
- Pinch cloves
- 2 cloves garlic
- ¼ cup (60 mL) brandy or cognac

IN A LARGE saucepan of boiling water, simmer the livers, celery seeds, peppercorns and half of the salt for 10 minutes or until the livers are cooked but still slightly pink inside. Drain in a sieve, reserving the peppercorns.

In a food processor, purée the livers, peppercorns, remaining salt, butter, mustard, nutmeg, cayenne and cloves. With the motor running, drop in the garlic. Blend in the brandy (or cognac).

Transfer to a 3-cup (750 mL) terrine or other serving dish; cover and refrigerate at least overnight and for up to 3 days. Serve at room temperature.

Ham and Cheese Squares

These savoury squares are easy, pretty, delicious to eat and can be made a day ahead. Be sure the ham and cheese slices are very thin and not too salty.

- One 10-oz (284 g) pkg fresh spinach
- 2 eggs
- One 14½-oz (411 g) pkg frozen puff pastry, thawed, divided
- 2 Tbsp (30 mL) Dijon mustard
- 1¼ lb (625 g) sliced cooked ham
- ¾ lb (375 g) sliced Swiss cheese
- 1 tsp (5 mL) milk or cream

REMOVE THE STEMS from the spinach. Wash the spinach and shake off excess water. With just the water that clings to the leaves, cook the spinach until wilted, about 5 minutes. Drain very well and squeeze to remove any moisture. Set aside.

Separate one of the eggs; set the yolk aside. Whisk together the white with the other whole egg. Set aside.

Roll half of the pastry into a rectangle to fit a 18 × 11½–inch (45 × 29 cm) jelly roll pan. Transfer to the pan; spread with the mustard.

Leaving a 1-inch (2.5 cm) border all around, top with half of the ham, then half the cheese. Top with the spinach and drizzle with the egg mixture. Layer the remaining meat and cheese slices on top. Fold the edges of the pastry over the filling. Beat the egg yolk with the milk to a make a glaze; brush some over the edges of the pastry. Cover the remaining glaze and refrigerate.

Roll the remaining pastry into a rectangle that's the same size and place on top. With the tines of a fork, press the edges together to seal well. Cover with plastic wrap and chill at least 1 hour, or up to 1 day.

About an hour before serving, brush with half the remaining glaze; let stand in the refrigerator for about 30 minutes. Brush again with the glaze, adding a bit more milk if necessary. With the tip of a sharp knife, cut a shallow pattern in the pastry top without going through the pastry. Cut 2 or 3 vent holes for steam.

Bake in a 425°F (220°C) oven for about 20 minutes or until puffed and golden brown. Let stand for 10 minutes before cutting into 1½-inch (4 cm) squares. Serve warm or at room temperature.

Baked Hazelnut Brie

Everyone will love this easy-to-make warm appetizer or snack. Provide butter knives so everyone can spread the warm cheese on the toast and apple slices.

- ¼ cup (60 mL) olive oil
- ⅓ cup (75 mL) fresh whole wheat breadcrumbs
- ⅓ cup (75 mL) finely chopped hazelnuts (filberts)
- 1 lb (500 g) Brie cheese
- Watercress or lettuce leaves
- 3 red apples (unpeeled), thinly sliced
- Fresh lemon juice
- Hot toast triangles

POUR THE OIL into a small bowl. In another small bowl, combine the breadcrumbs and hazelnuts. Cut the Brie into serving-size wedges; dip into the oil and roll gently in the breadcrumb mixture. Place in a shallow baking dish, leaving at least 1 inch (2.5 cm) between each wedge; drizzle with any remaining oil. Cover and refrigerate for at least 1 hour, or overnight.

Uncover and bake the cheese in a 325°F (160°C) oven for 10 to 15 minutes or until brown on the outside and soft and hot inside. (Don't worry if the cheese starts to ooze.)

Meanwhile, arrange the watercress on individual plates; fan the apple slices overtop. Sprinkle the apple with lemon juice. Make toast triangles and arrange on each plate, leaving just enough room for the cheese wedges.

With a metal spatula, transfer the cheese wedges to the plates; serve immediately.

BAKED HAZELNUT BRIE

Spiced Almonds

*Years ago, I needed to test
these toasted nuts for an
article I was doing with
Elizabeth Baird, so I made
them for a birthday party
I was throwing my friend
Sharon Boyd. She's been
making them ever since—and
receiving rave reviews from
guests.*

- 2 Tbsp (30 mL)
  unsalted butter
- 1 Tbsp (15 mL)
  Worcestershire sauce
- ½ tsp (2 mL) ground cumin
- Dash hot pepper sauce
- 1½ cups (375 mL)
  unblanched almonds
- 1 Tbsp (15 mL) pickling salt

IN A SMALL saucepan, melt the butter over low heat.
Stir in the Worcestershire sauce, cumin and hot pepper
sauce; simmer gently for 5 minutes. Stir in the almonds
to coat well.

Spread the nuts on a baking sheet; bake in a 325°F
(160°C) oven, stirring occasionally, for 15 to 20 minutes
or until toasted. Sprinkle with the salt. Serve warm.
(The nuts can be cooled and stored in an airtight
container for up to 2 weeks. Reheat in a 325°F/160°C
oven for about 4 minutes or just until warm.)

Smoked Salmon Mousse

MAKES 8 SERVINGS (ABOUT 1 CUP/250 ML)

*This quick-to-make creamy
mousse served with Melba
toast provides a very special
first course.*

- 6 oz (175 g)
  smoked salmon
- ½ tsp (2 mL) grated
  lemon zest
- 3 Tbsp (45 mL)
  fresh lemon juice
- ⅓ cup (75 mL)
  butter, melted
- ½ cup (125 mL) sour cream
- ¼ tsp (1 mL) pepper
- Capers
- Fresh dill sprigs

CUT THE SALMON into
small pieces. In a blender
or food processor, combine
the salmon, lemon zest
and juice. With the motor
running, gradually pour in
the butter and blend the
mixture to a purée.

Transfer the mixture to a bowl; fold in the sour
cream and pepper. Pack into a small bowl (or 8 individual ramekins if serving as a sit-down starter).

Garnish with capers and dill sprigs. (The mousse
can be covered and refrigerated for several hours or
overnight.)

Grilled Pita Pizzas

MAKES 16 HORS D'OEUVRES

*A pita is good simply cut in
two and brushed with olive
oil before grilling. Or, add the
following colourful topping,
grill and cut into wedges for
a quick, delicious outdoor
appetizer.*

- Two 6-inch (15 cm)
  pita breads
- ¼ cup (60 mL) chopped
  sun-dried tomatoes
  (packed in olive oil)
- 1 Tbsp (15 mL) finely
  chopped fresh oregano
  (or 1 tsp/5 mL dried)
- ½ cup (125 mL)
  feta cheese, rinsed
  and crumbled
- 2 Tbsp (30 mL) coarsely
  chopped black olives
- ½ cup (125 mL) shredded
  mozzarella cheese

CUT EACH PITA in half to
make 2 rounds. Drain the
tomatoes, reserving 2 Tbsp
(30 mL) oil; set the tomatoes aside. Brush both sides
of the pita rounds with
some of the oil; lay out on a
tray, outer sides down.

Sprinkle the pitas with the oregano and scatter with
the feta cheese. Scatter the tomatoes, then olives, then
mozzarella cheese overtop. Drizzle with any remaining
oil.

Place the pitas on a greased medium high–
temperature grill, or 4 inches (10 cm) from medium-hot
coals; grill for 1 to 2 minutes or until the undersides are
golden brown and the mozzarella is melted. Cut each
circle into 4 wedges and serve hot.

Quick Potato-Skin Snacks

MAKES 2 CUPS (500 ML)

When you're making mashed potatoes, prepare these nutritious snacks at the same time. Serve alone, with your favourite dip or as a garnish for Herbed Potato Soup (see p. 26).

- 2 lb (1 kg) baking potatoes (about 5)
- 2 tsp (10 mL) canola oil
- 1 clove garlic, crushed
- Coarse salt

SCRUB THE POTATOES well and dry. With a small sharp knife, peel off the skin lengthwise in ¾-inch (2 cm) wide strips, removing a thin layer of flesh with each strip. Reserve the potatoes in a bowl of cold water for another use.

Place the skins in a small bowl. Combine the oil and garlic; pour over the skins and toss to coat.

Arrange the strips, skin side up, in a single layer on a baking sheet. Bake in a 450°F (230°C) oven for 12 to 15 minutes or until crisp and golden. Toss with salt to taste.

Serve immediately or transfer to a rack to cool; store in an airtight container. Serve at room temperature or reheat in a 450°F (230°C) oven for 5 minutes.

Grilled Shrimp with Capellini and Pesto

MAKES 6 FIRST-COURSE SERVINGS

For this elegant-but-easy starter or light lunch dish, use homemade (see p. 14) or bottled pesto. Sprinkle some lemon rind on the coals or lava rocks for even more flavour when you grill the shrimp. Be sure to soak the wooden skewers in water for 30 minutes beforehand to avoid charring. If you have one, use the side element of your barbecue for the pasta.

PEEL THE SHRIMP, leaving the tails on; devein. Place in a sturdy plastic bag set in a bowl.

In a measuring cup, whisk together the lemon zest, 2 Tbsp (30 mL) of the lemon juice, mustard, pepper, hot pepper flakes, oregano, garlic and anchovy; gradually whisk in the oil. Pour into the bag, over the shrimp. Seal the bag and squeeze gently to coat the shrimp well. Refrigerate for 30 minutes. (Do not marinate longer or the shrimp will become mushy.)

Thread the shrimp onto soaked wooden skewers, pushing the skewer through each end of the shrimp but leaving the centre free. (The recipe can be prepared to this point, covered and refrigerated for up to 4 hours. If doing ahead, cover and refrigerate the marinade separately, brushing over the shrimp just before grilling.)

- 30 medium shrimp (about 1½ lb/750 g)
- 2 tsp (10 mL) grated lemon zest
- ¼ cup (60 mL) fresh lemon juice, divided
- 2 tsp (10 mL) dry mustard
- ¼ tsp (1 mL) pepper
- ¼ tsp (1 mL) hot pepper flakes
- ¼ tsp (1 mL) dried oregano
- 2 cloves garlic, minced
- 1 small anchovy, minced (or ½ tsp/2 mL anchovy paste)
- ⅓ cup (75 mL) olive oil
- ½ cup (125 mL) pesto
- ½ lb (250 g) capellini, spaghettini or linguine
- Lemon slices
- Basil leaves

Place the shrimp on a greased medium high–temperature grill, or about 3 inches (8 cm) from medium-hot coals; grill for 2 to 3 minutes per side or until bright pink (no longer opaque) and just cooked through. Do not overcook.

Meanwhile, stir together the pesto and remaining lemon juice; set aside. In a large pot of boiling salted water, cook the capellini until al dente (tender but still firm). Drain well and return to the pot; toss with three-quarters of the pesto mixture.

Arrange the pasta on 6 heated plates; place the shrimp skewers on top. Drizzle the remaining pesto on the shrimp. Garnish the plates with lemon slices and basil leaves.

Fiery Tex-Mex Popcorn

MAKES 4 SERVINGS

Hot-air poppers produce lovely light kernels without the aid of any oil. Here, I've added just a bit of melted butter along with some interesting and fun seasoning. Great with beer!

- ½ cup (125 mL) popcorn kernels
- 2 Tbsp (30 mL) butter, melted
- 1 tsp (5 mL) chili powder
- ½ tsp (2 mL) ground cumin
- ¼ tsp (1 mL) hot pepper flakes
- ⅓ cup (75 mL) freshly grated Parmesan cheese

POP THE POPCORN. Stir together the butter, chili powder, cumin and hot pepper flakes; drizzle over the hot popcorn and toss to coat well.

Sprinkle with the cheese; toss to coat and serve immediately.

Easy Pork Pâté

MAKES 3 CUPS (750 ML)

This simple version of a coarse, delicious pâté is made with chunks of lean pork that has been cooked for hours until it falls apart. It is combined with just enough fat to make it nicely spreadable. Accompany with cornichons, pickled garlic and slices of my easy No-Knead French Bread (see p. 40).

- 1 small onion, halved
- 2 whole cloves
- 12 sprigs fresh parsley
- 1 bay leaf
- 1 tsp (5 mL) dried thyme
- 1½ lb (750 g) pork shoulder, cut into 1-inch (2.5 cm) cubes
- ½ lb (250 g) pork back fat, cut into 1-inch (2.5 cm) cubes
- 2 cloves garlic, halved
- ½ tsp (2 mL) salt
- ¼ tsp (1 mL) pepper
- Pinch cinnamon
- Pinch allspice
- 4 cups (1 L) water

STICK THE ONION halves with a clove each. Tie the parsley, bay leaf and thyme in a square of rinsed cheesecloth to make a bouquet garni.

In a large heavy saucepan, combine the pork, pork fat, onion halves, bouquet garni, garlic, salt, pepper, cinnamon and allspice. Pour in the water; bring to a boil. Reduce heat, cover and simmer for 2½ to 3 hours or until the meat is falling apart.

Remove and discard the onion and bouquet garni. With a slotted spoon, remove the meat to a food processor, reserving the liquid and fat. Shred the meat but don't purée. Reduce the liquid by cooking, uncovered, over medium heat for 20 to 30 minutes or until the fat is slightly transparent. Let the fat cool a little, then mix in the shredded meat well. Taste and adjust the seasoning.

Pack into a 3-cup (750 mL) terrine or other suitable dish. Cover and refrigerate at least overnight, or for up to 3 days. Bring to room temperature to serve.

Satisfying Scotch Eggs

MAKES 4 EGGS

This is one of my favourite picnic staples, especially if I'm packing just finger foods. They're also great for brown baggers, just be sure that wherever you carry them you do so in an insulated bag with a small freezer pack or frozen box of juice.

- ½ lb (250 g) pork sausage meat
- ¼ tsp (1 mL) dried thyme
- Pinch dried sage
- 4 hard-cooked eggs, peeled
- 1 egg, beaten
- ½ cup (125 mL) dry breadcrumbs
- 2 Tbsp (30 mL) canola oil or butter (approx.)

IN A BOWL, mash the sausage meat with the thyme and sage; divide into 4 portions.

Wrap each portion of meat mixture evenly around an egg, sealing well. (Moist hands will make this easier.) Dip into the beaten egg; roll in the breadcrumbs.

In a medium-size skillet, heat the oil over medium-low heat. Fry coated eggs, turning frequently and adding more oil if necessary, until the sausage meat is cooked and browned on all sides, about 10 minutes. Let cool and refrigerate until serving.

Food Processor Gougère Ring

MAKES 6 SERVINGS

One of the most delightful French picnics I've had was in Burgundy, France, on a sunny Sunday in May with a couple of friends. We stopped at a tiny village to buy delicious ham, fruit and vegetables from the farmers' market and small shops. But it was the gougère, a rough cheese bread that we bought at the local boulangerie, that I remember most.

Gougère has become one of my favourite company appetizers to serve along with cucumber pickles or Pickled Cherries (see p. 182). I developed this easy recipe for a series of classes I was doing in Toronto for the Canadian writer Helen Gougeon.

- 6 or 7 eggs, divided
- ¾ tsp (4 mL) salt, divided
- 5 oz (150 g) Gruyère cheese
- ⅓ cup (75 mL) unsalted butter
- 1¼ cups (300 mL) water
- 1 tsp (5 mL) Dijon mustard
- 1 tsp (5 mL) granulated sugar
- ½ tsp (2 mL) dry mustard
- ¼ tsp (1 mL) pepper
- Dash hot pepper sauce
- 1¼ cups (300 mL) all-purpose flour

WITH A FORK, beat together one of the eggs and a pinch of the salt; set aside for the glaze.

Using the shredding disc in a processor or by hand, grate the cheese; set aside.

In a medium saucepan, bring the butter, water, Dijon mustard, sugar, remaining salt, dry mustard, pepper and hot pepper sauce to a boil, stirring to melt the butter. Remove from heat and immediately add the flour all at once; beat with a wooden spoon for 1 minute or until the mixture is well combined and leaves the side of the pan. Cook over medium heat for 2 minutes, stirring constantly.

Transfer the mixture to a processor fitted with the metal blade. Cool for 1 or 2 minutes. Add the remaining eggs and process, stopping once to scrape down the side of the bowl, until the eggs are completely incorporated and the mixture is very thick, smooth and shiny, about 30 seconds. If not shiny, process in another egg for 10 seconds. Add three-quarters of the reserved cheese and process for 5 seconds.

Grease a baking sheet and sprinkle with water, shaking off the excess. Using your finger and a 9-inch (23 cm) plate, draw a circle in the grease to use as a guide when forming the ring.

Using 2 large spoons, drop the dough by spoonfuls onto the circle so that the rounds touch to form a ring. With any remaining dough, form another ring of smaller rounds on top. Brush with the egg glaze. Sprinkle with the remaining cheese. (This can be done up to 30 minutes ahead and covered with an inverted bowl.)

Place in a 425°F (220°C) oven and immediately reduce the temperature to 400°F (200°C); bake for 25 minutes. Reduce the temperature to 375°F (190°C) and bake for another 20 minutes or until golden brown. Carefully remove the ring to a rack and cool for 5 minutes before placing on a large plate to cut into wedges and serve warm.

Caviar Mushrooms and Tomatoes

MAKES ABOUT 36 APPETIZERS

A little caviar provides a special start to a dinner or sparkle to a tray of finger cocktail food. Use whichever kind of caviar suits your taste and budget.

CLEAN THE MUSHROOMS and remove the stems, reserving for another use. Sprinkle the caps with the lime juice and set on a plate lined with paper towels. Cover tightly with plastic wrap and refrigerate.

Using a small sharp knife, cut the stem end from the tomatoes; hollow out by

- 16 large mushrooms
- Fresh lime juice
- 20 cherry tomatoes

FILLING

- ¼ lb (125 g) light cream cheese
- 2 Tbsp (30 mL) plain yogurt or light sour cream
- 1 tsp (5 mL) grated shallot or onion
- 1 tsp (5 mL) fresh lime juice
- ¼ tsp (1 mL) pepper
- 2 oz (50 g) caviar + extra for garnish (optional)
- Watercress or parsley sprigs

removing the seeds. Place upside down on a plate lined with paper towels, to drain. Refrigerate.

In a small bowl, beat the cream cheese; blend in the yogurt, shallot, lime juice and pepper. Cover and refrigerate if making ahead.

Shortly before serving, gently stir the caviar into the cheese mixture; spoon into the mushroom caps and tomatoes. Arrange on a thick bed of watercress or parsley on a serving plate. Garnish each appetizer with additional caviar, if desired.

SOOTHING SOUPS

....

WHEN I WAS a child, I studied music with a blind pianist who lived in a huge house in Collingwood, Ontario. Except for the light by the piano, the interior of that house was dark and gloomy indeed. I can still remember with great vividness how the only comforting thing about it was the pervasive aroma of homemade vegetable soup that the housekeeper would make every Saturday morning.

I never saw the housekeeper, nor had any of her soup, but I always thought of it when my mother filled one of her big kettles with the delicious, steaming vegetables and broth that she would always make from scratch.

There is something wonderfully soothing about soup whether it's hot or cold. In this chapter, you'll find hearty main-course soups to warm family and friends on the coldest winter's day, as well as a couple of quick and refreshing combinations to comfort a heated brow.

If you don't have homemade broth like my mother, use store-bought tetra packed, or canned beef or chicken broth (not the powdered kind, which could render a soup very salty).

Stock and broth are basically made the same way, but broth is the term usually used to apply to the liquid used in soups, and stock refers more to the base of sauces.

Hearty Beef Vegetable Soup

MAKES 8 SERVINGS

Quick chowders and soups are great, but sometimes it's very satisfying to throw chopped vegetables and beef together in a big pot and forget about them while they simmer for hours into an old-fashioned stick-to-your-ribs soup. The preparation time is next to nothing, and the enjoyment is great while the aroma fills not only your kitchen but the whole house. This thick soup freezes and reheats well, too.

- 2 lb (1 kg) beef shank
- 12 cups (3 L) water
- One 19-oz (540 mL) can tomatoes (undrained), chopped
- 4 carrots, coarsely chopped
- 2 leeks, sliced
- 2 parsnips, coarsely chopped
- 2 celery stalks with leaves, coarsely chopped
- 2 cloves garlic, chopped
- ½ cup (125 mL) uncooked pot barley
- 2 tsp (10 mL) salt
- 1 tsp (5 mL) granulated sugar
- 1 tsp (5 mL) dried savory
- 1 tsp (5 mL) dried marjoram
- 1 tsp (5 mL) dried thyme
- ½ tsp (2 mL) pepper

IN A LARGE kettle, combine the beef shank, water, tomatoes, carrots, leeks, parsnips, celery, garlic, barley and salt. Bring to a boil, skimming off any froth.

Stir in the sugar, savory, marjoram, thyme and pepper; reduce heat and simmer, partially covered, for 4 hours. Skim the fat from the surface. Remove the beef shank. Dice the meat and return to the pot; discard the bone. Serve in heated bowls.

Herbed Potato Soup

MAKES 6 TO 8 SERVINGS

Potato soup was so popular with early Canadian settlers that it was eaten even for breakfast. This hearty soup made from ingredients you have on hand will dispel winter chills any time of day.

IN A LARGE saucepan over medium heat, cook the potatoes, broth and marjoram for 10 to 15 minutes, or until the potatoes are tender. Without draining, coarsely mash in the pan. Set aside.

Meanwhile, in a medium skillet, fry the bacon over medium heat until crisp. Remove with a slotted spoon to a paper towel.

Pour off all but 2 Tbsp (30 mL) drippings in the skillet. Add the onion and garlic; cover and cook over low heat until softened but not browned, about 5 minutes. Stir in the flour and cook, stirring, for 2 minutes. Add to the potatoes and stir well to combine.

Gradually add the hot milk to the potato mixture; bring to a boil, stirring constantly. Boil gently for 1 minute.

Reduce heat to low and stir in the cream. Season with salt and pepper to taste. Stir in the parsley. Ladle into heated bowls. Garnish with the reserved cooked bacon.

- 6 potatoes, peeled and diced
- 2 cups (500 mL) chicken broth
- 1 tsp (5 mL) dried marjoram
- 5 slices smoked side bacon, diced
- 1 onion, coarsely chopped
- 2 cloves garlic, minced
- 2 Tbsp (30 mL) all-purpose flour
- 4 cups (1 L) hot milk
- ½ cup (125 mL) whipping cream
- Salt and pepper
- ½ cup (125 mL) chopped fresh parsley

Quick Chunky Minestrone

MAKES 4 TO 6 SERVINGS

For an interesting touch, omit the Parmesan cheese and top each serving with a big dollop of pesto (see p. 15). Serve with garlic toast: rub thick slices of Italian bread with cut garlic and toast under the broiler or in a toaster oven.

- 4 slices side bacon, diced
- 2 stalks celery, sliced
- 1 onion, chopped
- 1 carrot, thinly sliced
- 1 clove garlic, minced
- 5 cups (1.25 L) chicken broth

HERBED POTATO SOUP

If you don't have fresh green beans on hand, use 1 cup (250 mL) frozen.

IN A LARGE saucepan, cook the bacon over medium heat, stirring often, until crisp. Remove with a slotted spoon and set aside; pour off all but 1 Tbsp (15 mL) drippings.

In the same pan, cook the celery, onion, carrot and garlic for 5 minutes. Stir in the broth, tomatoes, sage and thyme, breaking up the tomatoes with the back of a spoon. Bring to a boil; reduce heat, cover and simmer for 5 minutes.

Add the chickpeas, green beans and macaroni; cook, uncovered, for about 10 minutes or until the beans are tender and the macaroni is tender but firm. Return the bacon to the pot. Season with salt and pepper to taste. (The soup can be cooled, covered and refrigerated for up to 2 days or frozen for up to 3 months.)

Ladle into heated bowls with lots of cheese.

- One 19-oz (540 mL) can tomatoes (undrained)
- ¼ tsp (1 mL) crumbled dried sage
- ¼ tsp (1 mL) dried thyme
- One 19-oz (540 mL) can chickpeas, drained and rinsed
- ¼ lb (125 g) green beans, sliced
- ⅓ cup (75 mL) uncooked macaroni
- Salt and pepper
- Freshly grated Parmesan cheese

Elegant Leek and Potato Soup with Crème Fraîche and Caviar

MAKES 4 TO 6 SERVINGS

Without the caviar, this is a lovely quick-and-easy soup to enjoy as an easy family supper with warm crusty bread, cheese and cold cuts. The same soup can be an exciting first course at a dinner party with the addition of a small amount of caviar. You don't have to use

- ¼ cup (60 mL) butter
- 4 leeks, thinly sliced
- 5 cups (1.25 L) chicken broth
- 4 potatoes, peeled and sliced
- Salt
- 2 cups (500 mL) coarsely chopped trimmed watercress
- Black pepper

expensive imported Iranian or Russian. A dab of rinsed lumpfish, Spanish mullet or a bit of Canadian golden white-fish is quite acceptable.

- ¼ cup (60 mL) crème fraîche (see sidebar) or sour cream
- 4 tsp (20 mL) caviar (optional)

IN A LARGE heavy saucepan, melt the butter over low heat; cook the leeks, stirring occasionally, for about 8 minutes or until softened but not browned.

Stir in the chicken broth, potatoes, and salt to taste; bring to a boil. Reduce heat and simmer partially covered for about 10 minutes, or until the potatoes are tender.

Using a fork, mash most of the potato slices against the side of the pan. Stir in the watercress and simmer, uncovered, for 1 minute longer. Season with lots of pepper.

Ladle into heated bowls. Garnish each serving with a dollop of crème fraîche. Place a mound of caviar (if using) on top of the cream.

CRÈME FRAÎCHE A cultured heavy cream that is sometimes available for sale in plastic tubs at the dairy counter, crème fraîche adds a tart and delicious accent to fruit or savoury dishes.

If you cannot find it for sale, whisk together equal quantities whipping cream and sour cream, cover and let sit in the refrigerator for a day or two or until thickened. Crème fraîche will keep in the refrigerator for 2 weeks.

Rainbow Salmon Chowder

MAKES 4 TO 6 SERVINGS

On a gray, misty day, a version of this quick and colourful soup dispelled any chills from the whale-watching boat I boarded with members of the British Columbia Fisheries Council.

- 2 Tbsp (30 mL) butter
- ½ cup (125 mL) chopped red or yellow onion
- ½ cup (125 mL) diced celery
- 1 clove garlic, minced
- 3 potatoes, peeled and diced

IN A LARGE saucepan, melt the butter over medium heat; cook the onion, celery and garlic for 5 minutes, stirring often.

Add the potatoes, carrots, broth and salt and pepper to taste; bring to a boil. Cover and reduce heat. Simmer for 15 to 20 minutes or until the vegetables are tender.

Reserving the liquid, drain the salmon and flake, mashing any bones; add to the chowder along with the liquid. Stir in the corn, milk, lemon juice and Worcestershire sauce; heat through. Stir in the parsley. Serve in heated bowls.

- 2 carrots, diced
- 2½ cups (625 mL) chicken broth
- Salt and pepper
- One 7½-oz (213 g) can salmon
- One 14-oz (398 mL) can cream-style corn
- 1 cup (250 mL) milk
- 1 tsp (5 mL) fresh lemon juice
- ½ tsp (2 mL) Worcestershire sauce
- ¼ cup (60 mL) chopped fresh parsley

Simply Superb Oyster Stew

MAKES 4 SERVINGS

This thin stew (actually a soup) has been one of the most popular ways of enjoying oysters since the 19th century. Thick chowders laden with vegetables and pork are appropriate for more strongly flavoured shellfish, such as clams, while oysters taste best with this simple preparation.

- ¼ cup (60 mL) butter
- 2 cups (500 mL) fresh oysters in their liquor
- 3 cups (750 mL) milk, scalded
- ½ cup (125 mL) whipping cream
- ¼ tsp (1 mL) white pepper
- Pinch nutmeg
- Salt
- Paprika

IN A LARGE heavy saucepan, melt the butter over low heat; simmer the oysters with their liquor until the edges begin to curl, about 3 minutes.

Stir in the scalded milk, cream, pepper, nutmeg and salt to taste. Heat through but do not boil.

Ladle into heated bowls. Sprinkle with paprika. Serve immediately.

Split Pea and Lentil Soup with Spiced Yogurt Garnish

MAKES ABOUT 8 SERVINGS

Instead of the usual ham, beef short ribs lend an extra heartiness to this nourishing soup that's almost like a stew. Warming and comforting, it's perfect to come home to on a cold winter's night. Although great as is, a little garnish of golden spiced yogurt turns it into terrific casual party fare.

- 2 lb (1 kg) beef short ribs
- 3 Tbsp (45 mL) olive oil, divided
- 1 Tbsp (15 mL) butter
- 2 parsnips, diced
- 1 celery stalk, diced
- 1 onion, diced
- 1 carrot, diced
- One 19-oz (540 mL) can tomatoes (undrained)
- 1 cup (250 mL) green lentils, rinsed
- 1 cup (250 mL) split peas, rinsed
- 8 cups (2 L) beef broth
- ½ tsp (2 mL) ground cumin
- Pinch dried oregano
- Pinch dried thyme
- Salt and pepper
- Spiced Yogurt (recipe follows)

IN A SHALLOW roasting pan, drizzle the short ribs with 1 Tbsp (15 mL) of the oil. Roast in a 450°F (230°C) oven for about 20 minutes or until browned all over, turning occasionally.

Meanwhile, in a large pot, heat the remaining oil and the butter over medium-high heat; sauté the parsnips, celery, onion and carrot until golden brown. Add the tomatoes, breaking up with the back of a spoon; reduce heat to low and simmer, uncovered, for 20 minutes. Stir in the lentils and peas.

Drain the ribs well and add to the pot along with the broth, cumin, oregano, thyme and salt and pepper to taste. Bring to a boil; reduce heat and simmer, covered, for about 1½ hours or until the lentils, split peas and ribs are tender. Taste and adjust seasoning.

Remove the ribs and cut off the meat in small cubes; return the meat to the soup. Serve in heated bowls; garnish with a dollop of Spiced Yogurt.

SPICED YOGURT

MAKES ½ CUP (125 ML)

IN A SMALL bowl, whisk together the yogurt, paprika, cumin, turmeric and cayenne. Cover and refrigerate for up to 3 days.

- ½ cup (125 mL) plain yogurt
- ½ tsp (2 mL) paprika
- ½ tsp (2 mL) ground cumin
- ¼ tsp (1 mL) turmeric
- Pinch cayenne

Quick Gazpacho

MAKES 1 SERVING.

This quick and refreshing soup, using some of fall's bounty, is great to carry to the office in a thermos packed alongside Melba toast, cheese and fruit. To share (or have extra on hand in the refrigerator), double the recipe.

IN A FOOD processor or blender, process the cucumber, onion, green pepper and garlic until chunky.

Blend in the juice, vinegar, oil, hot pepper sauce and salt and pepper to taste. Serve immediately or refrigerate until chilled.

- ¼ cucumber, peeled and seeded
- ¼ small onion
- ¼ sweet green pepper
- ½ small clove garlic
- ⅔ cup (150 mL) cocktail vegetable juice (V-8)
- 2 tsp (10 mL) white wine vinegar
- 1½ tsp (7 mL) olive oil
- Dash hot pepper sauce
- Salt and pepper

Italian Country Pasta and Bean Soup (Pasta e Fagioli)

MAKES 4 TO 6 SERVINGS

There are many versions of this healthy and hearty Italian soup, which is a staple of Tuscany. I've used Romano beans, but white or pink and white cranberry beans are also good. If starting with dried beans, use 6 cups (1.5 L) of their cooking liquid instead of chicken broth and purée half the beans with ¼ cup (60 mL) cooking liquid.

PURÉE HALF THE beans with ¼ cup (60 mL) of the broth; set aside.

In a large saucepan, heat the oil over medium-low heat; cook the onion, celery, carrot, garlic and hot pepper flakes for 10 minutes or until softened, stirring often. Add the tomatoes and salt; cook for 10 minutes.

Add the puréed and whole beans; cook for 3 minutes. Stir in the remaining broth and bring to a boil; add the macaroni and cook until tender but still firm, 10 to 15 minutes. Taste and add more salt if necessary. Serve immediately in heated bowls. Sprinkle with parsley and lots of cheese.

- One 19-oz (540 mL) can Romano beans, drained and rinsed
- 6 cups (1.5 L) chicken broth, divided
- 2 Tbsp (30 mL) olive oil
- 1 onion, chopped
- 1 celery stalk, chopped
- 1 carrot, chopped
- 2 cloves garlic, minced
- Pinch hot pepper flakes
- 1 cup (250 mL) chopped drained canned plum tomatoes
- ½ tsp (2 mL) salt (approx.)
- ¾ cup (175 mL) uncooked short tubular macaroni (tubetti or ditali)
- Fresh parsley, chopped
- Freshly grated Parmesan cheese

Hungarian Goulash Soup

MAKES 8 GENEROUS SERVINGS

Simmering for a long time with interesting spices and herbs gives this hearty soup lots of flavour, improved even more if the soup is made one day and reheated another. This is one of our family's all-time favourites.

IN A LARGE heavy-bottomed kettle, melt the lard over medium-high heat; cook the meat until

- 2 Tbsp (30 mL) lard or canola oil
- 1½ lb (750 g) lean beef, cut into ¾-inch (2 cm) cubes
- 2 onions, sliced
- ½ lb (250 g) mushrooms, sliced
- 2 Tbsp (30 mL) caraway seeds, crushed (see note)
- 1 Tbsp (15 mL) sweet paprika
- ½ tsp (2 mL) salt (approx.)

QUICK GAZPACHO

browned all over. Add the onions and mushrooms; cook until the onions are softened.

Remove from heat; stir in the caraway seeds, paprika and salt. Return to low heat; cover and cook for 20 minutes, stirring occasionally.

Stir in the tomatoes, basil, green peppers and water; bring to a boil. Reduce heat, cover and simmer for about 1 hour or until the meat is almost tender, adding a little water if necessary to prevent sticking.

Add the potatoes and broth; bring to a boil. Reduce heat, cover and cook until the potatoes and meat are tender, about 30 minutes. Taste and add more salt if necessary. Stir in the marjoram and pepper; cook for 2 minutes. (The recipe can be prepared to this point, cooled, covered and refrigerated. Reheat slowly, stirring often.)

Stir in the noodles; cook for about 7 minutes or until tender but firm. Ladle into heated bowls.

NOTE Crush the caraway seeds with a mortar and pestle, or place in a sturdy plastic bag and roll firmly with a rolling pin.

- One 19-oz (540 mL) can tomatoes (undrained), chopped
- 1¼ tsp (6 mL) dried basil
- 2 sweet green peppers, diced
- ¼ cup (60 mL) water
- 4 potatoes, peeled and diced
- 7 cups (1.75 L) beef broth
- 1¼ tsp (6 mL) dried marjoram
- ¾ tsp (4 mL) pepper
- ¼ lb (125 g) egg noodles

Family-Style Turkey Corn Soup

MAKES ABOUT 6 SERVINGS

For this quick-and-easy soup, use leftover turkey and stock from a big weekend dinner, or substitute cooked chicken and chicken broth. Either corn kernels cut from cooked ears or frozen kernels may be used.

IN A LARGE saucepan, bring the stock to a boil. Add the celery, onions, carrots and marjoram. Add salt and pepper to taste; return to a boil. Reduce heat, cover and simmer for 10 minutes or until the vegetables are tender.

In batches, purée in a food processor or blender, or use an immersion blender. Return to the saucepan. Stir in the turkey, corn and parsley. (The soup can be prepared to this point, covered and refrigerated.) Simmer until heated through.

Meanwhile, finely dice or crumble the cheese; place in heated bowls and pour the hot soup on top.

- 5 cups (1.25 L) turkey stock
- 3 celery stalks with leaves, chopped
- 2 onions, chopped
- 2 carrots, chopped
- ½ tsp (2 mL) dried marjoram
- Salt and pepper
- 1 cup (250 mL) diced cooked turkey
- 1 cup (250 mL) cooked corn kernels
- ¼ cup (60 mL) chopped fresh parsley
- 6 oz (175 g) mozzarella cheese

Chilled Red Pepper and Mushroom Bisque

MAKES 4 TO 6 SERVINGS

Your guests may not guess what's in this flavourful soup, but they'll certainly find it appealing. It's perfect as a starter at a dinner party on a warm fall evening.

IN A LARGE saucepan, melt the butter over medium-low heat; cook the red peppers, mushrooms, onion and garlic, stirring often, for 10 minutes or until softened.

Stir in the broth, paprika and sugar; bring to a boil. Reduce heat and simmer, uncovered, for 20 minutes.

Purée in batches in a blender, holding down the lid, then strain through

- ¼ cup (60 mL) butter
- 4 medium sweet red peppers, chopped
- 1 lb (500 g) mushrooms, finely chopped
- 1 onion, chopped
- 2 cloves garlic, minced
- 3 cups (750 mL) chicken broth (homemade or canned)
- 2 tsp (10 mL) paprika
- 1 tsp (5 mL) granulated sugar

a sieve into a large bowl. (Or pass through a food mill into a bowl, though a blender makes a smoother soup.) Stir in the lemon juice, cayenne and salt and pepper to taste. Chill, covered, at least 4 hours, or overnight.

- 2 Tbsp (30 mL) fresh lemon juice
- ¼ tsp (1 mL) cayenne
- Salt and pepper
- Mushroom or lemon slices for garnish

Taste and adjust seasoning. Serve in chilled bowls; garnish with mushroom or lemon slices.

BREADS, MUFFINS AND BREAKFAST STUFF

···

WHEN THE ONLY bread I could buy was the sponge-like cellophane-wrapped supermarket kind, I made all the bread for our family at home. I would find great satisfaction in kneading the soft dough and letting it rise like magic into a yeasty mountain. As it baked, the aroma alone would be worth the few minutes spent preparing the bread.

Now, with such a vast choice of good breads for purchase, I can buy soft crusty loaves of Portuguese, Italian or corn bread, or a whole variety of multigrain loaves, and I don't have to travel far (even in the small city where we live).

It's such an easy matter to round out a menu of homey stew with a purchased loaf of good bread that I have included only one of these yeast breads here, my No-Knead French Bread (see p. 40). It's worth doing yourself, as you can produce an extremely good loaf with only five minutes work.

I find such tremendous enjoyment in making pizzas and focaccia and smelling their wonderful homey fragrances as they bake, that I could not resist including a few recipes for these, too.

The remainder of the chapter is made up of soda bread, quick breads and biscuits that will make happy companions to my vast array of soups and stews. I've also included a few breakfast treats, which are always a most welcome way to greet houseguests on weekend mornings.

Puffed Pancake with Fresh Pears and Cardamom

MAKES 4 SERVINGS

Serve this unique pancake with tiny pork sausages for a satisfying but easy family breakfast.

IN A HEAVY ovenproof 8-inch (20 cm) skillet, melt the butter over medium heat; cook the pears, stirring often, for about 5 minutes or just until softened.

In a small bowl, whisk together 2 Tbsp (30 mL) of the sugar and ¼ tsp (1 mL) cardamom. Set aside.

Meanwhile, in a large bowl, combine the remaining ½ cup (125 mL) sugar with the flour, milk, eggs, vanilla, remaining ¼ tsp (1 mL) cardamom and salt; whisk just until blended.

Pour the batter over the pears in the skillet. Bake for about 15 minutes in a 425°F (220°C) oven, or until the batter sets.

Remove the skillet and reduce oven temperature to 350°F (180°C). Run a thin spatula around the edge of the skillet; invert the pancake onto a large plate and slide back into the skillet.

Sprinkle with the reserved sugar mixture; bake for another 10 to 15 minutes, or until puffy and golden brown and a tester inserted in the centre comes out clean. Cut into wedges to serve along with the syrup and/or cream (if using).

- ¼ cup (60 mL) unsalted butter
- 2 small pears, peeled, cored and thinly sliced
- ⅔ cup (150 mL) granulated sugar, divided
- ½ tsp (2 mL) ground cardamom, divided
- ½ cup (125 mL) all-purpose flour
- ½ cup (125 mL) milk
- 2 eggs
- ½ tsp (2 mL) vanilla
- ¼ tsp (1 mL) salt
- Maple syrup or sweetened whipped cream (optional)

VARIATION *Puffed Pancake with Fresh Apples and Cinnamon*
Substitute apples for the pears, and ½ tsp (2 mL) cinnamon and a pinch nutmeg for the cardamom.

Fiesta Cornbread

MAKES 8 GENEROUS SERVINGS

This spicy cornbread is very moist but still light in texture.

IN A LARGE bowl, stir together the cornmeal, flour, salt and baking soda. Stir in the cheese.

In a medium bowl, stir together the eggs, corn, buttermilk, oil and pepper. Add to the dry mixture and stir only enough to combine.

Pour into a greased 8-inch (2 L) square cake pan; bake in a 400°F (200°C) oven for about 35 minutes or until golden and a cake tester inserted in the middle comes out clean.

- 1¼ cups (300 mL) cornmeal
- ¾ cup (175 mL) all-purpose flour
- ½ tsp (2 mL) salt
- ½ tsp (2 mL) baking soda
- 1 cup (250 mL) shredded old Cheddar cheese
- 3 eggs, beaten
- One 10-oz (284 mL) can cream-style corn
- ¾ cup (175 mL) buttermilk
- ⅓ cup (75 mL) canola oil
- 2 Tbsp (30 mL) chopped pickled jalapeño pepper

Mike's Mom's Irish Soda Bread

MAKES 1 LOAF

For years I had such fond memories of the thick, buttered slices of warm soda bread I ate every morning during a visit to Ireland, and I spent much time trying to reproduce it. I came to the conclusion that the flour was different there and left it for a time, but later, armed with an authentic recipe from an Owen Sound friend's Irish mother-in-law, I made this version for a St. Patrick's Day party and it was a hit. It goes really well with soup or stew.

- 2 cups (500 mL) whole wheat flour
- ¾ cup (175 mL) all-purpose flour
- ⅓ cup (75 mL) granulated sugar
- ¼ cup (60 mL) rolled oats
- 1½ tsp (7 mL) baking soda
- 1 tsp (5 mL) baking powder
- ¾ tsp (4 mL) salt
- 1¼ cups (300 mL) buttermilk (approx.)

FIESTA CORNBREAD

RASPBERRY-WALNUT MUFFINS

IN A LARGE bowl, stir together the whole wheat and all-purpose flours, sugar, rolled oats, baking soda, baking powder and salt. Stir in the buttermilk to make a soft dough. Form into a ball.

On a greased baking sheet, flatten the dough with floured hands to a circle about 2 inches (5 cm) high; cut a cross ¾ inch (2 cm) deep in the centre. Place in a 475°F (240°C) oven; immediately reduce heat to 350°F (180°C) and bake for 45 minutes. Wrap in a damp clean tea towel and let cool on a rack for at least 5 hours to allow to set.

Fresh Mint Quick Bread

....

MAKES 4 LOAVES (ABOUT 16 SLICES EACH)

Nothing could be more refreshing than tiny slices of this bread spread with Lemon-Apricot Butter (see p. 176) and served with tea. Easy to make, the loaves can be refrigerated for one week or frozen for three months.

- ½ cup (125 mL) butter, softened
- 2 eggs
- 2¼ cups (550 mL) all-purpose flour
- 2 Tbsp (30 mL) granulated sugar
- 1 Tbsp (15 mL) baking powder
- 1 tsp (5 mL) ground ginger
- ½ tsp (2 mL) salt
- ½ cup (125 mL) fresh mint leaves
- ¾ cup (175 mL) milk

IN A LARGE bowl, beat the butter and eggs together well.

Sift or stir together the flour, sugar, baking powder, ginger and salt. Chop the mint and stir into the flour mixture. Add to the butter mixture alternately with the milk.

Spoon into 4 greased 4½ × 2½–inch (250 mL) loaf pans. Bake in a 350°F (180°C) oven for 30 minutes or until a cake tester inserted in the middle comes out clean.

Raspberry-Walnut Muffins

....

MAKES 12 MUFFINS

Use whatever jam (or marmalade) you have on hand for these easy muffins. No need to butter them either!

- 1½ cups (375 mL) all-purpose flour
- ½ cup (125 mL) finely chopped toasted walnuts
- ¼ cup (60 mL) packed brown sugar
- 1 Tbsp (15 mL) baking powder
- ½ tsp (2 mL) baking soda
- ½ tsp (2 mL) salt
- 1 egg
- 1 cup (250 mL) milk
- ¼ cup (60 mL) butter, melted
- ¼ cup (60 mL) raspberry jam

IN A LARGE bowl, stir together the flour, walnuts, sugar, baking powder, baking soda and salt; make a well in the centre.

Lightly beat together the egg, milk and butter; pour into the centre of the dry ingredients and stir lightly just to combine, being careful not to overmix.

Grease a 12-cup muffin tray and spoon just enough batter into each cup to cover the bottom. Top each with scant 1 tsp (5 mL) jam, then spoon in the remaining batter to fill the cups about three-quarters full.

Bake in a 400°F (200°C) oven for 18 to 20 minutes or until the tops are firm to the touch. Let cool in the pan for 3 to 4 minutes. Remove and serve warm or let cool completely on a rack. Store in an airtight container.

Banana Bread with Toasted Coconut

....

MAKES 1 LOAF

I purposely let bananas get overripe just for an excuse to make this delicious quick bread. Toasting the coconut and walnuts gives it an exceptional flavour.

SPREAD THE COCONUT and walnuts on a baking sheet; toast in a 350°F (180°C) oven for about 5 minutes or just until golden, watching carefully.

In a large bowl, cream the butter with the brown and granulated sugars until fluffy. Beat in the vanilla and eggs, one at a time. Stir in the banana, lemon zest and sour cream.

Sift or stir together the flour, baking powder, baking soda and salt; stir into the creamed mixture just until blended. Stir in the coconut and nuts.

Pour into a greased and floured 9 × 5–inch (2 L) loaf pan; bake in a 350°F (180°C) oven for about 1 hour and 15 minutes or until a cake tester inserted in the middle comes out clean. Let stand for 10 minutes in the pan; remove and let cool on a rack. Wrap well and store at room temperature for a day before cutting, or freeze for up to 3 months.

- 1 cup (250 mL) shredded coconut
- ½ cup (125 mL) chopped walnuts
- ⅔ cup (150 mL) butter, softened
- ½ cup (125 mL) packed brown sugar
- ½ cup (125 mL) granulated sugar
- 1 tsp (5 mL) vanilla
- 2 eggs
- 1 cup (250 mL) mashed banana (3 medium)
- 2 tsp (10 mL) grated lemon zest
- ¼ cup (60 mL) sour cream
- 2 cups (500 mL) all-purpose flour
- 1 tsp (5 mL) baking powder
- ½ tsp (2 mL) baking soda
- ½ tsp (2 mL) salt

No-Knead French Bread

....

MAKES 2 LOAVES

Over the years, I have had great fun teaching cooking in various schools and colleges throughout Ontario. Although I no longer have time to teach, I still enjoy the recipes generous students have shared with me. Lew Short, one of my students in Owen Sound, gave me the idea for this extremely easy bread. Although they take only 5 minutes of actual work, the loaves are beautiful and delicious.

Use a large stationary electric mixer with a dough hook if you have one. If not, use the mixer attachment, but use a rubber spatula to help get the dough up from the bottom edges and sides of the bowl.

COMBINE 1 CUP (250 mL) of the flour with the sugar, salt and yeast in a large mixing bowl; mix slowly until well combined. Add the oil, then drizzle in the water, mixing constantly at low speed. Increase to medium speed and mix for 3 minutes, scraping the sides of the bowl once.

Return to low speed and add 1 cup (250 mL) flour. Beat at the highest speed for 4 minutes, scraping the bowl occasionally. At the lowest speed, very gradually add enough of the remaining flour to make a soft dough that leaves the sides of the bowl and starts to become a ball. Remove the bowl from the machine; cover tightly with plastic wrap held on by an elastic band to secure the wrap while the dough rises. Let rest for 45 minutes.

With floured hands, remove the dough to a heavily floured surface and shape into a smooth oblong form. (The dough will be sticky.) Divide in half and form into 2 long, thin tapered loaves. Grease a baking sheet and sprinkle with cornmeal. Place the loaves on the sheet leaving plenty of room between them. Cover with a dry clean tea towel and let rest in a warm place (a heating pad on low works well) for 45 minutes or until doubled in bulk.

With a razor blade or very sharp knife, make 5 or 6 shallow diagonal cuts in the tops of the loaves, being careful not to press down on the loaves. Bake in a 400°F (200°C) oven for about 25 minutes or until loaves sound hollow when tapped on the bottom. Remove to cool on wire racks.

- 3 cups (750 mL) all-purpose flour (approx.)
- 4 tsp (20 mL) granulated sugar
- 1 tsp (5 mL) salt
- 1 pkg active dry yeast (or 2¼ tsp/11 mL)
- 2 Tbsp (30 mL) canola oil
- 1¼ cups (300 mL) very hot tap water
- ⅓ cup (75 mL) cornmeal

Make-Ahead Fully-Loaded French Toast

MAKES 4 TO 6 SERVINGS

This peanut-banana version of French toast will be a big hit with kids of all ages.

IN A FOOD processor or blender, process the peanuts until coarsely chopped. Remove half, cover and set aside.

Coarsely chop one of the bananas; add to the processor along with the eggs, egg white, milk and vanilla. Process until well blended. Transfer to a shallow dish.

Dip the bread slices into the egg mixture, pressing and turning until thoroughly soaked. Place on greased baking sheets. Spoon any remaining mixture overtop; sprinkle with the cinnamon. Cover with plastic wrap and refrigerate overnight.

Next morning, bake in a 475°F (240°C) oven for 5 to 10 minutes per side, or until golden brown. Transfer to warmed plates. Slice the remaining bananas and arrange around the toast; sprinkle with the reserved peanuts. Drizzle with honey.

- ¾ cup (175 mL) unsalted peanuts
- 3 large bananas, divided
- 4 eggs
- 1 egg white
- 1½ cups (375 mL) milk
- 1 tsp (5 mL) vanilla
- 9 slices French bread (approx. ¾ inch/2 cm thick each)
- Sprinkle of cinnamon
- Drizzle of liquid honey

Mary Lou's Blueberry Streusel Muffins

MAKES 24 MUFFINS

These moist, blueberry-rich muffins are the best you'll ever taste. From her family collection of recipes, Mary Lou Ruby Jonas makes them often for morning guests. If using frozen blueberries, do not thaw first.

STREUSEL TOPPING
- ¼ cup (60 mL) granulated sugar
- ¼ cup (60 mL) all-purpose flour
- ½ tsp (2 mL) cinnamon
- ¼ cup (60 mL) butter

STREUSEL TOPPING In a small bowl, combine the sugar, flour and cinnamon; cut in the butter until crumbly. Set aside.

MUFFINS In a large bowl, cream the butter with the sugar until fluffy; beat in the eggs, one at a time. Add the lemon zest.

Stir together the flour, baking powder and salt; alternating with the milk, add to the creamed mixture, stirring just to combine—do not overmix. Gently stir in the blueberries.

Spoon into 24 greased muffin cups. Sprinkle with the Streusel Topping. Bake in a 375°F (190°C) oven for 25 to 30 minutes or until tops are firm to the touch.

MUFFINS
- ½ cup (125 mL) butter, softened
- 1¼ cups (300 mL) granulated sugar
- 2 eggs
- 1 tsp (5 mL) grated lemon zest
- 4 cups (1 L) all-purpose flour
- 4 tsp (20 mL) baking powder
- ½ tsp (2 mL) salt
- 1¼ cups (300 mL) milk
- 4 cups (1 L) blueberries

Maple-Almond Granola

MAKES ABOUT 10 CUPS (2.5 L)

Maple syrup adds a subtle sweetness to this easy, healthy breakfast treat. The recipe is easily doubled if you want to have lots on hand to sprinkle over yogurt or ice cream for snacks, in addition to the usual morning bowl with milk.

IN A LARGE bowl, stir together the oats, almonds, sunflower seeds, wheat bran and oat bran.

In a small saucepan, heat together the maple syrup and oil to boiling; boil

- 3½ cups (875 mL) rolled oats
- 1½ cups (375 mL) coarsely chopped unblanched almonds
- 1 cup (250 mL) raw sunflower seeds
- 1 cup (250 mL) wheat bran
- ½ cup (125 mL) oat bran
- ¾ cup (175 mL) maple syrup
- ¼ cup (60 mL) canola oil
- ½ tsp (2 mL) vanilla
- 2 cups (500 mL) coarsely chopped dried apricots or golden raisins (or a combination of the two)

CLASSIC TEA BISCUITS

for 1 minute without stirring. Remove from heat and stir in the vanilla. Drizzle over the rolled oat mixture and toss well to coat.

Spread the mixture on a jelly roll pan; bake in a 350°F (180°C) oven for 15 minutes. Stir and reduce the temperature to 325°F (160°C); bake for 30 minutes longer or until evenly golden, stirring every 10 minutes.

Return to the bowl and stir in the dried fruit. Let cool, stirring occasionally. Store in an airtight container for up to 2 weeks at room temperature, or freeze for up to 2 months.

Classic Tea Biscuits

MAKES ABOUT 20 BISCUITS

When my mother disap-peared with a cup and came back with cream from the basement, we knew there would be flaky, hot tea biscuits for lunch. These aren't made with cream, but they are nice and tender. They're great with stews or on top of pot pies instead of pastry. If you wish, add your own favourite chopped herb or some grated cheese.

- 2 cups (500 mL) all-purpose flour
- 4 tsp (20 mL) baking powder
- 1 Tbsp (15 mL) granulated sugar
- ½ tsp (2 mL) salt
- ½ cup (125 mL) lard
- 1 egg, beaten
- ⅔ cup (150 mL) milk (approx.)

IN A LARGE bowl, sift or stir together the flour, baking powder, sugar and salt; cut in the lard until the mixture is like fine meal.

Stir together the egg and milk; add to the flour mixture all at once, stirring with a fork until the dough follows the fork around the bowl. (If too dry, add a bit more milk for a soft, sticky dough.)

Turn out onto a lightly floured surface; knead gently 20 times. Pat or roll to an even ½-inch (1 cm) thickness. Using a cookie cutter, cut into 2-inch (5 cm) circles.

Bake on ungreased baking sheets in a 450°F (230°C) oven for about 10 minutes or until golden brown.

Apple Cheddar Melt

MAKES 4 SERVINGS

For a quick and different lunch, enjoy this enlightened version of an old classic. The recipe can easily be halved or doubled for other numbers.

- 4 large slices rye bread, toasted
- 1 apple, peeled and minced
- 1 cup (250 mL) shredded Cheddar cheese
- ¼ cup (60 mL) light mayonnaise
- 2 Tbsp (30 mL) liquid honey
- 2 tsp (10 mL) Dijon mustard

PLACE THE TOAST on a baking sheet. In a small bowl, stir together the apple, cheese, mayonnaise, honey and mustard; spread over the toast, mounding in the centre.

Broil 4 inches (10 cm) from the heat for 2 to 3 minutes or until bubbly (or, cooking 2 slices at a time, place on a paper towel and microwave at medium power for 1 to 2 minutes).

COMFORTING MAIN COURSES

"WHAT'S FOR SUPPER?" When this question comes through the door with hungry children from school or a tired spouse from work, look to this chapter for comfort.

Because many people run out of ideas for family suppers I have, in fact, made this section the bulk of the book.

There are fast stir-frys, one-skillet sautés and quick pasta dishes, so that whole meals can materialize in minutes, often in one dish. While most of these meals centre around poultry, meat or seafood, there are some vegetarian ideas as well.

But don't pass over the quick-to-fix but long-simmering dishes that to me constitute the easiest cooking of all. My baked beans or updated pot roast may take hours to cook, but it's only a matter of minutes to put them together. Plus you'll have the pleasure of savouring their aroma throughout the afternoon, if you happen to be in the house.

Also included in this section are several easy ideas for casual entertaining—make-ahead, dressed-up stews and casseroles, incredibly easy roasts and simple but fancy grills.

Whether it's family fare or company food, this section puts forth a myriad of easy answers to the question "What's for supper?"

Chicken

SPICY WINGS WITH MANGO MUSTARD

Spicy Peanut and Citrus Grilled Chicken

MAKES 8 SERVINGS

You can use the same marmalade and method with eight thick pork chops instead of chicken, if that suits your fancy.

WIPE THE CHICKEN breasts and place in a shallow baking dish just big enough to hold them in a single layer.

Drop the onion and garlic into a food processor or blender, processing until finely chopped. Add the marmalade, peanut butter, lemon juice, oil, soy sauce and hot pepper flakes; process until smooth.

Pour the sauce over the chicken and coat well. Cover and refrigerate for at least 6 hours, or overnight, turning the breasts occasionally. Remove from the refrigerator 30 minutes before cooking.

Bake, uncovered, in a 350°F (180°C) oven for 30 minutes. Remove the chicken from the marinade, reserving the marinade in a small saucepan; bring to a boil and boil for 3 minutes.

Meanwhile, place the chicken on a greased medium high-temperature grill, or about 4 inches (10 cm) from medium-hot coals; grill, basting often with the marinade, for 15 to 20 minutes or until the chicken is no longer pink near the bone. Serve with the remaining sauce.

- 8 large bone-in, skin-on chicken breasts (about 4½ lb/2 kg total)
- 1 small onion
- 1 clove garlic
- ¾ cup (175 mL) Seville orange marmalade
- ¼ cup (60 mL) peanut butter
- 2 Tbsp (30 mL) fresh lemon juice
- 2 Tbsp (30 mL) canola oil
- 2 Tbsp (30 mL) low-sodium soy sauce
- Pinch hot pepper flakes

Spicy Wings with Mango Mustard

MAKES 8 APPETIZER SERVINGS OR 4 MAIN-COURSE SERVINGS

Because they're cooked at an unusually high temperature, these tangy wings are crusty on the outside but juicy and tender within. Watch them carefully for the last few minutes. They're great with beer. Just be sure to have lots of serviettes on hand.

WINGS Cut the tips from the wings and reserve for stock; separate the wings at the joint.

In a small bowl, stir together the garlic, dry mustard, paprika, thyme, ground coriander, cayenne pepper, black pepper, salt and cumin; blend in the lemon juice and brandy to make a paste.

Brush over the wings and arrange, meaty side down, on lightly greased foil-lined baking sheets. Add 1 tsp (5 mL) more lemon juice to the paste if it becomes too dry. Refrigerate for at least 30 minutes, or up to several hours.

MANGO MUSTARD Meanwhile, in a food processor or blender, purée the chutney with the mustard. Heat in a small saucepan until the chutney melts, stirring often; let cool.

ASSEMBLY Bake the wings, uncovered, in a 475°F (240°C) oven for 20 to 30 minutes or until brown and crisp, turning after 15 minutes. Serve hot with Mango Mustard for dipping.

WINGS
- 3 lb (1.5 kg) chicken wings
- 4 cloves garlic, minced
- 2 tsp (10 mL) dry mustard
- 2 tsp (10 mL) paprika
- 1 tsp (5 mL) dried thyme
- 1 tsp (5 mL) ground coriander
- ½ tsp (2 mL) cayenne pepper
- ½ tsp (2 mL) black pepper
- ½ tsp (2 mL) salt
- ½ tsp (2 mL) ground cumin
- 2 Tbsp (30 mL) fresh lemon juice (approx.)
- 2 Tbsp (30 mL) brandy

MANGO MUSTARD
- 1 cup (250 mL) sweet mango chutney
- ¼ cup (60 mL) Dijon mustard

Elegant Chicken Breasts with Sun-Dried Tomato Stuffing

MAKES 4 TO 6 SERVINGS

This impressive dish is easy to execute and can be made ahead. It can be doubled or tripled as needed, and is delicious served either hot or cold. Sun-dried tomatoes are available in grocery stores, but if you can only find dried, let them sit for a day or two in oil before using. Reserve oil to use in the recipe.

STUFFING In a bowl, blend together the cheese, egg, garlic, tomatoes, basil, lemon juice, oregano and salt and pepper to taste. Set aside.

CHICKEN Remove the bones from the chicken, but leave the skin on.

Loosen the skin from one side of each breast, leaving the edge of the skin attached on the other side; spoon a scant ⅓ cup (75 mL) stuffing into the pocket, spreading with a spatula. Tuck the skin and meat neatly under the breast, covering the stuffing completely. Form the breasts into a neat even round and place, skin side up, in a greased shallow baking dish just big enough to hold them in a single layer.

Brush the chicken lightly with some of the oil from the tomatoes and sprinkle with salt, pepper and paprika. (The breasts can be covered and refrigerated for a few hours or overnight. Remove from refrigerator

STUFFING
- ½ lb (250 g) low-fat ricotta cheese, drained (if necessary)
- 1 egg, lightly beaten
- 1 clove garlic, minced
- ⅓ cup (75 mL) chopped drained sun-dried tomatoes (reserving oil)
- 2 Tbsp (30 mL) chopped fresh basil (or 2 tsp/10 mL dried)
- 1 Tbsp (15 mL) fresh lemon juice
- 1½ tsp (7 mL) chopped fresh oregano (or ½ tsp/ 2 mL dried)
- Salt and pepper

CHICKEN
- 6 bone-in, skin-on chicken breast halves (about 3 lb/1.5 kg total)
- Salt and pepper
- Paprika

30 minutes before baking.)

Bake in a 400°F (200°C) oven for 25 to 30 minutes, or until the meat is no longer pink inside, basting once or twice after 15 minutes.

Honey-Curried Fast Family Chicken

MAKES 4 TO 6 SERVINGS

This quick and delicious chicken dish can be prepared early in the morning or just before baking. Add more curry powder for a hotter dish. Accompany with rice and colourful stir-fried vegetables.

- 6 or 7 bone-in, skin-on chicken breast halves (about 3 lb/ 1.5 kg total)
- ⅓ cup (75 mL) liquid honey
- ¼ cup (60 mL) Dijon or deli-style mustard
- 2 Tbsp (30 mL) butter, melted
- 4 tsp (20 mL) curry powder
- Pinch cayenne pepper

IN A GREASED shallow 13 × 9–inch (3.5 L) baking dish, arrange the chicken in a single layer, skin side down.

Combine the honey, mustard, butter, curry powder and cayenne in a small bowl; stir until smooth and blended. Pour over the chicken. Cover and refrigerate if preparing ahead.

Bake the chicken, uncovered, in a 375°F (190°C) oven for 20 minutes, basting once. Turn the chicken over and baste again; bake for 20 minutes longer or until the chicken is no longer pink inside.

Country Roast Chicken with Dried Fruit Stuffing

MAKES ABOUT 8 SERVINGS

In this fast-moving world, we yearn for comfort foods like the plump roast chicken that was so often the focus of Grandmother's Sunday supper. It's worth seeking out a big roasting chicken for this updated version.

HOW DO YOU TELL A YOUNG CHICK FROM AN OLD HEN?

....

In the poultry world, it's not a matter of wrinkles, it's a matter of weight.

Broilers are 2⅓ to 3 lb (1.2 to 1.5 kg) and are best broiled, fried or braised. Fryers, weighing in at 3 to 4 lb (1.5 to 2 kg), are basically used the same way as broilers.

Roasters, on the other hand, are the big males with more meat per pound than smaller birds. They weigh 4 to 6 lb (2 to 3 kg), and can be used for roasting.

Stewing hens are just that: older 3 to 7-lb (1.5 to 3.1 kg) gals that are only good for stews and soups and are tough without braising for a long time.

Free-range chickens are raised outside any confines and are generally firmer with richer chicken flavour, but they may not be quite as tender as supermarket poultry due to the extent of their travels and their unpredictable diets.

FRUIT STUFFING Soak the fruit in the stock for at least 30 minutes.

In a large skillet, melt the butter over medium heat; cook the onions and celery for 5 minutes, stirring often. Remove from heat; stir in the bread, parsley, sage, salt, pepper and fruit with the stock. Let cool.

CHICKEN Remove the neck and giblets from the chicken; pat dry inside and out. Rub with the lemon half inside and out. Stuff with the fruit stuffing and truss the bird.

In a small bowl, stir together the melted butter, mustard, paprika, garlic and sage and spread over the chicken.

Place the chicken on its side on a rack in a shallow roasting pan; roast, uncovered, in a 325°F (160°C) oven for 1 hour. Using oven mitts protected with foil, turn onto the other side; roast for 1 hour longer. Turn onto its back and roast for 30 to 60 minutes longer, or until the juices run clear when a thigh is pierced with a skewer and a meat thermometer registers 180°F (82°C).

Transfer the chicken to a cutting board. Cover loosely with foil and let stand for 15 minutes before carving. Remove the stuffing to a heated bowl.

FRUIT STUFFING

- 1 cup (250 mL) coarsely chopped dried fruit (pears, apples, apricots, prunes, etc.)
- 1 cup (250 mL) hot chicken stock
- 2 Tbsp (30 mL) butter
- 2 onions, chopped
- 1 cup (250 mL) chopped celery
- 6 cups (1.5 L) cubed slightly stale bread
- ¼ cup (60 mL) chopped fresh parsley
- ½ tsp (2 mL) crushed dried sage
- ½ tsp (2 mL) salt
- ¼ tsp (1 mL) pepper

CHICKEN

- 1 roasting chicken (about 8 lb/3.5 kg)
- ½ lemon (cut crosswise)
- 2 Tbsp (30 mL) butter, melted
- 2 Tbsp (30 mL) Dijon mustard
- 1 tsp (5 mL) paprika
- 2 cloves garlic, minced
- ½ tsp (2 mL) crushed dried sage

Hoisin Orange Chicken Legs

MAKES 4 SERVINGS

An easy, flavourful glaze gives a dark mahogany appearance to chicken. Serve with fried rice and snow or sugar snap peas.

WIPE THE CHICKEN dry; place in a shallow glass dish or sturdy plastic bag.

In a small bowl, stir together the hoisin sauce, orange zest, orange juice, garlic, ginger and oil; pour over the chicken. Cover and refrigerate for at least 3 hours, or up to 8 hours, turning occasionally. Remove from the refrigerator 30 minutes before cooking.

Remove the chicken from the marinade and pour the marinade into a small saucepan; bring to a boil and boil for 5 minutes. Stir in the marmalade; set aside on the edge of the grill.

Meanwhile, place the chicken on a greased medium high–temperature grill, or 6 inches (15 cm) from medium-hot coals; grill for 15 minutes, turning often. Brush the marinade liberally over the chicken and continue to grill, turning often and brushing with the marinade, for 10 to 20 minutes longer or until the juices run clear when the chicken is pierced with a fork.

- 4 chicken legs
- ¼ cup (60 mL) hoisin sauce
- 1 tsp (5 mL) grated orange zest
- ¼ cup (60 mL) fresh orange juice
- 2 cloves garlic, minced
- 1 Tbsp (15 mL) minced fresh ginger
- 1 Tbsp (15 mL) canola oil
- 1 Tbsp (15 mL) bitter orange marmalade

Thai Thighs

MAKES 4 SERVINGS

An easy marinade and a quick coating keeps these sprightly thighs nice and moist during baking. Accompany with rice and snow peas.

- 8 chicken thighs (about 2¾ lb/1.35 kg total)
- 1 cup (250 mL) low-fat plain yogurt

WIPE THE CHICKEN dry; pierce in several places with a fork.

In a shallow dish just big enough to hold the thighs in a single layer, stir together the yogurt, lime juice, garlic, ginger, ground coriander and cayenne. Add the chicken and roll to coat evenly. Cover and refrigerate for at least 2 hours, or up to 6 hours. Remove from the refrigerator 30 minutes before cooking.

Place the peanuts in a shallow dish. Remove the thighs from the marinade and let the excess drip off. Roll each thigh in the nuts patting to coat well. Place, meaty side up, on a greased baking sheet; bake, uncovered, in a 350°F (180°C) oven for 40 to 45 minutes or until the juices run clear when the chicken is pierced.

- 2 Tbsp (30 mL) fresh lime juice
- 2 cloves garlic, minced
- 1 Tbsp (15 mL) minced fresh ginger
- 1 tsp (5 mL) ground coriander
- ¼ tsp (1 mL) cayenne
- 1½ cups (375 mL) finely chopped peanuts

Elizabeth Baird's Chorizo and Chicken Paella

....

MAKES 6 TO 8 SERVINGS

My long-time friend Elizabeth Baird, former food director of Canadian Living Magazine, and I have gone on so many cooking, eating and food-learning explorations together that my book would not be complete without one of her favourite recipes. This one she describes as "a welcome dish for a buffet or dinner party... a paella that slips away from the traditional mix of seafood and meat."

IN A PLASTIC bag, combine the flour, salt

- ¼ cup (60 mL) all-purpose flour
- ½ tsp (2 mL) salt
- ¼ tsp (1 mL) pepper
- 5 chicken legs (about 2 lb/1 kg total)
- 2 Tbsp (30 mL) olive oil, divided
- 1 lb (500 g) smoked chorizo sausages
- 1 large onion, chopped
- 2 large cloves garlic, minced
- 2 zucchini (preferably yellow), coarsely chopped
- 1 large sweet red pepper, cubed

and pepper. Separate each chicken leg at the joint. Add to the bag and shake to coat; shake off the excess.

In a wide and heavy shallow saucepan or large skillet, heat half of the oil over medium-high heat and brown the chicken well on all sides. Remove chicken and set aside.

Cut the sausages into 2-inch (5 cm) lengths; add to the pan and cook until browned. Set aside with the chicken. Pour off and discard all fat.

Add the remaining oil to the pan and heat over medium heat; cook the onion, garlic, zucchini and peppers until softened, about 5 minutes. Stir in the paprika, thyme and cayenne; cook, stirring, for 2 minutes.

Meanwhile, steep the saffron in the stock for 5 minutes. Add the stock and saffron to the vegetable mixture along with the tomatoes and rice; bring to a boil. Nestle the chicken and sausages into the rice mixture. Cover and cook over medium-low heat until the rice is tender and the liquid absorbed, about 30 minutes. Sprinkle with the peas; cover and cook for about 2 minutes or until heated through.

To serve, sprinkle with the parsley and green onion. Cut the lemon lengthwise into wedges and arrange attractively on the paella.

- 1 large sweet green pepper, cubed
- 1 tsp (5 mL) paprika
- ¼ tsp (1 mL) dried thyme
- Pinch cayenne pepper
- ½ tsp (2 mL) saffron threads
- 3 cups (750 mL) hot chicken stock
- 3 cups (750 mL) chopped peeled tomatoes
- 2 cups (500 mL) parboiled long-grain rice
- 1 cup (250 mL) frozen peas
- ¼ cup (60 mL) minced fresh parsley
- 2 Tbsp (30 mL) chopped green onion or chives
- 1 lemon

Light Chicken Chili

....

MAKES ABOUT 4 SERVINGS

On a trip to Texas I discovered chili of every description, and there was much talk of "white chili" made with chicken and white beans instead of the usual beef and red beans. I came home to recreate this quick chicken chili, but I'm afraid I still like to use some chili powder, which does render the dish less than white. Serve with rice or tortillas and a green salad. You might like to accompany it with bowls of sour cream, salsa and grated Monterey Jack or mild Cheddar cheese.

IN A LARGE saucepan, heat 1 Tbsp (15 mL) of the oil over medium heat; cook the onion and celery for 5 minutes. Push to one side of the pan. Heat the remaining oil on the other side of the pan over high heat; brown the chicken on all sides, about 5 minutes.

Stir in the garlic, chilies, chili powder, cumin, oregano, black pepper and hot pepper flakes; cook, stirring for 1 minute. Stir in the stock and beans; bring to a boil. Cover and reduce heat; simmer for 15 minutes.

Uncover and simmer for 15 minutes longer. Taste and adjust seasoning, adding more hot pepper flakes if desired. Serve sprinkled with the fresh coriander.

- 2 Tbsp (30 mL) olive oil, divided
- 1 onion, chopped
- 1 stalk celery, sliced
- 1 lb (500 g) boneless, skinless chicken, cubed
- 2 cloves garlic, minced
- One 4-oz (125 g) can chopped mild green chilies, drained
- 1 Tbsp (15 mL) chili powder
- 1 tsp (5 mL) ground cumin
- 1 tsp (5 mL) crushed oregano
- Pinch black pepper
- Pinch hot pepper flakes
- 2 cups (500 mL) chicken stock
- One 19-oz (540 mL) can white kidney beans (undrained)
- ⅓ cup (75 mL) chopped fresh coriander (cilantro)

Teriyaki Chicken with Chunky Tropical Salsa

MAKES 2 SERVINGS

If you wish to serve this interesting chicken and its quick, fresh sauce just for one, merely cut the marinade and salsa in half.

TERIYAKI CHICKEN In a sturdy plastic bag, combine the soy sauce, sugar, ginger and garlic; add the chicken breasts and turn to coat. Let stand at room temperature for 20 minutes or refrigerate for up to 4 hours. Remove from the refrigerator 30 minutes before cooking.

Broil the chicken 6 inches (15 cm) from the heat for about 12 minutes, turning once, or until the chicken is no longer pink inside.

CHUNKY TROPICAL SALSA In a bowl, combine the mango, kiwifruit and vinegar; stir in the banana, green onion and red pepper. Season with salt, pepper and hot pepper flakes to taste. Serve with the chicken.

TERIYAKI CHICKEN
- 2 Tbsp (30 mL) low-sodium soy sauce
- ¼ tsp (1 mL) granulated sugar
- ¼ tsp (1 mL) ground ginger
- 2 cloves garlic, crushed
- 4 boneless, skinless chicken breasts (about 1 lb/500 g total)

CHUNKY TROPICAL SALSA
- 1 small mango, peeled and diced
- 1 kiwifruit, peeled and diced
- 2 Tbsp (30 mL) rice wine vinegar
- 1 banana, diced
- 1 green onion, sliced
- 2 Tbsp (30 mL) diced sweet red pepper
- Salt and pepper
- Hot pepper flakes

Chicken Pot Pie with Party Phyllo Crust

MAKES 4 TO 6 SERVINGS

A crisp light phyllo crust gives chicken pot pie a new twist. Serve with a crisp green salad for a quick make-ahead company meal.

IN A LARGE saucepan, melt 2 Tbsp (30 mL) butter over medium heat; cook the mushrooms, onion and garlic for 3 minutes. Stir in the flour and cook, stirring,

- ⅓ cup (75 mL) butter, divided
- ¼ lb (125 g) mushrooms, quartered
- 1 onion, chopped
- 1 clove garlic, minced
- ¼ cup (60 mL) all-purpose flour
- 3 cups (750 mL) hot chicken stock
- Salt and pepper

TERIYAKI CHICKEN WITH CHUNKY TROPICAL SALSA

for 2 minutes.

Gradually stir in the stock and bring to boil, stirring constantly. Cook for about 3 minutes or until thickened. Season with salt and pepper to taste; stir in the parsley and marjoram. Remove from heat.

Stir in the chicken, parsnips (or carrots) and peas. Pour into an ungreased 13 × 9–inch (3 L) baking dish. Refrigerate until cooled.

Melt the remaining butter. Cover the phyllo sheets with waxed paper and a damp tea towel to prevent drying out while you work. Place 1 phyllo sheet over the chicken mixture, folding excess pastry under the edges to fit inside the dish. Lightly brush the sheet with butter. Repeat with the remaining sheets and butter, making sure to brush the top sheet. (The recipe can be prepared to this point, covered and refrigerated for up to 12 hours. Remove from the refrigerator 30 minutes before cooking.)

Bake in a 375°F (190°C) oven for 25 to 30 minutes or until the pastry is golden and the filling bubbly.

- ¼ cup (60 mL) chopped fresh parsley
- 1 tsp (5 mL) dried marjoram
- 6 cups (1.5 L) diced cooked chicken
- 4 cups (1 L) cooked cubed parsnips or carrots
- 1 cup (250 mL) fresh or frozen peas
- 5 sheets phyllo pastry

One-Dish Stir-Fried Chicken with Asian Noodles

MAKES 6 SERVINGS

In this satisfying and simple main-dish stir-fry, the contrast of crisp green broccoli and soft egg noodles is a treat for both the eye and your taste buds.

IN A WOK OR large skillet, heat the oil over high heat; stir-fry the garlic and noodles for 1 minute to flavour the noodles. With a slotted spoon, remove the

- 2 Tbsp (30 mL) peanut or canola oil
- 4 cloves garlic, minced
- 1 lb (500 g) fresh Chinese egg noodles
- 4 boneless, skinless chicken breast halves, cut across the grain in thin strips (about 1 lb/500 g total)
- 8 cups (2 L) broccoli florets (about ½ lb/250 g), cut in narrow lengths

noodles to a large bowl and set aside.

Add the chicken and broccoli to the wok; stir-fry for 2 to 3 minutes or until the chicken is no longer pink inside. Add the stock and bring to a boil; reduce heat to low, cover and simmer for 2 minutes, or until the broccoli is tender-crisp. Stir in the noodles for the last few seconds.

Meanwhile, dissolve the cornstarch in the cold water. Increase heat of the wok to high and stir in the cornstarch mixture, oyster sauce, fish sauce, sugar and salt and pepper to taste; cook, stirring, until well blended and shiny. Serve immediately.

- ½ cup (125 mL) chicken stock
- 1 tsp (5 mL) cornstarch
- 1 Tbsp (15 mL) cold water
- 2 Tbsp (30 mL) oyster sauce
- 1 Tbsp (15 mL) fish sauce (nam plaa; see note)
- ½ tsp (2 mL) granulated sugar
- Salt and pepper
- coriander (cilantro)

NOTE Fish sauce is a thin, salty brown liquid indispensable in Southeast Asian cooking. It's milder than soy sauce and available in most supermarkets and Asian grocery stores.

Quick Honey-Garlic Chicken Wings

MAKES 4 SERVINGS

I've been doing chicken wings like this for many years. No matter how else I prepare them, my family likes it best. Serve these quick-and-easy braised wings with rice and green peas for a Friday night treat.

REMOVE THE TIPS from the wings and reserve for stock. Separate the wings at the joint. In a wok or skillet, heat the oil over high heat; stir-fry the wings for 3 to 4 minutes or until browned.

- 3 lb (1.5 kg) chicken wings
- 2 Tbsp (30 mL) peanut or canola oil
- ⅓ cup (75 mL) soy sauce
- 2 Tbsp (30 mL) liquid honey
- 2 Tbsp (30 mL) dry sherry
- 2 cloves garlic, crushed
- 1 Tbsp (15 mL) minced fresh ginger

Stir together the soy sauce, honey, sherry, garlic and ginger; pour over the wings and stir to coat well.

Reduce heat to low; cover and simmer for about 30 minutes or until tender, stirring often near end of cooking to make sure the glaze doesn't burn.

New-Style Chicken with Parsley Dumplings

....

MAKES 4 SERVINGS

This is an updated version of my mother's chicken and dumplings, for which she always used a large stewing hen. Chicken breasts are much more tender and far less greasy. Be sure to use a pot large enough to allow 3 inches (8 cm) of space for the dumplings to rise.

CHICKEN Sprinkle the chicken with salt and pepper; dust lightly with about 2 Tbsp (30 mL) flour.

In a large saucepan, melt the butter with the oil over medium heat; brown the chicken on all sides and remove to a plate.

Add the potatoes, parsnips, carrots, onions and celery to the pan; cook for 5 minutes. Cover with about 4 cups (1 L) water and bring to a boil, scraping up any brown bits from the bottom of the pan.

Return the chicken to the pan; add the thyme, salt, sage and bay leaves. Return to a boil; reduce heat, cover

CHICKEN

- 4 bone-in, skin-on chicken breast halves (about 3 lb/1.5 kg total)
- Salt and pepper
- 2 Tbsp (30 mL) all-purpose flour + extra for dusting
- 1 Tbsp (15 mL) butter
- 1 Tbsp (15 mL) canola oil
- 4 small red potatoes, quartered
- 2 parsnips, quartered
- 2 carrots, quartered
- 2 onions, quartered
- 2 stalks celery, diagonally sliced
- 4 cups (1 L) water
- ½ tsp (2 mL) dried thyme
- ½ tsp (2 mL) salt
- ¼ tsp (1 mL) crushed dried sage
- 2 bay leaves
- 1 cup (250 mL) frozen peas

PARSLEY DUMPLINGS

- 2 cups (500 mL) sifted cake-and-pastry flour
- 4 tsp (20 mL) baking powder
- ¾ tsp (4 mL) salt
- 2 Tbsp (30 mL) chopped fresh parsley

and simmer until the chicken is no longer pink inside, about 25 minutes. Remove and discard the bay leaves. Stir in the peas.

PARSLEY DUMPLINGS Mix or sift together the flour, baking powder and salt in a large bowl; stir in the parsley. Cut in the lard until you achieve the texture of meal. Stir in the milk, adding a few more drops if necessary to make a sticky dough.

Evenly dust a large plate with flour. With a tablespoon, cut out the dumplings and drop onto the floured plate. Quickly drop the dumplings onto the gently simmering stew, spacing evenly. Cover the pan tightly and simmer, without lifting the lid, for 15 minutes or until the dumplings are cooked.

- 2 Tbsp (30 mL) lard
- ⅔ cup (150 mL) milk (approx.)

Easy Grilled-Chicken Rice Salad

....

MAKES 4 SERVINGS

Everything, except grilling the chicken, can be done ahead for this full-flavoured main-course salad. Both hoisin sauce and rice vinegar are readily available in supermarkets.

IN A BOWL, stir together ¼ cup (60 mL) of the vinegar with the hoisin sauce, rice wine (if using), garlic and ginger; add the chicken and toss to coat well. Cover and refrigerate for at least 4 hours, or overnight, turning twice. Remove from the refrigerator 30 minutes before cooking.

Cook the rice according

- ½ cup (125 mL) rice vinegar, divided
- ¼ cup (60 mL) hoisin sauce
- 2 Tbsp (30 mL) rice wine or sherry (optional)
- 1 clove garlic, minced
- 1 Tbsp (15 mL) minced fresh ginger
- 4 boneless, skinless chicken breast halves (about 1 lb/500 g total)
- 1 cup (250 mL) parboiled long-grain rice
- ⅓ cup (75 mL) canola oil
- 2 Tbsp (30 mL) chopped fresh coriander (cilantro) or parsley + extra sprigs for garnish

to the package instructions. In a large bowl, stir together the oil, remaining rice vinegar, fresh coriander, curry powder, salt and sugar. Add the hot cooked rice; toss with a fork to coat well. Gently stir in the apricots and green onions. Cover and refrigerate for up to 2 days. Bring to room temperature before proceeding.

Place the chicken on a greased medium high–temperature grill, or 6 inches (15 cm) from medium-hot coals; grill for about 6 minutes per side or until no longer pink inside, turning once. (Alternatively, broil 4 inches/10 cm from medium-high heat for about 5 minutes per side.)

Stir the peas into the rice mixture; mound on a large platter. Cut each hot chicken breast into 3 strips; arrange around the rice mixture. Garnish with fresh coriander sprigs.

Make-Ahead Jambalaya

....

MAKES ABOUT 8 SERVINGS

A rice dish descended from Spanish paella, jambalaya is seasoned with chili powder as well as cayenne and, in view of its name (probably coming from the French "jambon" for ham), should always contain some ham. The rest of the ingredients can vary—sausage, shrimp, crawfish, oysters, pork. This make-ahead, easy version of the classic Creole stew has more sausage and chicken than anything else and is just right for casual entertaining.

- 1 tsp (5 mL) curry powder
- ½ tsp (2 mL) salt
- ½ tsp (2 mL) granulated sugar
- ½ cup (125 mL) sliced apricots (fresh or dried)
- 3 green onions, sliced
- 1 cup (250 mL) cooked green peas

- 1 Tbsp (15 mL) canola oil
- 6 oz (175 g) cooked ham, cubed
- 1 lb (500 g) hot Italian or chorizo sausage, cut into ½-inch (1 cm) thick slices
- 10 chicken thighs (about 2 lb/1 kg total)
- 3 onions, coarsely chopped
- 1 sweet red pepper, chopped
- 1 sweet green pepper, chopped
- ¼ cup (60 mL) chopped fresh parsley
- 4 cloves garlic, minced

Accompany with a green salad and crusty bread.

IN A LARGE heavy saucepan, heat the oil over medium-high heat; brown the ham and sausage for 8 to 10 minutes. With a slotted spoon, transfer to a bowl. Brown the chicken in batches; remove to a bowl.

Pour off all but 2 Tbsp (30 mL) drippings. Reduce heat to medium and cook the onions, red and green peppers, parsley, garlic and celery for 5 minutes. Stir in the bay leaves, thyme, chili powder, salt, pepper, oregano and cayenne; cook, stirring, for 2 minutes.

Return the chicken and meat to the pan along with any accumulated juices. Stir in the tomatoes and stock; bring to boil. Reduce heat to medium-low; cover and simmer for 35 to 45 minutes or until the juices run clear when the chicken is pierced, stirring occasionally. Remove and discard the bay leaves. (The recipe can be prepared to this point, covered and refrigerated for several hours or overnight.)

In a large pot of lightly salted boiling water, cook the rice for 6 minutes; drain through a fine sieve. Place the rice in a 16-cup (4 L) Dutch oven or shallow casserole; fluff with a fork.

Stir the green onions into the chicken mixture; spread over the rice. Cover and bake in a 350°F (180°C) oven for 25 minutes. Stick the shrimp down into the mixture; bake for 10 to 15 minutes or until the shrimp are pink and the casserole is bubbly.

- 4 stalks celery, sliced
- 2 bay leaves
- 1 tsp (5 mL) dried thyme
- ½ tsp (2 mL) chili powder
- ½ tsp (2 mL) salt
- ½ tsp (2 mL) pepper
- ½ tsp (2 mL) dried oregano
- ¼ tsp (1 mL) cayenne
- One 28-oz (796 mL) can tomatoes (undrained), chopped
- 2 cups (500 mL) beef stock
- 2 cups (500 mL) parboiled long-grain rice
- 6 green onions, sliced
- 12 large shrimp, peeled and deveined

MAKE-AHEAD JAMBALAYA

Oven-Fried Golden Crisp Chicken Legs

MAKES 4 SERVINGS

This is my favourite everyday way to cook chicken. I always pop potatoes (and perhaps some squash) into the oven to bake alongside. Accompany with Cider-Baked Applesauce (see p. 145) and green beans. If you don't have cornmeal in the house, substitute with an additional ¼ cup (60 mL) of all-purpose flour.

- 1 Tbsp (15 mL) butter
- 1 Tbsp (15 mL) canola oil
- ¼ cup (60 mL) all-purpose flour
- ¼ cup (60 mL) cornmeal
- 2 tsp (10 mL) paprika
- ¼ tsp (1 mL) salt
- ¼ tsp (1 mL) pepper
- ½ cup (125 mL) milk
- 4 chicken legs
- 2 Tbsp (30 mL) fresh lemon juice

IN A 13 × 9–inch (3.5 L) baking dish, melt the butter with the oil in a 375°F (190°C) oven; tilt the dish to evenly coat the bottom.

In a plastic bag, combine the flour, cornmeal, paprika, salt and pepper. Pour the milk into a shallow dish. Shake the chicken in the flour mixture, dip in the milk, then shake again in the flour mixture.

Place the chicken, skin side down, in the baking dish; drizzle with the lemon juice. Bake for 20 minutes; turn the chicken over. Bake for 20 to 25 minutes longer, or until the juices run clear when the chicken is pierced.

VARIATION *Sesame Oven-Fried Chicken*
Substitute sesame seeds for the cornmeal.

Make-Ahead Mediterranean Party Chicken with Saffron

MAKES 8 SERVINGS

This sunny French dish with Mediterranean flavours is perfect for casual entertaining, and even better after reheating. Serve with noodles, rice or just good crusty bread and a green salad.

CUT THE CHICKENS into serving pieces and pat dry; season with salt and pepper to taste.

In a heavy casserole, heat half of the oil over medium-high heat; brown the chicken in batches, adding more oil as necessary. Remove the chicken and keep warm.

Pour off all but 2 Tbsp (30 mL) pan drippings; cook the bacon, onions and garlic over medium heat, stirring, for 3 to 4 minutes or until the onion is softened. Do not let the garlic brown.

Sprinkle with the saffron; pour in the wine and cook over medium-high heat, stirring often, for about 5 minutes or until most of the wine has evaporated. Stir in the tomatoes, stock, half of the parsley, the anchovy paste, bay leaves, thyme, cayenne and orange zest.

Return the chicken to the pan and bring to a boil; reduce heat and simmer, covered, for 20 to 30 minutes or until the chicken is no longer pink inside and the juices run clear when the chicken is pierced. Remove the chicken; cover and keep warm.

Increase heat and boil the sauce until it reaches the desired thickness, about 15 minutes. Remove and discard the orange zest and bay leaves. Stir in the olives; taste and adjust seasoning.

Return the chicken to the pot and warm through if serving immediately. (Or, cover and refrigerate overnight, then reheat gently in the sauce.) Garnish with the remaining parsley to serve.

- 2 large chickens (fryers or roasters, 3 to 4 lb/ 1.5 to 2 kg each)
- Salt and pepper
- 2 Tbsp (30 mL) olive oil (approx.)
- 1 cup (250 mL) diced bacon
- 2 onions, chopped
- 12 cloves garlic, minced
- Pinch crumbled saffron
- 1 cup (250 mL) dry white wine
- Two 28-oz (796 mL) cans plum tomatoes, drained and chopped
- 2 cups (500 mL) chicken stock
- ⅓ cup (75 mL) finely chopped fresh parsley, divided
- 2 tsp (10 mL) anchovy paste
- 2 bay leaves
- ½ tsp (2 mL) dried thyme
- ¼ tsp (1 mL) cayenne pepper
- 2 strips (3 × 1 inch/ 8 × 2.5 cm) orange zest
- 30 good-quality pitted black olives

Mustard-Baked Chicken

MAKES 6 TO 8 SERVINGS

This quick and delicious chicken dish can be prepared early in the morning, then covered and refrigerated. If you wish, use one chicken, cut up, instead of breasts. In that case, you may have to bake the dish longer and turn the pieces halfway through baking.

- 8 bone-in, skin-on chicken breast halves (about 4½ lb/1.8 kg total)
- ¼ cup (60 mL) fresh lemon juice
- ¼ cup (60 mL) Dijon mustard
- 2 Tbsp (30 mL) butter, softened
- 2 cloves garlic, minced
- 1 tsp (5 mL) dried marjoram
- 1 tsp (5 mL) paprika

WIPE THE BREASTS dry; arrange in a single layer, skin side up, in a shallow baking dish.

Stir together the lemon juice, mustard, butter, garlic, marjoram and paprika; spread over the chicken. Bake, uncovered, in a 375°F (190°C) oven basting once or twice, for about 40 minutes or until no longer pink inside. Serve with the pan juices.

Pork

Maple Apricot Chops

....

MAKES 4 SERVINGS

When I want something easy but a bit special, I put these in the oven. Serve with a wild and white rice mixture and lemony green beans.

- 12 dried apricots
- ½ cup (125 mL) warm water
- 4 pork chops (loin or shoulder)
- Salt and pepper
- ½ tsp (2 mL) dried thyme
- ⅓ cup (75 mL) maple syrup

SOAK THE APRICOTS in the warm water for 20 minutes.

Meanwhile, remove any fat from the chops and render it in a large ovenproof skillet over medium-high heat to coat the pan well; discard the solid fat. Brown the chops on both sides; sprinkle with salt and pepper to taste.

Sprinkle the chops with the thyme; top with the apricots, reserving the soaking liquid. Stir the maple syrup into the liquid; pour around the chops in the pan.

Cover and bake in a 350°F (180°C) oven for 35 minutes. Uncover and bake for 10 minutes longer, or until the chops are tender.

Pork Medallions in a Double-Mustard Sauce

....

MAKES 4 SERVINGS

Serve this easy-but-impressive sauté with buttered fettuccine, green beans and tiny glazed carrots.

- 1½ lb (750 g) pork tenderloin
- Salt and pepper
- All-purpose flour
- 2 Tbsp (30 mL) butter, cut in bits, divided
- 1 Tbsp (15 mL) canola oil
- 3 Tbsp (45 mL) white wine vinegar
- ¾ cup (175 mL) chicken stock
- ½ cup (125 mL) whipping cream

CUT THE TENDERLOIN into ¾-inch (2 cm) thick slices; flatten between 2 sheets of waxed paper until ½ inch (1 cm) thick. Sprinkle with salt and pepper to taste and dust with flour.

- 2 Tbsp (30 mL) Dijon mustard
- Pinch dry mustard
- Watercress

In a large skillet, melt half of the butter with the oil over medium heat. Cook the pork, in 2 batches, for 4 to 5 minutes per side or until golden and tender, turning once. Transfer to a heated platter and keep warm.

Add the vinegar to the pan; bring to a boil, stirring to scrape up any brown bits in the pan. Add the stock and cream; simmer, stirring, for 5 minutes or until thickened.

Remove from heat; gradually stir in the remaining butter. Gradually blend in the Dijon and dry mustards. Taste and adjust seasoning. Spoon over the pork; garnish with watercress.

Grilled Basil Cream Pork Chops

....

MAKES 4 TO 6 SERVINGS

Cover pork chops with fresh basil and marinate them in a little cream for wonderfully moist, flavourful meat. Serve with buttered new potatoes, tiny fresh green beans and sliced tomatoes.

- 6 pork loin chops, 1-inch (2.5 cm) thick
- ¼ cup (60 mL) chopped fresh basil (or 2 Tbsp/30 mL dried)
- ¼ tsp (1 mL) pepper
- ¼ cup (60 mL) whipping cream

RUB THE PORK chops with the basil until well coated; sprinkle with the pepper.

Arrange the chops in a single layer in a plastic bag and place in a shallow dish. Pour the cream into the bag and over the chops, turning to coat well. Close the bag and let stand at room temperature for 30 minutes, turning occasionally. (Or, refrigerate for at least 4 hours, or overnight; remove from the refrigerator 30 minutes before grilling.)

Place the chops on a greased medium-temperature grill, or 5 inches (12 cm) from medium-hot coals; grill, turning frequently, for about 20 minutes or until the meat is tender and only slightly pink inside.

One-Dish Mexican Pasta and Pork Chops

MAKES 4 SERVINGS

Kids will love this easy pork chop casserole. Serve it right away or make it ahead of time for an instant answer when everyone rushes home asking "what's for supper?" If the chops are small, you might like to use six instead of four.

- 2 Tbsp (30 mL) canola oil, divided
- 1 onion, chopped
- 1 sweet green pepper, diced
- 2 cloves garlic, minced
- One 19-oz (540 mL) can tomatoes (undrained)
- 1 Tbsp (15 mL) chopped fresh parsley + extra sprigs for garnish
- 2 tsp (10 mL) chili powder
- 1 tsp (5 mL) ground cumin
- ½ tsp (2 mL) dried oregano
- Pinch hot pepper flakes
- 4 cups (1 L) boiling water
- ½ lb (250 g) spaghetti, broken in half
- 4 large pork chops
- Salt and pepper
- ¾ cup (175 mL) shredded Cheddar cheese

IN A LARGE saucepan, heat half of the oil over medium heat; cook the onion, green pepper and garlic for 3 minutes or until softened. Add the tomatoes, breaking them up with a fork. Stir in the chopped parsley, chili powder, cumin, oregano and hot pepper flakes.

Stir in the boiling water; bring to a boil and add the spaghetti. Reduce heat to medium-low; cover and simmer, stirring occasionally, for 20 to 25 minutes or until most of the liquid has been absorbed.

Meanwhile, trim any fat from the chops. In a large ovenproof skillet, heat the remaining oil over medium-high heat; cook the chops, without turning, for 10 minutes. Turn the chops over and sprinkle with salt and pepper to taste; cover and cook for 5 minutes longer, or until only slightly pink inside and still moist.

Remove the chops from the skillet and drain off any fat. Spread the spaghetti mixture in the skillet; top with the chops. (The recipe can be prepared to this point, cooled, covered and refrigerated for up to 6 hours. Heat, covered, in a 350°F/180°C oven for 20 minutes before continuing.) Sprinkle the cheese over the chops; bake, uncovered, in a 350°F (180°C) oven for 5 to 10 minutes or until the cheese melts. Garnish with parsley sprigs.

Sausage Skillet Dinner

MAKES 4 SERVINGS

Beer gives a simple everyday dish a special flavour. Accompany with colcannon (see p. 114) and steamed whole green beans. Follow with a warm Upside-Down Pear Gingerbread (see p. 148).

- 1 lb (500 g) farmer's sausages
- 2 cups (500 mL) boiling water
- 1 Tbsp (15 mL) canola oil
- 2 cups (500 mL) thinly sliced onions
- 1 cup (250 mL) peeled, cored and sliced apples
- 2 Tbsp (30 mL) all-purpose flour
- ½ tsp (2 mL) paprika
- 1 bottle lager or ale (11 oz/330 mL)
- 1 Tbsp (15 mL) Worcestershire sauce
- 6 peppercorns
- 1 bay leaf
- Salt

PIERCE THE SAUSAGES and pour boiling water over them to remove some of the fat; drain well and dry with paper towels. In a large skillet, heat the oil over medium-high heat; brown the sausage and remove to a warm platter.

Drain off all but 3 Tbsp (45 mL) drippings; cook the onions over medium heat for 3 minutes. Add the apples and cook for another 2 minutes. With a slotted spoon, transfer the onions and apples to a platter.

Stir the flour and paprika into the pan; cook, stirring, for 2 minutes. Remove from heat and gradually stir in the beer; cook, whisking constantly, until smooth and thickened, about 5 minutes. Stir in the Worcestershire sauce, peppercorns and bay leaf.

Return the sausage, onions and apples to the pan. Cover tightly and cook over low heat for about 20 minutes or until the sausage is cooked through. Taste and add salt if necessary. Discard the bay leaf.

Barbecued Spare Ribs with Apple-Sage Glaze

MAKES 8 SERVINGS

Cook the spare ribs, apply the flavourful rub to them and make the tangy-sweet sauce a day ahead for a carefree

SAUSAGE SKILLET DINNER

barbecue. Accompany with *New-Way Old-Fashioned Potato Salad (see p. 132) and a platter of crisp raw vegetables.*

IN A LARGE saucepan, cover the ribs with water and bring to a boil; reduce heat, cover and simmer for 45 to 60 minutes or until the meat is tender. Drain well and let cool slightly.

Meanwhile, stir together the garlic, sage, dry mustard, salt and pepper; rub all over the cooked ribs. Place in a sturdy plastic bag, close and refrigerate for up to 1 day. Remove from the refrigerator 30 minutes before cooking.

In a small saucepan, stir together the apple butter, water, vinegar, Dijon mustard, horseradish, brown sugar and cayenne; bring to a boil. Reduce heat and simmer, uncovered, for 15 minutes, stirring often. (The glaze can be cooled, covered and refrigerated for up to 1 day. Reheat before continuing.)

Place the ribs on a greased grill over slow coals or on low setting; place the glaze on the side of the grill. Barbecue the ribs for 30 to 45 minutes or until heated through, turning every 10 to 15 minutes and brushing with the glaze during the last 15 minutes. Cut between the bones to serve. Serve the remaining glaze as a sauce.

- 9 lb (4 kg) meaty pork spare ribs
- 4 cloves garlic, minced
- 2 Tbsp (30 mL) minced fresh sage (or 2 tsp/ 10 mL crumbled dried)
- 1 Tbsp (15 mL) dry mustard
- ½ tsp (2 mL) salt
- ¼ tsp (1 mL) pepper
- 2 cups (500 mL) apple butter
- ½ cup (125 mL) water
- ¼ cup (60 mL) cider vinegar
- 1 Tbsp (15 mL) Dijon mustard
- 1 Tbsp (15 mL) horseradish
- 1 Tbsp (15 mL) brown sugar
- ¼ tsp (1 mL) cayenne pepper

Ginger-Grilled Pork Loin

MAKES ABOUT 8 SERVINGS

I devised this flavourful marinade many years ago and still use it when I grill pork sirloins to keep them moist as they cook.

Sirloins are the fresh form of cured back bacon and can only be found at certain farmers' markets—particularly in the Waterloo area of Ontario, where I live. Since these great cuts are not available country-wide, this recipe is for a centre loin boneless roast. If you do happen to find sirloins, cook two for eight people, omitting the searing step and grilling about one hour, turning and basting often.

- 3 Tbsp (45 mL) finely chopped fresh thyme (or 1 Tbsp/15 mL crumbled dried)
- 1 Tbsp (15 mL) dry mustard
- 1 single boneless centre-cut pork loin (about 5 lb/2.5 kg)
- ½ cup (125 mL) green ginger wine (see note)
- ½ cup (125 mL) low-sodium soy sauce
- ¼ cup (60 mL) canola oil
- 3 large cloves garlic, crushed

IN A SMALL bowl or mortar, crush together the thyme and mustard with the tip of a spoon or pestle to form a paste; rub all over the pork.

Place the pork in a plastic bag set in a shallow dish. Stir together the wine, soy sauce, oil and garlic. Remove ¼ cup (60 mL), cover and refrigerate for brushing on later. Pour the remainder into the bag, over the pork. Seal the bag and turn to coat the meat well; refrigerate several hours or overnight, turning occasionally. Remove from the refrigerator 30 minutes before cooking.

Remove the pork and pat dry with a paper towel. Discard the marinade in the bag. Sear the pork on a greased high-temperature grill, or 4 inches (10 cm) from medium-hot coals. Grill, turning often, for 15 minutes.

Raise the grill 2 inches (5 cm) or reduce setting to medium. Cover with the lid or tent the pork with foil; grill, turning often and basting occasionally with the reserved marinade, for about 2 hours or until a meat thermometer inserted in the thickest part registers 160°F (70°C) and the juices run clear. (If cooking on a rotisserie, omit the searing and baste often.)

Transfer the roast to a carving board; cover loosely with foil and let stand for 10 minutes before slicing thinly.

NOTE Green ginger wine is available from a liquor store.

Currant-Glazed Company Pork Roast

MAKES 8 SERVINGS

For an elegant company meal, accompany this succulent roast with scalloped potatoes (see p. 116), Gingered Squash and Pear Purée (see p. 120) and Simple Garlic-Sautéed Green Beans (see p. 121).

IN A SMALL bowl, stir together the mustard, basil and pepper, crushing the basil finely with the back of a spoon. Stir in half of the sherry and half of the soy sauce to make a runny paste. Add the garlic.

Place the pork on a rack in a shallow roasting pan; spread the paste all over the roast. Cover and refrigerate for at least 2 hours, or up to 6 hours. Remove from the refrigerator 30 minutes before cooking.

- 1 tsp (5 mL) dry mustard
- 1 tsp (5 mL) crumbled dried basil
- ¼ tsp (1 mL) pepper
- 2 Tbsp (30 mL) dry sherry, divided
- 2 Tbsp (30 mL) soy sauce
- 2 cloves garlic, crushed
- 1 boneless double pork loin, rolled and tied (4 lb/2 kg)
- ¼ cup (60 mL) red currant jelly
- 1 cup + 2 Tbsp (280 mL) cold water, divided
- 1 Tbsp (15 mL) cornstarch

Roast the pork, uncovered, in a 325°F (160°C) oven for about 2 hours, or until a meat thermometer registers 160°F (70°C).

Meanwhile, in a small saucepan, stir together the remaining sherry and soy sauce with the red currant jelly; heat over medium heat, stirring, until the jelly melts. Spoon some of the mixture over the meat 2 or 3 times during the last 30 minutes of roasting.

Remove the pork to a carving board; cover loosely with foil and let stand for 10 minutes before carving.

Remove and discard any excess fat from the pan. Stir in about 1 cup (250 mL) water and bring to a boil, stirring to scrape up any brown bits from the bottom of the pan. Stir the cornstarch with 2 Tbsp (30 mL) cold water; add to the pan, stirring constantly, and cook over medium heat until smooth and thickened. Pass in a heated sauceboat with the pork.

Splendid Baked Glazed Ham

MAKES ABOUT 10 SERVINGS

"Fully cooked" smoked hams are greatly improved by a short cooking time to finish them off. A spicy fruit-honey mixture goes on for the last few minutes to give a seductive and delicious glaze to a ham that would be a perfect focus to any festive dinner table. Accompany with a mustard sauce, Sweet Potato Party Flan (see p. 118) and Three-Ingredient Creamy Coleslaw (see p. 136).

WITH A SHARP knife, remove any rind and excess fat from the ham. Place, fat side up, on a rack in a shallow pan.

With a sharp knife, score the outside layer of fat diagonally in both directions to make 2-inch (5 cm) diamonds. Do not cut too deeply. Insert whole cloves at the corners or in the centre of the diamonds. Bake in a 325°F (160°C) oven for 2 to 2½ hours, or until a meat thermometer registers 130°F (55°C).

- 1 fully cooked bone-in smoked ham (about 7½ lb/3.3 kg)
- Whole cloves
- ½ cup (125 mL) peach or apricot jam
- ¼ cup (60 mL) liquid honey
- 2 Tbsp (30 mL) fresh lemon juice
- 1 Tbsp (15 mL) cornstarch
- ¼ tsp (1 mL) ground cloves
- Pinch cinnamon

Meanwhile, in a small saucepan, stir together the jam, honey, lemon juice, cornstarch, cloves and cinnamon; bring to a boil over medium heat, stirring. During the last 30 minutes of cooking the ham, spoon some of the glaze onto the ham 2 or 3 times until all the glaze is used, basting with pan juices too.

Harvest Pork Stew

MAKES 6 TO 8 SERVINGS

This flavourful stew would be good company fare with crusty bread and a crisp green salad. Oven-browning the meat is not only easier but cuts down considerably on fat in the recipe.

IN A PAPER bag or bowl, toss the pork with the flour, salt and pepper. Spread the pork in a big shallow pan; roast in a 500°F (260°C) oven for about 15 minutes or until browned, stirring occasionally. Remove and reduce the oven temperature to 350°F (180°C).

Meanwhile, in a large Dutch oven or flameproof casserole, combine the wine, stock, garlic, red pepper, mustard, vinegar, sage, thyme, rutabaga and apples; bring to a boil. Add the browned meat; cover and return to a boil.

Transfer to the oven and bake, stirring occasionally, until the meat is fork-tender, about 1½ hours. Taste and adjust seasoning. Sprinkle with parsley to serve.

- 3 lb (1.5 kg) lean pork, cut into 1½-inch (4 cm) cubes
- ¼ cup (60 mL) all-purpose flour
- ½ tsp (2 mL) salt
- ¼ tsp (1 mL) pepper
- 1 cup (250 mL) dry white wine
- 1 cup (250 mL) chicken stock
- 12 cloves garlic, peeled
- 1 large sweet red pepper, finely diced
- 1 Tbsp (15 mL) Dijon mustard
- 1 Tbsp (15 mL) cider vinegar
- ½ tsp (2 mL) crushed dried sage
- ½ tsp (2 mL) dried thyme
- Half a rutabaga, peeled and cut into ¾-inch (2 cm) cubes
- 2 apples, peeled and thickly sliced
- Chopped fresh parsley

Impressive Chilled Pork Tenderloin Stuffed with Pistachio Nuts and Fruit

···

MAKES 4 TO 6 SERVINGS

This elegant make-ahead meat course is attractive to look at and delicious to taste. Serve with marinated asparagus and crusty French bread.

IN A SMALL bowl, combine the wine and dried fruits; set aside.

Slice the meat lengthwise through half its thickness; open like a book and flatten with the edge of a cleaver. Rub with the cut side of the garlic; set aside.

In a large skillet, melt the butter over medium heat; cook the onion and celery for 3 minutes or until softened (mincing and adding the garlic halves if desired). Remove from heat; stir in the bread, nuts, parsley, thyme, sage and salt and pepper to taste. Drain the fruits, reserving the wine; stir the fruits into the bread mixture.

Spread the stuffing evenly over the meat; roll up the meat. Using a trussing or darning needle and thin cord, sew all the edges of the meat closed. Place, seam side down, on a rack in a shallow roasting pan; brush with the mustard. Sprinkle with ½ tsp (2 mL) curry powder and salt and pepper to taste. Pour in the reserved wine. Roast, uncovered, in a 350°F (180°C) oven for 40 to 50 minutes, or until a meat thermometer registers 160°F (70°C), basting with pan juices and sprinkling with ½ tsp (2 mL) of the remaining curry powder twice during the roasting. Remove to a plate and let cool in the refrigerator until the steaming stops. Wrap tightly in foil and refrigerate overnight.

To serve, remove the cord; carve into thin slices and arrange on a platter garnished with watercress.

- ½ cup (125 mL) dry white wine or white grape juice
- ¼ cup (60 mL) chopped dried mixed fruits
- 2 lb (1 kg) pork tenderloin
- 1 small clove garlic, cut in half
- 2 Tbsp (30 mL) butter
- 2 Tbsp (30 mL) minced onion
- 2 Tbsp (30 mL) diced celery
- ½ cup (125 mL) finely diced stale bread
- 2 Tbsp (30 mL) coarsely chopped pistachios
- 2 Tbsp (30 mL) chopped fresh parsley
- ¼ tsp (1 mL) dried thyme
- Pinch dried sage
- Salt and pepper
- 2 tsp (10 mL) Dijon mustard
- 1½ tsp (7 mL) curry powder, divided
- Watercress

Beer-Glazed Picnic Shoulder

···

MAKES 6 TO 8 SERVINGS

This easy smoked picnic shoulder is delicious served hot. Barbecue foil packets of sliced potatoes and onions to serve along with green peas that have been cooked in the kitchen or on a side element on the barbecue. Any leftover meat is good served cold in sandwiches.

- ⅔ cup (150 mL) packed brown sugar
- ¼ tsp (1 mL) ground cloves
- 1 boneless fully cooked smoked picnic shoulder (3 lb/1.5 kg)
- ½ cup (125 mL) beer
- 1 Tbsp (15 mL) all-purpose flour
- 1 Tbsp (15 mL) dry mustard
- 2 Tbsp (30 mL) white vinegar

IN A SMALL bowl, stir together the brown sugar and cloves. Place the picnic shoulder on a piece of heavy-duty foil large enough to enclose it, set in a foil pan. Press half the sugar mixture on top and drizzle with the beer.

Wrap the meat completely with the foil and set the pan on a medium high–temperature grill, or over medium-hot coals. Cover with the barbecue lid and cook for 1 hour, turning the wrapped meat once.

Meanwhile, stir the flour and mustard into the remaining sugar mixture. Blend in the vinegar. Set aside for the glaze.

Remove the ham from the foil and pan and place right on the greased grill. Brush with some of the glaze and cook another 15 minutes, brushing often with the glaze and turning once.

Easy Pork Scaloppine with Fresh Red Pepper Relish

MAKES 4 SERVINGS

Where I live, all the local taverns feature pork schnitzel as one of their specialties. It's traditionally served with applesauce and sauerkraut—two great accompaniments if you don't have a red pepper on hand. This relish, however, is a bright, fresh tart-sweet sauce that particularly complements the meat. It would also go along happily with veal, chicken or turkey scaloppine if you cooked them like this. The relish can be made ahead and reheated.

RED PEPPER RELISH

- 1 Tbsp (15 mL) olive oil
- 1 large sweet red pepper, finely diced
- 1 clove garlic, minced
- ¼ cup (60 mL) red wine vinegar
- 2 tsp (10 mL) granulated sugar
- Salt and pepper
- 1 Tbsp (15 mL) chopped fresh parsley

PORK SCALOPPINE

- 1 lb (500 g) pork cutlets
- Salt and pepper
- ¼ cup (60 mL) all-purpose flour
- 2 eggs
- ¾ cup (175 mL) dry breadcrumbs
- 2 Tbsp (30 mL) canola oil (approx.)
- Lemon wedges

RED PEPPER RELISH In a small skillet, heat the oil over medium heat and cook the red pepper for 7 to 10 minutes, or until softened. Stir in the garlic, vinegar, sugar and salt and pepper to taste; bring to a boil. Reduce heat and simmer, uncovered and stirring often, for 10 minutes or until thickened. Stir in the parsley.

PORK SCALOPPINE Meanwhile, if the cutlets are not already thin, pound them as thinly as possible between 2 pieces of waxed paper. Sprinkle with salt and pepper to taste; dust with the flour.

With a fork, beat the eggs in a shallow dish. Place the crumbs on waxed paper. Dip the floured cutlets in the egg, then coat well with crumbs. (The cutlets can be covered and refrigerated for up to 3 hours. Remove from the refrigerator 30 minutes before cooking.)

In a large skillet, heat the oil over medium-high heat; cook the cutlets in batches, adding more oil if necessary, for about 2 minutes per side or until golden brown, turning once. Place on paper towels. Serve immediately with lemon wedges and the Red Pepper Relish.

Maple-Glazed Back Bacon

MAKES 8 SERVINGS

For a special brunch, a glazed roast of back bacon is a nice change from baked ham, especially with this tangy glaze.

Accompany with a crisp green salad and poached eggs on toasted French bread. It's also great for a family supper with scalloped potatoes (see p. 116) and green peas. Any leftovers make nice sandwiches.

PLACE THE BACON on a rack in a small shallow roasting pan or baking dish. Pour the boiling water into the pan and roast, uncovered, in a 325°F (160°C) oven for 1½ hours.

- 1 back bacon roast (3 lb/1.5 kg)
- ½ cup (125 mL) boiling water
- ½ cup (125 mL) maple syrup
- 2 Tbsp (30 mL) all-purpose flour
- 1 Tbsp (15 mL) Dijon mustard
- 1 Tbsp (15 mL) fresh lemon juice
- Pinch ground cloves

In a small saucepan, stir together the maple syrup, flour, mustard, lemon juice and cloves; bring to a boil over medium heat, stirring constantly. Pour and spread over the bacon; roast for 20 minutes longer, basting occasionally with the glaze until the meat is tender and nicely glazed. (For a darker glaze, increase the oven temperature to 375°F/190°C for the last 20 minutes of baking.) Remove from the oven and cover loosely with foil; let stand for a few minutes before carving.

Beef and Veal

....

Sassy Skillet Shepherd's Pie

MAKES 3 OR 4 SERVINGS

On a cold night, don't you sometimes yearn for a steaming, comforting helping of old-fashioned shepherd's pie? This one, which cooks in a matter of minutes on top of the stove, uses raw ground beef instead of left-over roast beef, but it still relies on mashed potatoes left over from the night before. Roasted red peppers are available in jars in most supermarkets.

- 2 tsp (10 mL) canola oil
- 1 onion, chopped
- 1 lb (500 g) lean ground beef
- ⅔ cup (150 mL) beef stock
- 2 Tbsp (30 mL) tomato paste
- 4 tsp (20 mL) chili powder
- ½ tsp (2 mL) dried oregano
- ½ tsp (2 mL) ground cumin
- One 10-oz (284 mL) can kernel corn, drained
- Salt and pepper
- 1 cup (250 mL) coarsely diced roasted red peppers
- 3 cups (750 mL) mashed potatoes
- ¼ cup (60 mL) milk
- 1 egg

IN A 10-INCH (25 cm) oven-proof skillet, heat the oil over medium heat; cook the onion for 3 minutes. Add the beef, breaking it up with a spoon; cook for 5 minutes or until browned. Drain off any fat.

Stir in the beef stock, tomato paste, chili powder, oregano, cumin and corn; cook for 5 minutes. Season with salt and pepper to taste. Spread out in the pan evenly; sprinkle with the roasted red peppers.

Beat the potatoes with the milk and egg; spoon over the meat mixture. Place in the bottom third of the oven and broil for 7 to 8 minutes or until the potatoes are golden.

Oven-Baked Party Beef Stew

MAKES 8 TO 10 SERVINGS

Serve this flavourful make-ahead beef dish with Three-Ingredient Creamy Coleslaw (see p. 136) and a full-bodied red wine.

IN A LARGE heavy skillet, heat half of the oil over medium-high heat; cook the onions, carrots, celery, mushrooms and garlic until the onions are golden brown, about 5 minutes. With a slotted spoon, remove the vegetables to a large bowl.

Trim and cut the meat into 1-inch (2.5 cm) cubes. In a plastic bag, combine the flour, salt and pepper. In batches, shake the cubes in the flour mixture, then brown in the skillet, adding remaining oil as needed. Transfer to a separate bowl.

Add any remaining flour mixture to the skillet; cook, stirring, until browned. Gradually stir in the hot stock, stirring to scrape up any brown bits from the bottom of the pan; bring to a boil. Stir in the wine, tomato paste, vinegar, Worcestershire sauce and bay leaves. Taste and adjust seasoning.

In a 12-cup (3 L) casserole, layer the meat and vegetables alternately; pour the sauce over everything while still hot. Cover and bake in a 300°F (150°C) oven for 3 hours or until the beef is very tender. Remove and discard the bay leaves. (The stew can be prepared to this point and refrigerated or frozen; thaw in the refrigerator before proceeding, and heat in a 350°F/180°C oven for 20 minutes before adding the crust.)

- ¼ cup (60 mL) canola oil (approx.), divided
- 10 small pearl onions
- 8 carrots, quartered
- 4 stalks celery, cut into large pieces
- ½ lb (250 g) small button mushrooms
- 2 large cloves garlic, minced
- 2½ lb (1.25 kg) lean boneless beef
- ⅓ cup (75 mL) all-purpose flour
- ½ tsp (2 mL) salt
- ½ tsp (2 mL) pepper
- 2½ cups (625 mL) hot beef stock or consommé
- ⅔ cup (150 mL) dry red wine
- 2 Tbsp (30 mL) tomato paste
- 2 Tbsp (30 mL) tarragon vinegar
- 2 Tbsp (30 mL) Worcestershire sauce
- 2 bay leaves

PIQUANT CRUST

- ¼ cup (60 mL) unsalted butter
- 3 large cloves garlic, minced
- French bread slices (½-inch/1 cm thick) to cover casserole
- 1 Tbsp (15 mL) Dijon Mustard

SASSY SKILLET SHEPHERD'S PIE

PIQUANT CRUST In a large skillet, melt the butter over low heat; stir in the garlic. Spread the bread with the mustard and arrange in the garlic butter. Heat gradually, turning the slices over, until the butter is absorbed; arrange on top of the baked stew. Bake, uncovered, in a 350°F (180°C) oven for about 30 minutes or until the stew is bubbly and the crust is golden.

Super Easy One-Dish Spaghetti

MAKES ABOUT 4 SERVINGS

Family supper couldn't be easier or better. Everyone's favourite meal cooks in one pot. My friend Jean Medley made it often for her family, but she called it "Glop." Enjoy with a green salad and crusty bread.

IN A LARGE deep skillet or shallow Dutch oven, combine the beef, garlic, basil, oregano, paprika, sugar, salt, pepper and hot pepper flakes; cook over medium heat, breaking up the beef with a wooden spoon, for about 5 minutes or until browned.

Stir in the water, tomato sauce, tomatoes, parsley and ¼ cup (60 mL) of the Parmesan cheese; bring to a boil, breaking up the tomatoes with a spoon. Reduce heat; cover and simmer for 45 minutes. (The recipe can be prepared to this point, covered and refrigerated or frozen. Bring to a simmer before continuing.)

Stir in the spaghetti, making sure all the pasta is covered with sauce. Cover and simmer, stirring

- 1 lb (500 g) lean ground beef
- 1 clove garlic, minced
- 1 tsp (5 mL) dried basil
- 1 tsp (5 mL) oregano
- 1 tsp (5 mL) paprika
- 1 tsp (5 mL) granulated sugar
- ½ tsp (2 mL) salt
- ¼ tsp (1 mL) pepper
- ¼ tsp (1 mL) hot pepper flakes
- 2 cups (500 mL) water
- One 14-oz (398 mL) can tomato sauce
- One 14-oz (398 mL) can tomatoes (undrained)
- ¼ cup (60 mL) chopped fresh parsley
- ¾ cup (175 mL) freshly grated Parmesan cheese (approx.), divided
- ½ lb (250 g) spaghetti, broken

occasionally, for 10 to 15 minutes or until the pasta is tender but firm. Serve in bowls. Serve the remaining Parmesan cheese separately.

Beef Cheese Casserole

MAKES 8 SERVINGS

Everyone loves lasagna, but there isn't always time to make it. This easy casserole, somewhat like lasagna in flavour, can be prepared ahead, then reheated. Serve with crusty Italian bread and a salad of Romaine lettuce and avocado with lemon vinaigrette.

IN A LARGE skillet over medium-high heat, cook the beef and half of the onions until the beef is browned, breaking up the meat with a spoon. Drain off any fat.

Stir in the tomato sauce, basil and salt and pepper to taste; simmer, uncovered, over medium-low heat for 15 minutes.

- 2 lb (1 kg) lean ground beef
- 2 large onions, chopped, divided
- One 14-oz (398 mL) can tomato sauce
- 1 tsp (5 mL) dried basil
- Salt and pepper
- ½ lb (250 g) uncooked broad egg noodles (about 6 cups/1.5 L), divided
- ¾ lb (375 g) mozzarella cheese, cubed (about 3½ cups/875 mL)
- 1 sweet green pepper, chopped
- ½ cup (125 mL) sour cream or plain yogurt
- ¾ cup (175 mL) freshly grated Parmesan cheese

Meanwhile, in a saucepan of boiling water, cook the noodles until tender but firm; drain well.

Combine the mozzarella cheese, green pepper, sour cream and remaining chopped onion; set aside.

In a greased 12-cup (3 L) shallow casserole, spread half of the noodles. Top with the mozzarella mixture, then half of the meat mixture. Cover with the remaining noodles; top with the remaining meat mixture. Sprinkle with the Parmesan cheese. (The recipe can be covered and refrigerated for up to 6 hours. Remove from the refrigerator 30 minutes before cooking.)

Bake, covered, in a 350°F (180°C) oven for about 30 minutes or until hot and bubbly.

ONE-POT FAMILY SUPPERS

....

As time goes on, I find myself preparing simpler food both for family meals and when entertaining. I don't rely on sodium- or chemical-laden mixes, nor do I think that everything that comes out of a microwave oven is marvellous. (Mind you, it's great for countless things and will make life much easier if you have one.) I don't know why everyone wants something quick. Quick is good, but easy is great.

I prefer a long-simmering or roasted meal in the oven or on top of the stove—one that I can pop in and forget about while I read the paper. I guess I don't care how long it takes to cook as long as it's easy to make.

There's a certain satisfaction, too, in cooking sturdy, real food in your own kitchen, rather than heading for the nearest fast food establishment or running to the telephone to order in. Food that simmers for a long time on the stove is a comfortable kind of cooking, a soothing escape from the pressures of life.

I particularly like one-pot suppers. They're very easy to prepare and to serve, both to family and to good friends.

Almost-Cabbage-Rolls Casserole

MAKES 4 TO 6 SERVINGS

With the flavour of cabbage rolls but a fraction of the work, this easy casserole is delicious served with sour cream on the side.

- 1 lb (500 g) lean ground beef
- ¾ cup (175 mL) long-grain rice
- 1 large onion, chopped
- 2 cloves garlic, minced
- ½ tsp (2 mL) salt
- ¼ tsp (1 mL) pepper
- One 28-oz (796 mL) can tomato sauce
- ¼ cup (60 mL) apple cider vinegar
- 2 Tbsp (30 mL) packed brown sugar
- 1 Tbsp (15 mL) dry mustard
- 1 tsp (5 mL) Worcestershire sauce
- 8 cups (2 L) coarsely chopped cabbage (half a head), divided

IN A LARGE bowl, mix together the beef, rice, onion, garlic, salt and pepper. In a small bowl, stir together the tomato sauce, vinegar, brown sugar, mustard and Worcestershire sauce.

Layer one-third of the cabbage in a 12-cup (3 L) deep casserole. Cover with one-third of the tomato sauce. Arrange half of the beef mixture on top. Cover with another one-third of the cabbage. Cover with another one-third of the sauce. Top with the remaining beef mixture and the remaining cabbage.

Pour the remaining tomato sauce mixture overtop, but do not stir. (The casserole will be quite full.) Cover and let stand at room temperature for 20 minutes. Bake in a 325°F (160°C) oven for 2 hours, without stirring.

New-Style Peppery Pot Roast

MAKES 6 TO 8 SERVINGS

Pour a thin liquid mixture over a beef roast, add a few vegetables and everything roasts to a comforting one-dish meal—with the added bonus of an intriguing sauce, no added fat and very little effort. Use homemade or canned stock, not powdered concentrate.

- 1 chuck or blade beef roast (4 lb/2 kg)
- One 28-oz (796 mL) can tomato sauce
- 2½ cups (625 mL) beef stock
- 1 cup (250 mL) dry red wine
- ¼ cup (60 mL) low-sodium soy sauce
- 2 Tbsp (30 mL) packed brown sugar
- 2 bay leaves
- ½ tsp (2 mL) hot pepper flakes
- ½ tsp (2 mL) pepper
- 1 whole head garlic, separated into cloves and peeled
- 1 butternut squash, peeled and cut into large pieces
- 6 to 8 potatoes, peeled
- 6 to 8 wedges green cabbage

PLACE THE ROAST in a very large roasting pan. In a large bowl, stir together the tomato sauce, beef stock, wine, soy sauce, sugar, bay leaves, hot pepper flakes and pepper; pour over the roast. Add the garlic. Cover and roast in a 325°F (160°C) oven for 1½ hours.

Add the squash, potatoes and cabbage; cover and roast for 1 to 1½ hours, or until the meat and vegetables are very tender. Remove the meat and vegetables to a heated platter; cover and set aside to keep warm.

Remove the bay leaves. Boil the liquid in the pan until desired consistency for the sauce is reached, 5 to 10 minutes. Slice the beef and serve the sauce in a heated sauceboat.

Grilled Party-Style Flank Steak with Mustard Horseradish

MAKES 4 TO 6 SERVINGS

Extremely lean flank steak should not be overlooked for both family meals and entertaining. This easy marinade renders the meat fork-tender, while adding a piquant flavour due to the large amount of pepper. Accompany with rice and steamed broccoli.

MUSTARD HORSERADISH In a small bowl, stir together the mustard and horseradish. Cover and refrigerate for up to 1 day.

STEAK Remove any membrane from the flank steak's surface. With a sharp knife, score the steak by cutting very shallow grooves on both sides. Rub the cut side of the garlic all over the steak; reserve the garlic. Sprinkle the steak all over with the pepper; lay flat in a shallow dish.

In a small bowl, combine the sherry, soy sauce, oil, lemon juice and ginger. Mince the reserved garlic and add to the mixture; pour over the meat. Cover and refrigerate for at least 3 hours, or overnight. Remove from the refrigerator about 30 minutes before cooking.

Broil the meat 3 inches (8 cm) from high heat, or barbecue on a greased high-temperature grill or 4 inches (10 cm) from hot coals, turning only once, for 3 to 5 minutes per side for rare meat. Don't overcook. Slice thinly across the grain on the diagonal. Serve with the Mustard Horseradish.

Mystery-Marinated Steak

MAKES 4 SERVINGS

No one will guess the source of this marinade's interesting flavour—strong coffee—but everyone will love the tender, delicious results.

SCORE BOTH SIDES of the steak at 2-inch (5 cm) intervals; place in a sturdy plastic bag. Add the onion and garlic.

Stir together the coffee, soy sauce, Worcestershire sauce, vinegar, oil and pepper; pour into the bag, over the steak. Close the bag and refrigerate for at least 6 hours, or overnight. Remove from the refrigerator

MUSTARD HORSERADISH

- ¼ cup (60 mL) Dijon mustard
- ¼ cup (60 mL) well-drained prepared horseradish

STEAK

- 1½ lb (750 g) flank steak
- 1 large clove garlic, halved
- 1 tsp (5 mL) black pepper
- ⅓ cup (75 mL) dry sherry
- ¼ cup (60 mL) soy sauce
- 2 Tbsp (30 mL) canola oil
- 4 tsp (20 mL) fresh lemon juice
- 1 Tbsp (15 mL) minced fresh ginger

30 minutes before grilling.

Place the steak on a greased medium high–temperature grill, or 4 inches (10 cm) from medium-hot coals; grill for 4 to 6 minutes per side or until rare. Do not overcook. Meanwhile, heat the marinade in a small saucepan on the grill or side barbecue element for 5 minutes.

Transfer the steak to a cutting board and pour the marinade overtop; tent with foil and let stand for 5 minutes. Thinly slice on the diagonal.

Everybody's Favourite Classic Chili

MAKES 6 TO 8 SERVINGS

Everyone loves robust chili in which red kidney seems to be the classic bean.

IN A LARGE saucepan, heat the oil over medium heat; cook the mushrooms for 5 minutes. Remove with a slotted spoon and set aside.

Add the beef, celery, onion and green pepper; cook over high heat, stirring to break up the beef, until the meat is no longer pink, about 7 minutes. Stir in the tomato sauce and 1 tomato-sauce can of water; add the tomatoes (breaking them up with a spoon), chili powder, cumin, salt, pepper, oregano, hot

- 1½ lb (750 g) flank steak
- 1 onion, chopped
- 2 cloves garlic, minced
- ½ cup (125 mL) strong brewed coffee
- ⅓ cup (75 mL) low-sodium soy sauce
- 1 Tbsp (15 mL) Worcestershire sauce
- 1 Tbsp (15 mL) cider vinegar
- 1 Tbsp (15 mL) canola oil
- ½ tsp (2 mL) pepper

- 1 Tbsp (15 mL) canola oil
- ½ lb (250 g) small button mushrooms
- 2 lb (1 kg) lean ground beef
- 2 stalks celery, sliced
- 1 large onion, chopped
- 1 sweet green pepper, diced
- One 7½-oz (213 mL) can tomato sauce
- One 19-oz (540 mL) can tomatoes (undrained)
- 1 Tbsp (15 mL) chili powder
- 1 tsp (5 mL) ground cumin
- ½ tsp (2 mL) salt
- ½ tsp (2 mL) pepper
- ½ tsp (2 mL) dried oregano
- ½ tsp (2 mL) hot pepper flakes
- ¼ tsp (1 mL) cayenne pepper

CHILI CHEESEBURGERS

pepper flakes, cayenne and garlic.

Return the mushrooms and any accumulated liquid to the pan; stir in the beans. Bring to a boil; reduce heat and simmer, covered, for 1 hour, stirring occasionally. Taste and adjust seasoning if necessary. (The chili can be refrigerated immediately and slowly reheated the next day. Or, cool in the refrigerator and freeze for up to 3 months.)

- 2 cloves garlic, minced
- Two 19-oz (540 mL) cans red kidney beans (undrained)

Chili Cheeseburgers

Keep the cheese in the centre of these big juicy patties by sealing the meat around the edges and chilling well. Serve open face–style on top of crispy fried tortillas and sprinkle with additional grated cheese, slivers of hot pepper, chopped lettuce and a dollop of sour cream, guacamole or taco sauce. You can also present the patties on toasted kaiser rolls with all the traditional trimmings.

- 1½ lb (750 g) ground beef
- 2 Tbsp (30 mL) minced onion
- 2 Tbsp (30 mL) ketchup
- 1 Tbsp (15 mL) chili powder
- ½ tsp (2 mL) salt
- ½ tsp (2 mL) dried oregano
- 1 egg
- 1 cup (250 mL) shredded mild Cheddar cheese
- 1 Tbsp (15 mL) diced jalapeño pepper (pickled or fresh)

IN A LARGE bowl, combine the beef, onion, ketchup, chili powder, salt, oregano and egg; mix gently but well. Shape into 8 patties, ¼ inch (5 mm) thick and 5 inches (12 cm) wide.

Stir together the cheese and jalapeño pepper; mound in the centre of 4 patties. Top with the remaining patties, pressing the meat around the edges to seal well. With a spatula, arrange in a single layer on a large plate; cover with plastic wrap and refrigerate until chilled, or overnight.

Place the patties on a greased medium-temperature grill, or 4 inches (10 cm) from medium-hot coals; grill

for 7 minutes. Turn and grill for 6 to 8 minutes longer, or until no longer pink inside.

Marinated Beef and Vegetable Salad

Turn leftover grilled steak or cold roast beef into a delicious main-course make-ahead salad that will leave your kitchen cool on hot nights. It will become one of your favourite summer suppers or company lunches just as it is at our house.

- ⅓ cup (75 mL) tarragon vinegar
- 1 clove garlic, minced
- 1 tsp (5 mL) dry mustard
- ½ tsp (2 mL) Worcestershire sauce
- Salt and pepper
- ⅔ cup (150 mL) canola oil
- 1 lb (500 g) cold cooked roast beef or steak, cut into strips (about 4 cups/1 L)
- ½ lb (250 g) small mushrooms
- 2 large potatoes, cooked and cubed
- 1 cup (250 mL) sliced celery
- 8 cherry tomatoes
- 1 small red onion, thinly sliced
- 1 large dill pickle, sliced
- ½ cup (125 mL) pitted black olives
- 1 Tbsp (15 mL) chopped fresh parsley
- Lettuce leaves

IN A LARGE bowl, whisk together the vinegar, garlic, mustard, Worcestershire and salt and pepper to taste. Gradually whisk in the oil.

Add the beef, mushrooms, potatoes, celery, tomatoes, onion, pickle, olives and parsley; toss gently to coat. Cover and chill for at least 6 hours, or up to 24 hours, stirring occasionally.

To serve, line individual plates with lettuce. With a slotted spoon, mound the salad on top.

Three-Cheese Meat Loaf

Bake potatoes and squash alongside this moist, flavourful meat loaf and accompany with a spinach salad.

GREASE A 9 × 5–inch (2 L) loaf pan and sprinkle lightly with breadcrumbs.

In a large bowl, soak the bread in the milk for 5 minutes; with your hands, squeeze out any excess moisture. Break up the beef with a spoon and add to the bowl; add the onion, green pepper, Parmesan, tomato paste, parsley, egg, salt, pepper and sage; with moistened hands, mix together.

Press one-third of the meat mixture evenly into the prepared pan; sprinkle the mozzarella evenly on top. Press another one-third of the meat mixture on top; sprinkle with the Swiss cheese. Cover with the remaining meat mixture.

Bake in a 350°F (180°C) oven for about 1 hour, or until a meat thermometer registers 170°F (75°C). Slice to serve.

- Dry breadcrumbs
- 2 slices Italian-style bread, cubed
- ⅓ cup (75 mL) milk
- 1 lb (500 g) lean ground beef
- 1 small onion, chopped
- 1 sweet green pepper, chopped
- ¼ cup (60 mL) freshly grated Parmesan cheese
- 2 Tbsp (30 mL) tomato paste or ketchup
- 1 Tbsp (15 mL) chopped fresh parsley
- 1 egg, lightly beaten
- ¾ tsp (4 mL) salt
- ¼ tsp (1 mL) pepper
- ¼ tsp (1 mL) dried sage
- ½ cup (125 mL) diced mozzarella (about 3 oz/90 g)
- ½ cup (125 mL) diced Swiss cheese (about 3 oz/90 g)

Skillet Steak Stroganoff

MAKES 4 SERVINGS

Serve with egg noodles and green peas for a fast and easy supper.

IN A LARGE skillet, heat the oil over medium-high heat; cook the steak just until browned. Add the mushrooms, red pepper

- 2 Tbsp (30 mL) canola oil
- 1 lb (500 g) sirloin steak, slivered
- 2 cups (500 mL) sliced or tiny whole mushrooms
- 1 sweet red pepper, cut into small strips
- 2 cloves garlic, minced

and garlic; cook, stirring, for 4 minutes, or until the pepper is tender-crisp.

Reduce heat to low; stir in the mustard, Worcestershire sauce and sour cream. Season with salt and pepper to taste; heat through.

- 4 tsp (20 mL) Dijon mustard
- 1 Tbsp (15 mL) Worcestershire sauce
- ⅔ cup (150 mL) light sour cream
- Salt and pepper

Santa Fe Braised Short Ribs

MAKES 4 SERVINGS

Serve these crisp, spicy ribs with barbecue-roasted potatoes, corn and a green salad.

PLACE THE RIBS in a sturdy plastic bag in a shallow glass dish just big enough to hold them. Stir together the salsa, lime juice, oil, garlic and onion; pour into the bag, over the ribs. Close the bag and refrigerate for at least 2 hours, or up to 4 hours. Remove from the refrigerator 30 minutes before cooking.

- 3 lb (1.5 kg) lean beef short ribs, trimmed
- 1 cup (250 mL) hot salsa
- ½ cup (125 mL) fresh lime juice
- 1 Tbsp (15 mL) canola oil
- 2 cloves garlic, minced
- 1 small onion, finely chopped

Wrap the ribs and marinade in heavy-duty foil; place on a medium-temperature grill, or 6 inches (15 cm) from medium-hot coals. Cover the barbecue and cook, turning often, for about 1 hour or until the ribs are tender.

Remove the ribs to a greased grill, reserving the marinade in a small saucepan on the grill or side element over medium heat. Lower the grill over hot coals or increase heat to high; grill, turning and basting occasionally with the marinade, for 10 to 15 minutes or until crisp and brown on the outside. Serve any remaining sauce with the ribs.

TIMELY TIPS FOR QUICK COOKS

- If you have one, use your food processor to chop vegetables. For even results, place 1½-inch (4 cm) chunks in the work bowl and pulse three times. Scrape down the sides and pulse two or three more times.
- Grate or shred cheese in a food processor and store in the freezer.
- Chop parsley in larger quantities to have on hand for garnishing. Remove the stems and wash and dry thoroughly; process until finely chopped. Store, covered, in the refrigerator for up to one week.
- Wash greens as soon as you get home from shopping. Dry well and wrap loosely in paper towels in a plastic bag to store in the crisper.
- Start water boiling for pasta before preparing other parts of a pasta supper.
- Speed up preparation with prepared vegetables from the produce section—more expensive but handy in a pinch and perhaps without as much waste.
- Plan your cooking steps and move back and forth between recipes, working on one while part of another dish cooks.
- Cook enough potatoes, rice or pasta for two meals; serve hot the first night and use the rest for salads, soups and desserts, like Easy Rice Pudding (see p. 143). You can also reheat them the next night into creative dishes like stir-fried rice, home fries or potato patties.

Veal and Onion Ragout with Gremolata Garnish

MAKES 6 TO 8 SERVINGS

This delicious stew gains flavour when it's reheated. With buttered fettuccine, crusty bread and a salad of mixed greens, it's elegant enough for company. Gremolata is a mixture of lemon zest, garlic and parsley that is added to osso buco (braised veal shanks). Here, I've used it as a special garnish for an easy stew.

VEAL AND ONION RAGOUT

- 2 lb (1 kg) boneless veal
- Salt and pepper
- ¼ cup (60 mL) all-purpose flour
- ¼ cup (60 mL) olive oil (approx.)
- 1 tsp (5 mL) sweet paprika
- 1 cup (250 mL) dry vermouth
- 1 cup (250 mL) chicken stock
- 1 tsp (5 mL) crushed dried rosemary
- Pinch dried thyme
- ¾ lb (375 g) baby carrots, scrubbed
- 10 oz (284 g) small pearl onions, peeled
- 2 cups (500 mL) frozen peas

GREMOLATA GARNISH

- 1 clove garlic, minced
- 1 Tbsp (15 mL) chopped fresh parsley
- 1 tsp (5 mL) coarsely grated lemon zest

VEAL AND ONION RAGOUT Trim the veal; cut into 2-inch (5 cm) cubes. Sprinkle with salt and pepper to taste; dredge with the flour.

In a large heavy saucepan (preferably nonstick), heat half of the oil over medium-high heat; brown the meat in batches, adding more oil as needed. Transfer the meat to a plate and sprinkle with the paprika.

Drain the fat from the pan. Add the vermouth and stock; bring to a boil, stirring to scrape up any brown bits. Return the meat and any accumulated juices to the pan; stir in the rosemary and thyme. Reduce heat and simmer, covered, for 45 minutes.

Add the carrots and onions; simmer for about 15 minutes or until the vegetables are tender. (The recipe can be prepared to this point, cooled, covered and refrigerated for up to 2 days or frozen. Reheat before continuing.) Stir in the peas; heat through. Taste and adjust seasoning.

GREMOLATA GARNISH Stir together the garlic, parsley and lemon zest; sprinkle over the stew.

Veal Scaloppine with Cheese and Tomato

MAKES 4 TO 6 SERVINGS

You can stretch this easy dish if extra people come along by just adding more veal. Try it also with chicken, turkey or pork cutlets (or pork scaloppine). A vegetarian version can be made with browned eggplant or zucchini. If you don't have homemade tomato sauce on hand, substitute a 14-oz (398 mL) can. Serve with buttered noodles or garlic bread and a green salad.

- 1½ lb (750 g) veal cutlets or scaloppine (5 to 8 cutlets)
- 2 Tbsp (30 mL) all-purpose flour
- Salt and pepper
- 3 Tbsp (45 mL) olive oil, divided
- 2 cups (500 mL) tomato sauce (see p. 179)
- 1½ cups (375 mL) shredded mozzarella cheese (about 6 oz/175 g)
- ½ cup (125 mL) freshly grated Parmesan cheese

DUST THE CUTLETS with the flour and sprinkle with salt and pepper to taste.

In a large skillet, heat 2 Tbsp (30 mL) of the oil over medium heat; fry the cutlets, in batches, for 1 minute on each side or until browned. Remove to a plate and keep warm.

Pour off any excess oil in the pan; pour in the tomato sauce and bring to a simmer. Arrange the cutlets in one crowded layer on top of the sauce, spooning sauce over each piece. Sprinkle with the mozzarella and Parmesan; drizzle with the remaining olive oil.

Cover tightly and cook over very low heat for 8 minutes, or until the cheese has melted and the meat is tender.

Special-Occasion Garlic Roast Veal

MAKES 10 TO 12 SERVINGS

This simple garlic-studded roast stays succulent and moist under its coating of butter and mustard. A round roast makes an elegant cut, but an excellent and less expensive substitute is a rolled, boned shoulder.

- 4½ lb (2 kg) boneless roast of veal
- 4 cloves garlic, slivered
- ¼ cup (60 mL) Dijon mustard
- ¼ cup (60 mL) butter, at room temperature
- 1 tsp (5 mL) crushed dried rosemary
- Pepper
- ¾ cup (175 mL) dry white wine
- ½ cup (125 mL) chicken stock
- 1 Tbsp (15 mL) cornstarch
- 2 Tbsp (30 mL) cold water

PIERCE THE MEAT in several places around the roast; insert the garlic slivers. Set on a rack in a shallow roasting pan just large enough to hold it comfortably. Stir together the mustard and butter; spread all over the roast. Sprinkle with the rosemary and pepper to taste. Pour the wine into the pan.

Roast, uncovered and basting often in a 350°F (180°C) oven for 2 hours and 15 minutes, or until a meat thermometer registers 150 to 155°F (65 to 68°C). Transfer to a cutting board; cover loosely with foil and let stand for 20 minutes.

Meanwhile, pour the stock into the pan; bring to a boil on the stove top, stirring to scrape up any brown bits. Dissolve the cornstarch in the cold water; add to the pan and cook, stirring, until smooth and bubbly, about 3 minutes.

Carve the roast into thin slices; arrange on a warm platter. Serve the sauce in a warm sauceboat.

Lamb

. . . .

Stir-Fried Lamb with Baby Corn and Snow Peas

MAKES 4 SERVINGS

If you don't have a can of baby corn on hand, this quick low-cal supper is also good with crunchy strips of fennel or celery. You can substitute lean beef for the lamb. Serve on hot rice.

- 1 lb (500 g) lean lamb (loin, tenderloin or leg)
- 2 Tbsp (30 mL) low-sodium soy sauce
- 1 Tbsp (15 mL) dry sherry
- 1 Tbsp (15 mL) fresh lemon juice
- 1 Tbsp (15 mL) minced fresh ginger
- 1 clove garlic, minced
- ½ tsp (2 mL) pepper
- 2 Tbsp (30 mL) peanut or canola oil, divided
- ¼ lb (125 g) snow peas, trimmed
- 1 sweet red pepper, cut into ¼-inch (5 mm) strips
- ½ tsp (2 mL) granulated sugar
- 2 Tbsp (30 mL) cold water, divided
- 1 tsp (5 mL) cornstarch
- One 14-oz (398 mL) can whole baby corn, drained

CUT THE LAMB across the grain into ¼-inch (5 mm) thick strips; place in a sturdy plastic bag or a bowl.

Stir together the soy sauce, sherry, lemon juice, ginger, garlic and pepper; pour into the bag, over the lamb. Close the bag and squeeze to coat lamb, or stir to coat and cover the bowl. Marinate at room temperature for 30 minutes or up to 4 hours in the refrigerator.

In a wok or large skillet, heat half of the oil over high heat; stir-fry the meat for 2 minutes or until no longer pink. With a slotted spoon, remove to a warm platter and keep warm.

Heat the remaining oil over high heat; stir-fry the peas and red pepper for 1 minute. Stir in the sugar and 1 Tbsp (15 mL) of the water. Cover and reduce heat to medium; cook for 30 seconds or until the vegetables are tender-crisp.

Stir the cornstarch with the remaining water. Increase heat to high and return the lamb to the wok; add the corn. Pour the cornstarch mixture into the pan; cook, stirring constantly, for 1 minute or until the liquid is clear and thickened. Serve immediately.

Lemon-Tarragon Roast Leg of Lamb

MAKES ABOUT 8 SERVINGS

I have been developing hundreds of lamb recipes over a number of years and still consider it one of my favourite meats. A simple glaze gives a fresh flavour to this succulent roast. Serve with buttered fiddleheads or asparagus and mashed potatoes.

- 1 bone-in leg of lamb (about 4 lb/2 kg)
- 1¼ tsp (6 mL) crumbled dried tarragon, divided
- 1 tsp (5 mL) coarse salt
- ¼ tsp (1 mL) pepper
- ½ cup (125 mL) lemon marmalade
- 2 Tbsp (30 mL) fresh lemon juice

PLACE THE LAMB, flat side down, on a rack in a shallow roasting pan. In a small bowl, mix together ¼ tsp (1 mL) of the tarragon, the salt and the pepper; rub all over the leg.

Roast, uncovered, in a 450°F (230°C) oven for 10 minutes. Reduce heat to 325°F (160°C); roast for 55 minutes.

Stir together the marmalade, remaining tarragon and the lemon juice; drizzle some over the lamb. Roast, drizzling with the marmalade mixture every few minutes until used, for 20 to 25 minutes for rare, or until a meat thermometer registers 140°F (60°C). Cover loosely with foil and let stand for 15 to 20 minutes before carving.

Warm Lamb Salad with Ratatouille Vinaigrette

MAKES 6 TO 8 SERVINGS

When I served this warm salad at a dinner party I was giving for a number of my "food" friends, they all wanted the recipe. It's impressive, delicious and easy to make for company because

- 1 boneless leg of lamb (about 3 lb/1.5 kg)
- ⅓ cup (75 mL) olive oil, divided
- ¼ cup (60 mL) dry red wine

its various components can be made ahead of time. Serve this with lots of crusty Italian or French bread.

OPEN OUT THE lamb and place in a shallow glass dish. Combine 2 Tbsp (15 mL) of the olive oil, the wine, half of the thyme, the anchovy paste, garlic and pepper; pour over the lamb and turn to coat. Cover and refrigerate for at least 4 hours, or up to 12 hours.

Meanwhile, trim and thinly slice the eggplants. Place in a colander and sprinkle lightly with salt; toss and let drain for 30 minutes. Rinse and pat dry; place in a greased shallow roasting pan. Sprinkle with the parsley and the remaining thyme; drizzle with the remaining oil. Roast in a 450°F (230°C) oven for 25 minutes or until cooked through, stirring once. Transfer to a bowl. Whisk together half of the balsamic vinegar and 2 Tbsp (30 mL) of the tomato paste. Pour over the eggplant and toss to coat. (Refrigerate, covered, if making several hours ahead. Bring to room temperature before serving.)

Reserving the marinade, remove the lamb and pat dry. Roast, meaty side up, on a rack in a shallow pan in the 450°F (230°C) oven for 1 hour, or until a meat thermometer registers 140°F (60°C). Transfer to a cutting board and tent with foil; let rest for 10 minutes before carving.

Pour the marinade and remaining vinegar into the roasting pan. Set the pan on the stove and bring the liquid to a boil, scraping up any brown bits. Stir in the remaining tomato paste (add 1 Tbsp/15 mL or so of water if too dry), diced tomato and pepper. Remove from heat.

Arrange slices of lamb across the centre of a platter.

- 2 Tbsp (30 mL) chopped fresh thyme (or 2 tsp/ 10 mL dried), divided
- 1 Tbsp (15 mL) anchovy paste
- 3 cloves garlic, crushed
- ¼ tsp (1 mL) pepper
- 6 small eggplants, preferably Italian (1 lb/500 g total)
- Salt
- 1 Tbsp (15 mL) chopped fresh parsley
- ¼ cup (60 mL) balsamic vinegar, divided
- 3 Tbsp (45 mL) tomato paste, divided
- 1 tomato, finely diced
- 1 sweet yellow pepper, finely diced
- Arugula or watercress

Pile the eggplant on either side. Place arugula alongside the eggplant at the ends of the platter. Drizzle some of the tomato mixture down the centre of the meat, serving the remainder in a sauceboat.

Quick Lamb Chop Curry

....

MAKES 4 SERVINGS

Accompany this fast supper dish with bottled chutney, Carrot Pilaf (see p. 124), cherry tomatoes and a cucumber salad.

IN A HEAVY saucepan, heat 4 tsp (20 mL) of the oil over medium heat; cook the onion, stirring, about 3 minutes or until softened. Add the celery, apple, garlic, raisins and curry powder; cook for 3 minutes. Stir in the stock and tomato sauce and add the bay leaf. Bring to a boil, reduce heat and simmer for 10 minutes. Discard the bay leaf.

- 2 Tbsp (30 mL) olive oil, divided
- 1 onion, chopped
- 2 stalks celery, chopped
- 1 large apple, peeled and chopped
- 1 clove garlic, minced
- ½ cup (125 mL) raisins
- 2 Tbsp (30 mL) curry powder
- 1 cup (250 mL) beef stock
- ½ cup (125 mL) tomato sauce
- 1 bay leaf
- 8 loin lamb chops (1½ lb/ 750 g total)

Meanwhile, slash the edges of the chops and brush with the remaining oil. Grill or broil on a greased medium-temperature grill, over hot coals or under the broiler for 3 to 4 minutes per side for medium-rare, or to desired doneness. Arrange on warm plates and pour the sauce over the lamb, or serve the lamb on the sauce.

Honey Mustard Lamb Chops

....

MAKES 3 OR 4 SERVINGS

Lamb chops are incredibly delicious and fast to cook. This simple recipe, which includes many of my favourite seasonings with lamb, is best on the barbecue but fares very well under the broiler, too.

SLASH THE CHOPS at the edge. In a small bowl, stir together the honey, mustard, garlic, thyme and rosemary; spread over both sides of the chops. Let stand at room temperature for at least 15 minutes, or up to 30 minutes.

Place on a greased medium high–temperature grill, 4 inches (10 cm) above medium-hot coals or on a greased broiler rack; barbecue or broil for about 5 minutes on each side for rare, turning once. For best flavour, do not overcook.

- 8 loin lamb chops
- 2 Tbsp (30 mL) liquid honey
- 2 Tbsp (30 mL) Dijon mustard
- 1 large clove garlic, crushed
- ½ tsp (2 mL) dried thyme
- ½ tsp (2 mL) dried rosemary

Easy Bistro-Style Lamb Pot Roast with Beans

MAKES 6 SERVINGS

A classic French bistro dish, the combination of beans and lamb is a winner. I've used lima beans here, but white navy or great Northern beans are also good. The pot roast can be prepared ahead and reheated slowly at serving time.

SORT AND RINSE the beans. Cover with three times their volume in cold water and let them soak overnight in the refrigerator. (Or cover with three times their volume in cold water and bring to a boil; boil for 2 minutes. Cover and let stand for 1 hour.) Drain and set aside.

Sprinkle the lamb with

- 1 lb (500 g) dried lima beans
- 1 boneless lamb shoulder (2 to 3 lb/1 to 1.5 kg)
- 1 tsp (5 mL) dried thyme
- Salt and pepper
- 3 slices smoked side bacon, diced
- 4 carrots, thickly sliced
- 3 onions, coarsely chopped
- 2 stalks celery, sliced
- 1 cup (250 mL) dry white wine (optional)
- 1 cup (250 mL) chicken stock (2 cups/500 mL if omitting the wine)
- 2 Tbsp (30 mL) tomato paste
- ¼ cup (60 mL) chopped fresh parsley, divided
- 2 cloves garlic, minced
- 2 bay leaves

some of the thyme and salt and pepper to taste. Roll up and tie at intervals with twine to make a compact roast.

In a large saucepan, cook the bacon over medium-high heat until crisp. Remove with a slotted spoon to a paper towel and set aside. Add the lamb and brown on all sides in the drippings. Remove to a plate.

In the same pan, cook the carrots, onions and celery over medium heat for 10 minutes, stirring often. Stir in the wine, stock, tomato paste, half of the parsley, the garlic, bay leaves and beans; bring to a boil.

Place the lamb on top; cover and roast in a 325°F (160°C) oven for 1½ to 2 hours or until the lamb and beans are tender, stirring occasionally and adding more stock if necessary to keep the beans covered.

Stir in the remaining parsley, reserved bacon and salt and pepper to taste. Discard the bay leaves. Slice the lamb.

Grilled Lamb Shanks (Rundles' Style)

MAKES 4 SERVINGS

I learned about the goodness of lamb shanks prepared this way from Neil Baxter, chef of Rundles Restaurant in Stratford, Ontario. Lamb shanks are braised ahead of time to a melting tenderness, cooled in their liquid and then grilled over a hot fire. The braising juice then becomes a wonderful sauce to serve with an accompanying pasta. Toss a crisp green salad to go alongside. The shanks are also delicious when hot right after they are braised.

- 2 Tbsp (30 mL) olive oil
- 4 lamb shanks (about 1¾ lb/875 g)
- 1 carrot, diced
- 1 onion, chopped
- 12 cloves garlic (unpeeled)
- 2 cups (500 mL) beef stock
- ¼ cup (60 mL) chopped fresh parsley
- ½ tsp (2 mL) dried thyme
- 1 bay leaf
- Salt and pepper

IN A LARGE saucepan, warm the oil over medium-high heat; brown the shanks on all sides. Remove the lamb from the pan and set aside.

Reduce heat to medium; cook the carrot, onion and

garlic for 5 minutes, stirring often. Stir in the stock, parsley, thyme, bay leaf and salt and pepper to taste; bring to a boil.

Return the lamb to the pan; cover and cook in a 325°F (160°C) oven for 2½ hours, turning the meat occasionally. Let cool until the steaming stops; cover and refrigerate overnight.

Remove the lamb from the braising mixture, reserving the mixture. Place the lamb on a greased high-temperature grill, or 4 inches (10 cm) from very hot coals; grill for 15 minutes without turning. Turn the lamb and grill until a crust forms on the other side and the shanks are warmed through.

Meanwhile, remove any fat from the the braising liquid and heat the liquid and vegetables; push the vegetables through a sieve and boil with the liquid for 5 minutes until reduced and thickened. Serve with the lamb.

Lemon-Herb Grilled Leg of Lamb

MAKES 6 TO 8 SERVINGS

One of the most delicious things you'll ever barbecue is lamb. This already-tender meat requires a relatively short time over the coals— just long enough to add a smokiness to its distinct flavour. A boneless leg needs little in the way of a marinade, but this simple one adds a certain interesting flavour. Accompany with minted new potatoes, grilled sweet peppers and a cucumber salad.

- 1 boneless leg of lamb (about 3 lb/1.5 kg)
- ⅓ cup (75 mL) fresh lemon juice
- ¼ cup (60 mL) canola oil
- 1 tsp (5 mL) dried rosemary
- ¼ tsp (1 mL) dried thyme
- ¼ tsp (1 mL) pepper
- 2 large cloves garlic, minced

MAKE SEVERAL SLASHES in the thickest part of the meat (on the meaty side); place in a shallow glass dish. In a measuring cup, stir together the lemon juice, oil, rosemary, thyme, pepper and garlic. Remove ¼ cup (60 mL) of the marinade, cover and refrigerate for

brushing on the lamb as it cooks. Pour the remainder over the lamb. Cover and refrigerate at least 2 hours, or up to 6 hours. Remove from the refrigerator 30 minutes before cooking.

Place the lamb on a greased medium high–temperature grill, or 6 inches (15 cm) from medium-hot coals; grill for 15 to 20 minutes per side, turning once and brushing with the reserved marinade, until a meat thermometer registers 140°F (60°C) for rare. (Alternatively, broil 4 inches/10 cm from heat for 12 to 15 minutes per side.)

Transfer to a cutting board; cover loosely with foil and let stand for 10 minutes before carving.

Hearty Low-Cal Lamb Stew

MAKES 6 SERVINGS

When you brown mild, tender, trimmed lamb cubes under the broiler, less fat is required and any accumulated fat is drained off, producing a stew high in flavour but low in calories. Serve with crusty country bread and a green salad.

- 1½ lb (750 g) boneless lamb shoulder, trimmed
- 2 Tbsp (30 mL) all-purpose flour
- ¼ tsp (1 mL) salt
- ¼ tsp (1 mL) pepper
- 2 cups (500 mL) beef stock
- 1 Tbsp (15 mL) tomato paste
- 2 cloves garlic, minced
- 1 small sweet red pepper, diced
- ½ tsp (2 mL) dried rosemary
- 6 small potatoes, unpeeled and quartered
- 3 carrots, coarsely diced
- 1½ cups (375 mL) coarsely diced peeled rutabaga
- ¾ cup (175 mL) pearl onions
- ¾ cup (175 mL) frozen peas

CUT THE MEAT into 1½-inch (4 cm) cubes. Broil on a broiler rack in a single layer for 10 to 15 minutes or until brown on all sides. Remove with a slotted spoon to a large ovenproof stove-top casserole dish, or a large roasting pan.

Sprinkle the meat with the flour, salt and pepper; bake, uncovered, in a 450°F (230°C) oven for 12 to 15 minutes or until the flour browns.

Place over high heat on the top of the stove. Stir in the stock, tomato paste, garlic, red pepper and rosemary; bring to a boil, stirring to scrape up any brown bits on the bottom of the pan. Cover and return to a 350°F (180°C) oven for 45 minutes. (Or, simmer on top of the stove, stirring often.)

Stir in the potatoes, carrots, rutabaga and onions; cover and bake for 1 hour or until the vegetables and meat are tender. Stir in the peas; bake for 10 minutes or until the peas are cooked.

Fish and Seafood

Grilled Cod with Lemon-Dill Mayonnaise

MAKES 3 OR 4 SERVINGS

A simple mayonnaise mixture coats fish to keep it moist during barbecuing and then becomes a refreshing accompanying sauce. Use the same marinade for other types of fillets and for fish steaks. If you can cook the fish right on the grill or in a hinged basket, the flavour is better than placing foil underneath. Stand right over the grill and move the fish with two spatulas. Do not over-cook. Serve with asparagus and oven-fried potatoes.

- 1 lb (500 g) cod fillets
- ½ cup (125 mL) light mayonnaise
- 2 Tbsp (30 mL) plain yogurt
- 1 tsp (5 mL) grated lemon zest
- 2 Tbsp (30 mL) fresh lemon juice
- 1 tsp (5 mL) dried dill
- ¼ tsp (1 mL) pepper

PAT THE FISH very dry and place in a shallow dish. Stir together the mayonnaise, yogurt, lemon zest, lemon juice, dill and pepper. Using about one-third of the mixture, generously brush on all sides of the fish.

Place the fish on a clean greased high-temperature grill, or 4 inches (10 cm) from hot coals; grill for about 5 minutes or until the fish flakes easily when tested with a fork, turning thicker pieces over. (Alternatively, broil 3½ inches/9 cm from heat.) Serve with the remaining mayonnaise mixture.

Marvellous Mussels

MAKES 4 SERVINGS

Plain steamed mussels are a Friday night treat that's simple and cheap when you want something special for your family or an easy dish for entertaining. Accompany with French bread and spoons so that everyone can enjoy the broth after the mussels are gone.

- 4 lb (2 kg) mussels
- 1 cup (250 mL) dry white wine or chicken stock
- ½ cup (125 mL) chopped shallots, leeks or onions
- ½ cup (125 mL) diced celery
- ½ cup (125 mL) diced carrot
- ½ cup (125 mL) chopped fresh parsley, divided
- 1 bay leaf
- Salt and pepper
- 2 Tbsp (30 mL) butter

WITH A STIFF brush, scrub the mussels under cold running water. Remove any beards by pulling up toward the rounded end of the shell, or cut them off. Firmly tap mussels and discard any that do not close.

In a large heavy saucepan, combine the wine, shallots, celery, carrot, half of the parsley and the bay leaf; bring to a simmer. Add the mussels; cover and simmer over medium heat for 4 to 7 minutes or until the shells open and the meat is loosened. Discard any mussels that do not open. Discard the bay leaf.

Sprinkle with the remaining parsley; season with salt and pepper to taste. Dot with the butter. Serve in heated wide soup or pasta bowls.

Hot Seafood Salad

MAKES 6 SERVINGS

Serve this quick-and-easy casserole with whole wheat rolls and a salad of orange slices and watercress. Since it makes a delicious company casserole, feel free to double it.

- 1½ cups (375 mL) medium shell pasta
- 2½ cups (625 mL) cooked seafood (crabmeat, lobster, shrimp, scallops or a mixture)
- 1 cup (250 mL) diced celery
- ¾ cup (175 mL) coarsely chopped sweet green pepper
- ¾ cup (175 mL) finely chopped onion
- ¼ cup (60 mL) chopped fresh parsley
- ¼ lb (125 g) small button mushrooms
- ¼ cup (60 mL) toasted slivered almonds

COOK THE PASTA until just tender; drain well. (There should be about 2 cups/500 mL.)

If using canned seafood, rinse thoroughly in cold water and drain well. In a large bowl, combine the pasta, seafood, celery, green pepper, onion, parsley, mushrooms, almonds and cheese.

In a medium bowl, stir together the mayonnaise, yogurt, lemon zest, sherry, lemon juice, mustard and salt and pepper to taste. Blend gently but thoroughly into the seafood mixture. Pour into a greased 8-cup (2 L) casserole.

Combine the crumbs with the melted butter; spread evenly over the casserole. (The casserole can be prepared to this point, covered and refrigerated for up to 3 hours.) Bake, uncovered, in a 350°F (180°C) oven for 30 to 35 minutes or until heated through.

- 1½ cups (375 mL) coarsely shredded Swiss cheese
- 1 cup (250 mL) light mayonnaise
- ½ cup (125 mL) low-fat plain yogurt
- 2 tsp (10 mL) grated lemon zest
- ¼ cup (60 mL) dry sherry
- ¼ cup (60 mL) fresh lemon juice
- ½ tsp (2 mL) dry mustard
- Salt and pepper
- 1 cup (250 mL) fresh breadcrumbs
- 2 Tbsp (30 mL) butter, melted

Mediterranean Tomato and Fish Stew

MAKES 4 TO 6 SERVINGS

This bright, fresh stew is just right for inexpensive, casual entertaining, as well as family meals. If you wish, add a dozen mussels and a pinch of saffron to the stew for the last 3 to 5 minutes. Accompany with spiced olives, crusty Italian bread and beer, and follow it with a salad of leaf lettuce, red onion and goat cheese.

IN A LARGE heavy saucepan, heat the oil over medium heat; cook the onion, garlic and sweet pepper until softened,

- 2 Tbsp (30 mL) olive oil
- 1 large onion, chopped
- 4 cloves garlic, minced
- 1 sweet pepper (green, red or yellow), diced
- One 28-oz (796 mL) can tomatoes (undrained)
- One 8-oz (237 mL) bottle clam juice
- ½ tsp (2 mL) dried thyme
- ½ tsp (2 mL) fennel seeds
- ¼ tsp (1 mL) pepper
- ¼ tsp (1 mL) hot pepper flakes
- 2 bay leaves
- 1½ lb (750 g) haddock or cod fillets
- 1 Tbsp (15 mL) butter

about 5 minutes.

Add the tomatoes, crushing them with a potato masher. Stir in the clam juice, thyme, fennel seeds, pepper, hot pepper flakes and bay leaves; bring to a boil. Reduce heat and cook, uncovered and stirring occasionally, for 12 to 15 minutes or until thickened slightly. (The stew can be prepared to this point, cooled and refrigerated for up to 2 days. Bring to a simmer before proceeding.)

Cut the fish into 2-inch (5 cm) pieces; add to the tomato mixture. Cover and cook over medium-low heat for about 5 minutes or until the fish flakes easily when tested with fork. Do not stir, but baste with the tomato mixture periodically. Discard bay leaves.

Dot with the butter. Heat, uncovered, for 1 minute longer. Serve immediately sprinkled with the parsley and green onion.

- ¼ cup (60 mL) chopped fresh parsley
- 2 Tbsp (30 mL) chopped green onion

Terrific Teriyaki Salmon

MAKES 4 SERVINGS

Salmon lends itself happily to these Asian flavours. Serve with fluffy rice and steamed spinach or broccoli.

STIR TOGETHER the soy sauce, rice wine, sugar, garlic, ginger and pepper until the sugar is dissolved.

Place the salmon in a shallow glass dish; pour on the marinade. Cover and let stand in the refrigerator for at least 2 hours, and no more than 4 hours, turning occasionally. Remove from the refrigerator 30 minutes before cooking.

Place the salmon on a greased broiler rack or

- ¼ cup (60 mL) low-sodium soy sauce
- ¼ cup (60 mL) Japanese rice wine or dry sherry
- 2 Tbsp (30 mL) granulated sugar
- 2 cloves garlic, minced
- 1 Tbsp (15 mL) minced fresh ginger
- ½ tsp (2 mL) pepper
- 4 salmon steaks (about 6½ oz/185 g each)
- Thin strips peeled cucumber

medium high–temperature barbecue grill, 4 inches (10 cm) from heat or above medium-hot coals; cook, turning once, until the fish flakes easily when tested with a fork, 3 to 5 minutes per side.

Serve hot, garnished with cucumber strips.

Lime-Grilled Salmon

. . . .

MAKES 4 SERVINGS

An easy marinade and quick grilling produce juicy, flavourful fish without adding a great deal of fat. Try the same marinade for other fish steaks and fillets, but grill fillets for less time.

- 4 salmon steaks (about 6½ oz/185 g each)
- 1 tsp (5 mL) grated lime zest
- ¼ cup (60 mL) fresh lime juice
- 1 Tbsp (15 mL) canola oil
- 1 clove garlic, minced
- ¼ tsp (1 mL) hot pepper flakes
- Pinch dried oregano
- Fresh Tomato-Cucumber Salsa (see p. 176)

PAT THE STEAKS dry and place in a shallow glass dish.

Stir together the lime zest and juice, oil, garlic, hot pepper flakes and oregano; pour over the salmon. Cover and refrigerate for 1 hour.

Place the steaks on a greased medium-high grill, or 4 inches (10 cm) above medium-hot coals (or under the broiler); cook for 5 to 6 minutes per side, turning once with a spatula until fish flakes easily when tested with a fork. Serve with Fresh Tomato Cucumber Salsa.

Quick and Nutritious Salmon Loaf

. . . .

MAKES 4 SERVINGS

When you think there's nothing in the house for supper, remember that a couple cans of salmon from the cupboard make a quick and nutritious loaf. If you wish, accompany with a sauce made from ½ cup (125 mL) plain yogurt or low-fat cream, with 2 Tbsp (30 mL) chopped fresh dill. Round off the menu with baked potatoes, a crunchy cucumber salad and steamy glazed carrots. Slices of cold salmon loaf make a great salad with greens.

IN A LARGE bowl, soak the crumbs in the milk for 5 minutes. Stir in the salmon with its juice, mashing to crush bones and flake the salmon. Stir in the celery, eggs, lemon juice, salt, pepper, paprika and cayenne.

Pack firmly into a greased 9 × 5–inch (2 L) loaf pan; set the pan in a bigger pan of hot water. Bake in a 350°F (180°C) oven for 40 minutes or until golden on top. Cover loosely with foil and let stand for 5 minutes before slicing.

- 1½ cups (375 mL) cracker crumbs (about 36 soda crackers)
- ½ cup (125 mL) milk
- Two 7½-oz (213 g) cans salmon
- ¼ cup (60 mL) finely diced celery
- 2 eggs, lightly beaten
- 2 Tbsp (30 mL) fresh lemon juice
- ¼ tsp (1 mL) salt
- ¼ tsp (1 mL) pepper
- ¼ tsp (1 mL) paprika
- Pinch cayenne pepper

Crunchy Oven-Fried Haddock

. . . .

MAKES 3 OR 4 SERVINGS

Everyone loves crunchy deep-fried battered fish. This is an oven-baked low-fat version the kids are sure to enjoy. Bake a sheet of potato slices alongside and accompany with green peas and raw carrot sticks.

- 1 lb (500 g) haddock fillets (or other lean white fish)
- Salt and pepper
- Paprika
- All-purpose flour
- 2 cups (500 mL) cornflakes
- 1 egg, beaten
- 1 Tbsp (15 mL) canola oil (approx.)

CUT THE FILLETS into serving-size pieces. Sprinkle lightly with salt, pepper and paprika. Dust lightly with flour.

Place the cornflakes in a sturdy plastic bag and roll gently with a rolling pin to crush finely. In a shallow bowl, beat the egg with 1 Tbsp (15 mL) oil.

Dip each fish piece into the egg mixture, then coat evenly with the cornflake crumbs, pressing firmly to make the crumbs adhere. Place on a well-greased baking sheet. (The recipe can be prepared to this point, covered and refrigerated for up to 6 hours.)

Drizzle the fish lightly with oil; bake, uncovered, in a 450°F (230°C) oven for 6 minutes. Turn and bake for 2 to 3 minutes longer or until crispy and the fish flakes easily when tested with fork.

Saucy Spinach and Tuna Casserole

....

MAKES 4 TO 6 SERVINGS

This easy, low-cost family supper has lots of flavour. Enjoy it with crusty bread and a green salad.

- 2 Tbsp (30 mL) olive or canola oil
- 1 onion, sliced
- 1 clove garlic, minced
- One 19-oz (540 mL) can tomatoes (undrained)
- 1 cup (250 mL) water
- One 7½-oz (213 mL) can tomato sauce
- ½ tsp (2 mL) dried basil
- ½ tsp (2 mL) granulated sugar
- ½ tsp (2 mL) salt
- ¼ tsp (1 mL) pepper
- ¼ lb (125 g) medium egg noodles
- One 10-oz (284 g) pkg fresh spinach, rinsed
- Two 6½-oz (185 g) cans tuna
- ½ cup (125 mL) freshly grated Parmesan cheese

IN A LARGE saucepan, heat the oil over medium heat; cook the onion and garlic until softened, about 5 minutes.

Stir in the tomatoes, breaking them up with the back of a spoon; stir in the water, tomato sauce, basil, sugar, salt and pepper; simmer, uncovered, for 15 minutes or until thickened. Taste and adjust seasoning.

Add the noodles and wet spinach leaves; return to a simmer. Cook, making sure the noodles are immersed, for 15 to 20 minutes or until noodles are tender but firm.

Drain the tuna and break into large chunks; add to the tomato mixture. Transfer to a shallow 6-cup (1.5 L) casserole and sprinkle with the cheese. (The casserole can be prepared to this point, covered and refrigerated for up to 8 hours. Remove from the refrigerator 30 minutes before cooking.) Bake in a 375°F (190°C) oven for 20 to 25 minutes, or until hot and bubbly.

Egg Dishes,
Beans and Pizzas

....

COLOURFUL HARVEST FRITTATA

Colourful Harvest Frittata

MAKES 3 OR 4 SERVINGS

This quick meatless main course is lightened with a couple of extra egg whites. Serve with chili sauce and toast triangles for a quick lunch, brunch or light supper.

- 4 eggs
- 2 egg whites
- ½ tsp (2 mL) salt
- Pinch pepper
- 1 Tbsp (15 mL) butter
- 1 Tbsp (15 mL) canola oil
- 1 onion, sliced
- 1 small zucchini, sliced
- ½ sweet red pepper, diced
- 1 clove garlic, minced
- 1½ cups (375 mL) cooked corn kernels, cut from cob (or a 12-oz/341-mL can, well drained)
- ½ tsp (2 mL) dried basil
- 1½ cups (375 mL) shredded Swiss cheese

IN A BOWL, whisk together the eggs, egg whites, salt and pepper; set aside.

In a large heavy oven-proof skillet, melt the butter with the oil over medium heat; cook the onion and zucchini for 6 to 7 minutes or until light brown. Add the red pepper and garlic; cook for 4 minutes or until softened. Stir in the corn and basil. Remove from heat.

Spread the mixture evenly over the bottom of the skillet; pour the egg mixture overtop. Cook over medium heat for 1 minute then sprinkle with the cheese. Bake in a 400°F (200°C) oven for 15 to 20 minutes or until golden brown and set. Cut into wedges to serve.

Light Eggs Benedict

MAKES 4 SERVINGS

Prosciutto and a butterless Hollandaise make a lighter version of this classic brunch dish.

LIGHT HOLLANDAISE SAUCE
- 3 eggs
- 3 Tbsp (45 mL) fresh lemon juice
- ¼ cup (60 mL) hot water
- ¼ tsp (1 mL) white pepper
- Dash hot pepper sauce

LIGHT HOLLANDAISE SAUCE In a large heatproof bowl, whisk together the eggs, lemon juice and hot water. Place over a pan of simmering, not boiling, water; whisk until fluffy and thickened, 3 to 4 minutes.

Whisk in the pepper and hot pepper sauce; cover and keep warm over hot water for up to 30 minutes.

EGGS BENEDICT
- 4 English muffins or slices French bread
- 2 Tbsp (30 mL) unsalted butter
- ¼ lb (125 g) prosciutto ham, slivered or sliced
- 8 poached eggs

EGGS BENEDICT Split the muffins; toast and place on hot plates. Keep warm.

In a small skillet, melt the butter; sauté the prosciu-tto just until heated through. Place on top of the muffins; top each with a poached egg. Spoon the sauce overtop.

Incredibly Easy Ham and Cheese Strata

MAKES 8 SERVINGS

When I have houseguests, I always enjoy serving a one-dish breakfast that needs no last-minute attention.

- 8 slices firm white homemade-style bread
- 2 tsp (10 mL) Dijon mustard
- ¼ cup (60 mL) butter, melted
- 8 slices Black Forest ham, slivered
- 1 cup (250 mL) shredded mild Cheddar or Swiss cheese
- ¼ cup (60 mL) chopped fresh parsley
- 3 eggs
- ½ tsp (2 mL) salt
- 1½ cups (375 mL) milk
- ½ cup (125 mL) sour cream
- Dash hot pepper sauce
- 2 Tbsp (30 mL) butter

REMOVE THE CRUSTS from the bread; diagonally cut each slice in half. Spread each with mustard; dip one side in the melted butter.

Arrange half of the slices, butter side down, in an ungreased 13 × 9–inch (3.5 L) baking dish. Sprinkle evenly with half each of the ham, cheese and parsley. Top with the remaining bread, butter side up, and repeat with the remaining ham, cheese and parsley.

In a bowl, beat together the eggs, salt, milk, sour cream and hot pepper sauce; pour evenly over the strata. Dot with the butter. Cover with foil and refrigerate overnight.

Bake, covered, in a 350°F (180°C) oven for 30 minutes; uncover and bake for about 10 minutes longer or until puffed and golden. Let stand for 5 minutes before cutting.

Maple Baked Beans

MAKES 6 SERVINGS

On a chilly day, I often get hungry for a big pot of old-fashioned baked beans. They make such a satisfying but easy supper with chili sauce. I stick some slices of side pork (pork belly) in a pan to bake alongside for an hour until it's crisp and brown, then I add a creamy cabbage salad to the meal.

- 2 cups (500 mL) dried white navy (pea) beans (1 lb/ 500 g)
- 1½ tsp (7 mL) dry mustard
- 1 tsp (5 mL) salt
- 1 tsp (5 mL) pepper
- 1 onion, minced
- ¼ lb (125 g) salt pork
- ¾ cup (175 mL) maple syrup (preferably dark cooking)
- 2 Tbsp (30 mL) molasses

SORT AND RINSE the beans. In a medium saucepan, cover the beans with 6 cups (1.5 L) cold water and let soak overnight in the refrigerator. (Or, cover with water and bring to a boil; boil for 2 minutes. Remove from heat; cover and let stand for 1 hour.)

Drain the beans. Cover again with cold water and bring to a boil; reduce heat and simmer, covered, for 40 minutes.

Reserving the liquid, drain and transfer the beans to a bean pot or heavy casserole dish. Stir in the mustard, salt, pepper and onion. Rinse the salt pork; dice and add to the beans. Stir in enough of the reserved cooking liquid to reach the top of the beans.

Cover and bake in a 350°F (180°C) oven for about 5 hours or until the beans are very tender, stirring occa-sionally and adding more cooking liquid or water if necessary to ensure the beans do not become too dry.

Half an hour before serving, stir in the maple syrup and molasses; cook, uncovered.

Bean Burritos

MAKES 4 SERVINGS

These easy burrito sand-wiches make a terrific carry-away lunch. Enjoy them cold, or microwave on high for 35 seconds or until heated through; serve with sour cream if you wish. Look for refried beans in the grocery store with the other Mexican ingredients.

- 4 tsp (20 mL) canola oil
- ½ cup (125 mL) chopped onion
- 2 cloves garlic, minced
- ½ sweet green or red pepper, diced
- 1 can (455 mL) refried beans
- 1 Tbsp (15 mL) chopped pickled or fresh jalapeño pepper
- ¼ tsp (1 mL) ground cumin
- ¼ tsp (1 mL) dried oregano
- 4 flour tortillas (9 or 10 inch/23 or 25 cm)
- 1 cup (250 mL) shredded Cheddar or skim milk mozzarella cheese
- 2 green onions, chopped

IN A LARGE skillet, heat the oil over medium heat; cook the onion, garlic and green pepper until tender but not browned, about 5 minutes.

Stir in the beans, jala-peño pepper, cumin and oregano; cook for about 2 minutes or until the beans are heated through and the flavours blended.

Spoon about ½ cup (125 mL) of the filling just below the centre of each tortilla; sprinkle with one-quarter of the cheese and green onion. Fold the lower edge over the filling, then fold in the sides and roll up. (Burritos can be wrapped in plastic and refrigerated for up to 3 days.)

DRIED BEANS

....

Had it not been for dried beans and peas, many of our early settlers would have starved during the long Canadian winters. Indigenous peoples first introduced beans to French settlers, who quickly made them a staple of their diet. They especially liked them as a convenience food for sailing, which is how white dried beans got the nickname "navy."

Now beans and lentils are chic and appear in all the best restaurants. But they have a lot more going for them than fashion. Containing no preservatives or chemicals, they're real and nutritious food that's always available. They're also a cheap source of protein that's a complete protein if combined with grains. And it's protein without the amount of fat that animal sources contain.

Dried beans are, of course, more economical than canned, but canned beans of various varieties are handy to have in the cupboard for instant nutrition. Canned beans are better drained and rinsed, with the exception of kidney beans.

To rehydrate dried beans, pick them over and rinse in a sieve under cold running water. Using 3 parts water to 1 part beans, either let them sit overnight in the refrigerator or bring them to a full boil for 2 minutes, removing them from the heat and letting them stand, covered, for 1 hour. Drain, add fresh water and cook for 40 to 60 minutes depending on the type of bean and recipe. Whatever method of cooking you choose, be sure to bring beans to a full boil at some point in their cooking.

The Star's Quick Cassoulet

MAKES 4 TO 6 SERVINGS

A number of years ago, my husband and I spent a little time at a farm near Bergerac, France, an area famous for its confit (preserved goose) and for the casserole that farm wives make with confit and dried beans (along with a number of other meats like lamb and pork). Of course, I came home from that visit inspired to make a true cassoulet, which I did for the following New Year's Eve. The dish was wonderful, but I had worked four days on it.

When Marion Kane (then the Toronto Star Food Editor) asked me to develop a cheap and cheerful casserole recipe for an article on reces-sion-proof recipes, I came up with the following updated, easy cassoulet. Marion subse-quently chose it as one of her favourite recipes of 1990, and referred to it as "a terrific version of the labour-intensive French bistro classic." Thanks Marion. I think it is still relevant today.

- 1 lb (500 g) garlic farmer's sausage
- 3 chicken thighs (¾ lb/375 g)
- 1 Tbsp (15 mL) canola oil (optional)
- 3 cloves garlic, minced
- 2 onions, coarsely chopped
- One 19-oz (540 mL) can tomatoes (undrained), chopped
- 1¼ cups (300 mL) chicken stock (approx.), divided
- ½ tsp (2 mL) dried thyme
- 2 bay leaves
- Pinch granulated sugar
- Pinch dried savory
- Salt and pepper
- Two 19-oz (540 mL) cans white navy (pea) beans
- 2 cups (500 mL) fresh breadcrumbs
- ½ cup (125 mL) finely chopped fresh parsley
- ¼ cup (60 mL) butter, melted

CUT THE SAUSAGE into ½-inch (1.25 cm) thick rounds. Remove the chicken meat from the bones; cut into large chunks.

In a large flameproof casserole dish, brown the sau-sage over medium-high heat for 5 to 7 minutes, adding the oil if necessary. With a slotted spoon, remove to paper towels. Brown the chicken for 5 minutes; remove to paper towels.

Discard all but 1 Tbsp (15 mL) of the drippings; cook the garlic and onions, stirring, for 5 minutes. Stir in the tomatoes, ½ cup (125 mL) of the stock, the thyme, bay leaves, sugar, savory and salt and pepper to taste.

Return the sausage and chicken to the pot; bring to a boil. Reduce heat and simmer, uncovered, for 30 minutes or until nearly all moisture has evaporated, stirring often. Discard the bay leaves.

Drain and rinse the beans; stir into the tomato mixture. Add enough of the remaining chicken stock to make a very moist, but not soupy mixture.

Toss together the breadcrumbs, parsley and melted butter; sprinkle over the casserole. Bake, uncovered, in a 350°F (180°C) oven for about 45 minutes or until a gold-en-brown crust has formed and the casserole is bubbly.

(The cassoulet can be cooled, covered and refrigerat-ed up to 2 days. Let stand for 30 minutes at room temperature before reheating.)

Friday Night Family Pizza

MAKES 4 SERVINGS

This quick-and-easy pizza is a fun way to celebrate the week's end. For extra conve-nience, you can pick up a good prepared pizza shell.

- ¾ lb (375 g) Italian sausage
- 3 Tbsp (45 mL) olive oil, divided
- ½ lb (250 g) mushrooms, sliced
- ½ sweet green pepper, cut into chunks
- Pizza Dough (see p. 100)
- ½ lb (250 g) mozzarella cheese, shredded, divided
- ½ tsp (2 mL) dried Italian herb seasoning
- Pinch hot pepper flakes
- One 7½-oz (213 mL) can pizza sauce

CUT THE SAUSAGE into ½-inch (1 cm) thick rounds. In a large skillet, brown the sausage over medium heat, stirring often and adding some oil if needed, until no longer pink, about 8 minutes. Add the mush-rooms for the last 5 minutes. Stir in the green pepper; cook for 1 minute.

Meanwhile, grease a 12-inch (30 cm) pizza pan with oil; top with the pizza dough. Brush with some of the oil

FRIDAY NIGHT FAMILY PIZZA

and sprinkle with half the cheese. Stir the Italian herb seasoning and hot pepper flakes into the pizza sauce; spread over the dough.

Drain off any fat from the sausage mixture and arrange on the sauce. Sprinkle with the remaining cheese and drizzle with the remaining oil. Bake in the lower third of a 500°F (260°C) oven for about 15 minutes or until the crust is golden brown.

Pizza Dough

MAKES ONE 12-INCH (30 CM) CRUST

You can prepare this ahead of time, to ensure that it's ready and waiting when the urge to have pizza hits. The dough can be rolled out, wrapped and refrigerated on the pan for up to eight hours, or frozen. Or wrap the risen dough in plastic wrap, then in a plastic bag. Thaw before rolling out. Recipe can be doubled.

- Pinch granulated sugar
- ⅔ cup (150 mL) warm water
- 2 tsp (10 mL) active dry yeast
- 2 Tbsp (30 mL) canola oil
- 1½ cups (375 mL) all-purpose flour
- ½ tsp (2 mL) salt

IN A SMALL bowl, combine the sugar and water; sprinkle with the yeast and let stand in a warm place until bubbly and doubled in volume, about 5 minutes. Stir in the oil.

In a large bowl, mix together the flour and salt. Make a well in the centre of the flour mixture; pour in the yeast mixture. With a fork, gradually blend together the flour and yeast mixtures to form the dough. With floured hands gather into a ball.

Turn out onto a lightly floured surface; knead for about 5 minutes, adding just enough extra flour to make a soft, slightly sticky dough. Place in a greased bowl, turning once to grease all over. Cover the bowl with greased waxed paper and a tea towel. Let stand in a warm draft-free place until tripled in size, 1½ to 3 hours.

Punch down the dough and form into a ball. Turn out onto a lightly floured surface and cover with the bowl; let stand for 10 minutes. Roll out the dough into a 12-inch (30 cm) circle.

Asparagus and Prosciutto Pizza with Gruyère

MAKES 2 OR 3 SERVINGS

Celebrate asparagus season by teaming the fresh stalks with these two happy ingredients.

- ½ lb (250 g) asparagus
- 2 Tbsp (30 mL) olive oil, divided
- Pizza Dough (see p. 100)
- ½ tsp (2 mL) dried oregano
- ¼ tsp (1 mL) pepper
- 2 cups (500 mL) shredded Gruyère cheese, divided
- 6 oz (175 g) thinly sliced prosciutto ham, cut into 1-inch (2.5 cm) strips

TRIM THE ASPARAGUS; arrange in a single layer on a 12-inch (30 cm) pizza pan. Drizzle with 2 tsp (10 mL) of the oil; roast in a 500°F (260°C) oven for 4 minutes. Cut each stalk into 3 diagonal pieces; set aside.

Press the dough into the same pan; brush lightly with some of the remaining oil. Sprinkle with the oregano, pepper and two-thirds of the cheese.

Arrange the asparagus and prosciutto on top; sprinkle with the remaining cheese. Drizzle with the remaining oil. Bake in the lower third of the 500°F (260°C) oven for 12 to 15 minutes or until the crust is golden brown.

Prosciutto, Roasted Garlic and Red Pepper Pizza

MAKES 2 OR 3 MAIN-COURSE SERVINGS

This flavourful pizza is well worth a trip to your local grocery store for the prosciutto, cheese and roasted peppers. The garlic can be roasted ahead of time when you happen to have the oven on for something else.

- 2 heads garlic
- ¼ cup (60 mL) olive oil, divided
- 1 tsp (5 mL) dried thyme, divided
- Pizza Dough (see p. 100)
- 3 cups (750 mL) shredded mozzarella

CUT THE TOPS from the garlic heads just to expose the top of the cloves; place on greased foil. Drizzle with a dash of the olive oil and sprinkle with a pinch of the thyme. Fold up the foil to enclose the garlic; bake in a 350°F (180°C) oven for 1½ hours. Let cool and press the garlic out of the skins.

Place the dough on a greased 12-inch (30 cm) pizza pan. Brush lightly with some of the oil; sprinkle with two-thirds of the cheese. Dot with the garlic and sprinkle with remaining thyme.

Arrange the peppers and prosciutto on top; sprinkle with the remaining mozzarella. Drizzle with the remaining oil. Bake in the lower third of a 500°F (260°C) oven for 12 to 15 minutes or until the crust is golden brown.

Pear and Brie Pizza with Caramelized Red Onions on a Walnut Crust

....

MAKES 2 OR 3 MAIN-COURSE SERVINGS

Pears and Brie complement each other so well that I couldn't resist combining them with tart caramelized onions in a pizza. The dough gets a toasted walnut flavour by kneading in a few of the nuts.

CORE AND SLICE the pear. In a skillet, melt the butter over medium heat; cook the pear for 5 minutes. Sprinkle with the thyme and generously with pepper. With a slotted spoon, remove pears to a bowl.

- or fontina cheese or a combination, divided
- One ½-cup (125 mL) jar roasted red peppers, drained and sliced
- 2 oz (50 g) thinly sliced prosciutto ham, cut into 1-inch (2.5 cm) strips

- 1 pear (unpeeled)
- 2 tsp (10 mL) butter
- ½ tsp (2 mL) dried thyme
- Pepper
- 1 Tbsp (15 mL) olive oil (approx.)
- 1 small red onion, thinly sliced in rings
- 1½ tsp (7 mL) red wine vinegar
- ½ tsp (2 mL) salt
- Pinch granulated sugar
- Pizza Dough (see p. 100)
- ¼ cup (60 mL) finely chopped toasted walnuts
- 6 oz (175 g) Brie cheese (unpeeled)

In the same skillet, heat the oil over low heat; cook the onion, covered, for 5 minutes. Stir in the vinegar, salt and sugar; cover and cook for 5 minutes.

Meanwhile, punch down the dough; knead in the walnuts and form into a ball. Turn out onto a lightly floured surface and cover with the bowl; let stand for 10 minutes. Press into a 12-inch (30 cm) pizza pan and brush lightly with more of the oil. Scatter evenly with the onion and pear mixtures.

Cut the cheese (including rind) into ½-inch (1 cm) cubes. Scatter over the pizza. Drizzle with any juice from the skillet. Bake in the lower third of a 500°F (260°C) oven for 12 to 15 minutes or until the crust is golden brown.

Sage-Onion Focaccia

....

MAKES 4 SERVINGS

This wonderful Italian flatbread is a tribute to my father, who loved Spanish onion sandwiches. Serve as an appetizer to a light dinner or as an accompaniment to a main-course soup. Prepare the pizza dough just to the point where you punch it down, then use in this recipe.

IN A SMALL bowl, combine the onion, vinegar and honey; let stand for at least 30 minutes, but no longer than 1 hour, stirring occasionally.

- 1 very small Spanish onion, thinly sliced
- ¼ cup (60 mL) white vinegar
- 2 Tbsp (30 mL) liquid honey
- Pizza Dough (see p. 100)
- ¾ cup (175 mL) freshly grated Parmesan cheese, divided
- Cornmeal
- 1 tsp (5 mL) crumbled dried sage
- 2 Tbsp (30 mL) canola oil

Punch down the dough; blend in ¼ cup (60 mL) of the cheese and form into a ball. Turn out onto a lightly floured surface and cover with the bowl; let stand for 10 minutes. Roll out into a 10-inch (25 cm) circle. Transfer to a baking sheet lightly sprinkled with cornmeal.

Make indentations all overtop with your fingertips.

Drain the onion and scatter over the dough. Sprinkle with the remaining cheese, the sage and the oil.

Sprinkle all over with 1 tsp (5 mL) cold water; bake in a 425°F (220°C) oven for 20 to 25 minutes or until golden. Cut into wedges to serve warm.

Tuna and Fresh Tomato Pizzas

....

MAKES 4 SERVINGS

These little pizzas are made with ingredients you probably already have on hand. You can make your own pizza dough rounds by doubling the Pizza Dough recipe on page 100, or you can buy them at a super-market or bakery.

- Cornmeal
- Four 7-inch (18 cm) pizza dough rounds
- ¼ cup (60 mL) olive oil, divided
- ¾ lb (375 g) mozzarella cheese, thinly sliced
- 1 tsp (5 mL) dried thyme
- 2 cloves garlic, minced
- Two 6½-oz (185 g) cans tuna, drained and flaked
- 2 tomatoes, thinly sliced
- ¼ cup (60 mL) freshly grated Parmesan cheese

SPRINKLE 2 BAKING sheets with cornmeal; place the pizza rounds on top. Brush the rounds with half of the oil.

Divide the mozzarella among the pizza rounds, leaving a small border on the outsides; sprinkle the thyme and garlic over the cheese.

Arrange the tuna and tomato on the pizzas, sprinkle with the Parmesan and drizzle with the remaining oil. Bake in the lower third of a 500°F (260°C) oven for 10 to 15 minutes or until the bottoms are golden brown.

Pasta

CHÈVRE AND FRESH TOMATO PASTA

Chèvre and Fresh Tomato Pasta

MAKES 4 TO 6 SERVINGS

The heat of this pasta will bring out the sunny flavour of garden-fresh tomatoes and the creamy goodness of fresh goat cheese. The flavour is also delightful with a good-quality feta and dried basil. To seed tomatoes, cut them in half crosswise, squeeze gently and help out seeds with the end of a sharp knife. There's no need to peel.

- 2 lb (1 kg) ripe plum or regular tomatoes, seeded and diced
- ¾ cup (175 mL) coarsely chopped pitted black olives
- ¼ cup (60 mL) loosely packed slivered fresh basil
- ¼ cup (60 mL) olive oil
- 1 Tbsp (15 mL) slivered lemon zest
- 1 clove garlic, minced
- ¼ tsp (1 mL) pepper
- ¾ lb (375 g) fresh goat cheese (chèvre), crumbled (about 1½ cups/375 mL)
- ½ cup (125 mL) freshly grated Parmesan cheese
- 4 cups (1 L) corkscrew pasta or penne

IN A LARGE bowl, stir together the tomatoes, olives, basil, oil, lemon zest, garlic and pepper; gently stir in the goat cheese and Parmesan.

In a large pot of boiling salted water, cook the pasta until al dente (tender but firm). Drain well and add to the sauce. Toss and serve immediately.

Spicy Penne with Clams and Fresh Tomatoes

MAKES 4 SERVINGS

Canned fish or seafood is always handy to have in the cupboard for quick-and-easy pasta sauces like this one. It's perfect for tomato season.

- 4 tomatoes, seeded and diced (1½ lb/750 g total)
- 1 clove garlic, minced
- 2 Tbsp (30 mL) chopped fresh parsley
- 1 Tbsp (15 mL) anchovy paste

IN A LARGE bowl, stir together the tomatoes, garlic, parsley, anchovy paste, oregano, salt, pepper, hot pepper flakes and oil; stir in the clams.

In a large pot of boiling salted water, cook the pasta until al dente (tender but firm). Drain well and toss with the tomato-clam mixture. Serve immediately with the Parmesan cheese.

- 1 Tbsp (15 mL) chopped fresh oregano (or 1 tsp/ 5 mL dried)
- ½ tsp (2 mL) salt
- ¼ tsp (1 mL) pepper
- ¼ tsp (1 mL) hot pepper flakes
- ¼ cup (60 mL) olive oil
- One 5-oz (142 g) can baby clams, drained and rinsed
- ¾ lb (375 g) penne or linguine
- Freshly grated Parmesan cheese

Jiffy Mac and Cheese

MAKES 3 OR 4 SERVINGS

This easy version of old-fashioned macaroni and cheese will be ready in a matter of minutes. Serve with warm stewed tomatoes and toast for instant comfort at lunch or dinner.

- 4 cups (1 L) corkscrew pasta
- 2 Tbsp (30 mL) butter
- 1 Tbsp (15 mL) Dijon mustard
- ½ tsp (2 mL) pepper
- ½ tsp (2 mL) Worcestershire sauce
- ¼ tsp (1 mL) salt
- 2 cups (500 mL) shredded old Cheddar cheese
- ¼ cup (60 mL) light sour cream

IN A LARGE pot of boiling salted water, cook the pasta until tender but firm. Drain in a colander.

In the pasta pot, melt the butter over low heat; stir in the mustard, pepper, Worcestershire sauce and salt. Return the pasta to the pot and toss to coat.

Remove from heat. Add the cheese and sour cream; toss to combine. Let the cheese melt and serve.

Mom's Oven-Baked Macaroni and Cheese with Tomatoes

MAKES 6 TO 8 SERVINGS

Occasionally, I get a real craving for a big dish of macaroni and cheese just like my mother used to bake. You can divide this recipe between two 6-cup (1.5 L) casserole dishes and reduce the baking time to 35 minutes. Freeze the second one to have on hand when the craving strikes again.

- ½ lb (250 g) elbow macaroni (2 cups/500 mL)
- 1 lb (500 g) Cheddar cheese, preferably old
- One 28-oz (796 mL) can tomatoes, diced
- 1 tsp (5 mL) granulated sugar
- 1 tsp (5 mL) Worcestershire sauce
- ½ tsp (2 mL) dried summer savory
- ½ tsp (2 mL) salt
- ½ tsp (2 mL) Tabasco
- ¼ tsp (1 mL) pepper
- 2 eggs, beaten
- 1 cup (250 mL) milk

IN A LARGE pot of boiling salted water, cook the macaroni until just tender, about 8 minutes; do not overcook. Drain well and transfer to a well-buttered 12-cup (3 L) casserole.

Meanwhile, shred half of the cheese and set aside. Thinly slice the remainder; set aside.

Drain ¾ cup (175 mL) of the juice from the tomatoes and reserve for another use. Pour the tomatoes and remaining juice into a bowl; chop the tomatoes if not already diced. Stir in the shredded cheese, sugar, Worcestershire sauce, savory, salt, Tabasco and pepper; pour over the macaroni and mix well. Top with the cheese slices.

In a small bowl, blend the eggs with the milk; pour over the cheese-covered macaroni but do not stir. Bake in a 350°F (180°C) oven for 40 to 50 minutes or until the top is golden brown.

Quick Hot or Cold Pasta with Fresh Tomato Sauce

MAKES 4 SERVINGS

The uncooked tomato sauce has to be made ahead for flavours to mingle. Serve on hot pasta or as a cold pasta salad with tossed greens and crusty rolls.

PEEL, SEED AND chop the tomatoes. In a bowl, combine the tomatoes, ham, garlic, basil, parsley, oregano, vinegar, salt, sugar and pepper. Cover and refrigerate for at least 1 hour, or overnight.

In a large pot of boiling salted water, cook the pasta until tender but firm. Drain well and toss with the olive oil, tomato sauce and zucchini. Serve with the cheese.

- 4 large ripe tomatoes (about 2 lb/1 kg)
- ½ lb (250 g) cooked smoked ham, turkey or chicken, julienned
- 2 cloves garlic, minced
- ⅓ cup (75 mL) chopped fresh basil (or 1 Tbsp/15 mL dried)
- ⅓ cup (75 mL) chopped fresh parsley
- 2 Tbsp (30 mL) chopped fresh oregano (or 1 tsp/ 5 mL dried)
- 1 tsp (5 mL) red wine vinegar
- ½ tsp (2 mL) salt
- ½ tsp (2 mL) granulated sugar
- ¼ tsp (1 mL) pepper
- 6 cups (1.5 L) corkscrew pasta
- 2 Tbsp (30 mL) olive oil
- 2 small zucchini, shredded
- Freshly grated Parmesan cheese

Fettuccine with Creamy Rosemary Shrimp

MAKES 4 SERVINGS

Serve this quick, delicious main course as a celebration meal with hot crusty rolls and a green salad.

IN A LARGE pot of boiling salted water, cook the pasta until tender but firm; drain well.

Meanwhile, in a skillet, melt the butter over low heat; cook the green onion

- 1 lb (500 g) fettuccine
- 2 Tbsp (30 mL) butter
- 2 Tbsp (30 mL) chopped green onion
- 1 lb (500 g) shrimp, peeled and deveined
- ½ cup (125 mL) whipping cream
- 2 tsp (10 mL) minced fresh parsley
- 2 tsp (10 mL) minced fresh rosemary (or

PASTA PRESTO

....

Fresh pasta will take as little as 2 minutes to cook; dried will take 7 to 10 minutes or more. Use a large pot with about 16 cups (4 L) of cold, salted water for every pound (500 g) of pasta, but fill the pot no more than two-thirds full of water.

Bring to a full boil before adding the pasta a bit at a time. Cover to bring back to a boil, but remove the lid as soon as you hear a rolling boil again. Start timing and stir often, preferably with a wooden fork. Pasta is cooked when it's al dente, tender but still firm to the bite and not mushy.

Save energy and cut back on clean-up time, too, by trying to use the same bowl or pot for more than one purpose: for example, cook a vegetable with the pasta.

TORTELLINI TOSS WITH BROCCOLI AND ROASTED RED PEPPERS

until softened, about 3 minutes. Add the shrimp and increase heat to medium-low; cook for 5 minutes, turning until just pink all over.

Reduce heat to low; stir in the cream, parsley and rosemary. Increase heat to medium and bring to a boil, stirring often. Add the vermouth and mix gently. Serve immediately on the hot pasta.

Tortellini Toss with Broccoli and Roasted Red Peppers

MAKES 4 SERVINGS.

Broccoli florets cook in the colander as you drain hot pasta over them for an easy and colourful pasta supper. Bottled roasted red peppers are available in most supermarkets.

- ½ cup (125 mL) drained bottled roasted red peppers, cut into strips
- ¼ cup (60 mL) olive oil
- ¼ cup (60 mL) chopped fresh parsley
- ¼ cup (60 mL) freshly grated Parmesan cheese (approx.)
- 2 cloves garlic, minced
- ½ tsp (2 mL) pepper
- 1 lb (500 g) tortellini with meat
- 4 cups (1 L) small broccoli florets (about ¼ lb/125 g)

IN A LARGE bowl, stir together the red peppers, oil, parsley, cheese, garlic and pepper.

In a large pot of boiling salted water, cook the pasta until al dente (tender but firm).

Place the broccoli in a colander; drain the pasta over the broccoli. Add to the bowl and toss to combine. Serve immediately with more Parmesan cheese.

Monda Rosenberg's Easy Spicy Lasagna

MAKES 8 SERVINGS

Monda Rosenberg, my long-time good friend and former Food Editor at Chatelaine magazine, knew her readers wanted great tasting food without having to spend hours in the kitchen. Monda's spicy lasagna is an excellent example of this. Accompany with crusty bread and a green salad.

- ½ tsp/2 mL dried)
- ¼ cup (60 mL) dry vermouth

- 2 Tbsp (30 mL) canola oil
- 2 lb (1 kg) hot or mild Italian sausage, casings removed
- One 28-oz (796 mL) can meatless spaghetti sauce
- 2 cloves garlic, crushed
- 12 lasagna noodles
- 1 lb (500 g) ricotta, drained if necessary
- 2 eggs
- ½ lb (250 g) mozzarella cheese, grated

IN A LARGE heavy-bottomed saucepan, heat the oil over medium heat; cook the sausage, breaking it up with a fork, until no longer pink. Drain off any fat.

Stir in the spaghetti sauce and garlic; bring to a boil. Cover, reduce heat and simmer for 15 minutes, stirring occasionally.

Meanwhile, cook the lasagna noodles according to the package directions until tender but firm. Drain and lay flat on clean tea towels.

If not using smooth tub ricotta, whirl it with the eggs in a food processor or blender until fairly smooth. If the ricotta is already smooth, just beat the eggs in a bowl and stir in the ricotta.

To assemble, spread 1 cup (250 mL) meat sauce in a 13 × 9–inch (3 L) baking dish. Cover with a layer of noodles, half of the ricotta mixture, one-third of the remaining meat sauce and one-third of the mozzarella. Repeat layers, ending with noodles, meat sauce and mozzarella. (The recipe can be prepared to this point, covered and refrigerated or frozen. Thaw in the refrigerator before proceeding and remove from the refrigerator 30 minutes before cooking.)

Bake, uncovered, in a 350°F (180°C) oven for 30 to 45 minutes or until bubbly around the edges.

Pasta with Flavourful Spinach Pesto

MAKES 4 SERVINGS

One of my favourite no-cook sauces is pesto made with fresh basil leaves. However, if your basil crop is not as plentiful as you would like, try this version of pesto, which is especially good with fresh-market bunch spinach. Enjoy with a fresh tomato salad and crusty bread.

- 4 cups (1 L) loosely packed stemmed spinach
- ½ cup (125 mL) loosely packed stemmed fresh parsley
- ½ cup (125 mL) freshly grated Parmesan cheese (approx.)
- ⅓ cup (75 mL) coarsely chopped walnuts
- ¼ cup (60 mL) olive oil
- 2 cloves garlic
- Salt and pepper
- 1 lb (500 g) pasta

IN A FOOD processor or blender, chop the spinach and parsley; add the cheese, walnuts and oil. With the motor running, drop in the garlic. Season with salt and pepper to taste. (The recipe can be prepared to this point, covered and refrigerated for up to 2 days.)

In a large pot of boiling salted water, cook the pasta until al dente (tender but firm). Reserving ¼ cup (60 mL) of the cooking water, drain the pasta well. Blend the hot liquid into the spinach purée; toss with the hot pasta. Serve immediately with additional cheese.

Short-Cut Rotini with Broccoli and Clams

MAKES 2 SERVINGS

Fresh broccoli cooks in less time than it will take the frozen variety to thaw. You can usually buy pre-cut broccoli florets in produce departments for this quick and pretty dish, and the recipe is easily divided in half for one person. Freeze the other half can of clams for another night.

IN A LARGE pot of boiling salted water, cook the rotini for 4 minutes. Add the broccoli and cook for 2 minutes, or until the rotini is tender but firm.

Meanwhile, in a large skillet, melt the butter with the oil over low heat; cook the garlic and hot pepper flakes for 3 minutes. Reserving the liquid, add the clams to the skillet and heat through; stir in the liquid.

Drain the broccoli and pasta well and stir into the skillet. Increase heat to high; cook until the pasta has absorbed most of the liquid, stirring often, about 4 minutes. Sprinkle generously with pepper. Serve on warmed plates. Sprinkle with lots of cheese and serve immediately.

- 1⅓ cups (325 mL) uncooked rotini or other pasta (about ¼ lb/125 g)
- 2 cups (500 mL) small broccoli florets (about ¼ lb/125 g)
- 1 Tbsp (15 mL) butter
- 1 Tbsp (15 mL) olive oil
- 2 cloves garlic, minced
- Pinch hot pepper flakes
- One 3-oz (85 g) can clams (preferably pink)
- Pepper
- Freshly grated Parmesan cheese

1959 photo: I was 18 years old, in our farm kitchen where my mother taught me to cook on both a wood and an electric stove. The whole family is there . . . as you look at it (from left to right): my sister Muriel, my father George, my brother Allen, myself, my sister Helen, my mother Josephine and my brother John on the floor. We are on the cot where my father had a nap every day after lunch . . . or, as he said, where he "just rested his eyes."

SIMPLE SIDES

....

WHEN LOCALLY GROWN produce is fresh and in season, a simple treatment is best. Little needs to be done to dewy-fresh corn or sun-ripe tomatoes right off the vine. Even storage vegetables, like carrots or rutabaga, have such wonderful real flavour that a straightforward preparation is all that's necessary. The important thing to remember is not to overcook any of these good things.

The recipes in this chapter are short, simple and delicious little twists on the common dishes that often accompany main courses, with many make-ahead ideas for festive meals (with the potato, one of my all-time favourite foods, taking the spotlight).

Fast Oven-Roasted Asparagus

MAKES 4 SERVINGS

One year, when I was doing a lot of work with asparagus, I discovered that oven roasting at a high temperature was not only fast but also easy, and provided a new dimension to asparagus. It becomes nuttier and of a more substantial texture. I do it often for guests, and it never fails to impress them. This recipe can be doubled easily.

- 1 lb (500 g) asparagus spears
- 1 Tbsp (15 mL) canola oil
- Salt and pepper

SPREAD THE ASPARAGUS in a single layer in a large baking pan. Drizzle with the oil; sprinkle with salt and pepper to taste.

Roast, uncovered, in a 500°F (260°C) oven for about 8 minutes, stirring once, until tender but still slightly firm.

Do-Ahead Mashed Potato Casserole with Parsley Crumb Topping

MAKES 8 SERVINGS

I always prepare potatoes in a make-ahead casserole like this for special holiday dinners. It eliminates peeling and mashing potatoes when visiting is more important.

- 8 potatoes, peeled
- ¼ cup (60 mL) butter, divided
- ½ lb (250 g) cream cheese, in bits
- ¾ cup (175 mL) light sour cream
- Salt and pepper
- ¼ cup (60 mL) fine fresh breadcrumbs
- ¼ cup (60 mL) chopped fresh parsley

IN A SAUCEPAN of boiling salted water, cover and cook the potatoes for about 30 minutes or until tender. Drain well and return to the heat briefly to dry.

Mash the potatoes with half of the butter. Add the cream cheese, sour cream and salt and pepper to taste. With an electric hand mixer, beat the potato mixture until creamy. Spoon into a greased 8-cup (2 L) casserole.

Melt the remaining butter; stir together with the breadcrumbs and parsley. Sprinkle evenly over the potato mixture. Let cool, cover and refrigerate overnight.

Bake, covered, in a 350°F (180°C) oven for 20 minutes. Uncover and bake for 10 minutes longer or until heated through.

Lean but Comfortable Colcannon

MAKES 4 SERVINGS

One of the most comforting vegetable dishes ever whipped up, colcannon is a favourite Irish recipe that is topped off with a little pool of melted butter. I've updated an old favourite by removing most of the butter and beating in yogurt, but you'll be glad to know it's still as comfortable as ever.

- 5 potatoes, peeled
- ½ small cabbage, coarsely shredded
- 1 small onion, chopped
- 1 Tbsp (15 mL) butter
- 4 green onions, finely sliced
- ½ cup (125 mL) low-fat plain yogurt, at room temperature
- ¼ tsp (1 mL) nutmeg
- Salt and pepper

QUARTER THE POTATOES. In a saucepan with a small amount of boiling salted water, cover and cook the potatoes for 20 minutes. Add the cabbage and onion; cook for about 10 minutes or until the potatoes are tender. Drain well in a colander.

Meanwhile, in the same saucepan, melt the butter over medium heat; cook the green onions until softened, about 3 minutes. Add the potato mixture and mash well.

Whisk in the yogurt, nutmeg and salt and pepper to taste until light and fluffy. Serve immediately.

FAST OVEN-ROASTED ASPARAGUS

Dilled New-Potato Kabobs

MAKES 4 SERVINGS

Tiny new waxy potatoes are on the market before you know it in the spring. One of my favourite ways of enjoying them is to boil them until just tender, then grill them for a few minutes to reheat and give them a barbecued taste. These are particularly good with grilled fish.

- 16 small new potatoes (unpeeled)
- 3 Tbsp (45 mL) canola oil
- 2 Tbsp (30 mL) finely chopped fresh dill (or 2 tsp/ 10 mL dried dill)
- 1 green onion, minced
- ½ tsp (2 mL) salt
- Pinch hot pepper flakes

SCRUB THE POTATOES. In a saucepan of boiling salted water, cover and cook the potatoes until barely tender, about 10 minutes; drain well.

In a small bowl, stir together the oil, dill, onion, salt and hot pepper flakes; add the potatoes and toss well. (The potatoes can be prepared to this point and left at room temperature for up to 4 hours.)

Thread 4 skewers with 4 potatoes each. Pour the remaining marinade over the potatoes and lay the skewers on a greased, medium-high grill, or 4 inches (10 cm) above medium-hot coals. Barbecue, turning often, for 3 to 4 minutes, or until the skins are crisp and the potatoes are heated through.

New Potatoes Roasted with Olive Oil and Garlic

MAKES ABOUT 4 SERVINGS

When available, I love to buy waxy little new potatoes at the farmers' markets, toss them with olive oil, garlic and herbs and roast them until they're tender but crusty on the outside.

- 12 small new potatoes (about 2 lb/1 kg), unpeeled
- 4 cloves garlic, crushed
- 2 Tbsp (30 mL) olive oil
- 2 tsp (10 mL) finely chopped fresh rosemary or thyme (or ½ tsp/ 2 mL dried)

SCRUB AND DRY the potatoes. In a small roasting pan, toss together the potatoes, garlic, oil, rosemary and paprika.

- 1 tsp (5 mL) paprika
- Salt and pepper

Cover and roast in a 375°F (190°C) oven until tender, 30 to 40 minutes, stirring occasionally. Season with salt and pepper to taste.

Easy Down-Home Scalloped Potatoes

MAKES 4 SERVINGS

When I make scalloped potatoes, I make a thin layer of potatoes and onions, then sprinkle them with flour, salt and pepper, repeating until the dish is full. I pour in milk until I can see it from the top, then I dot with butter and bake. The following method is just as easy (although it does dirty a bowl and a wooden spoon), and it gives novice cooks some idea of the quantities involved without having to just eyeball it.

- 2 lb (1 kg) potatoes (about 8), washed and peeled
- 2 Tbsp (30 mL) all-purpose flour
- 1 tsp (5 mL) salt
- ¼ tsp (1 mL) pepper
- 1 small onion, thinly sliced
- 2 Tbsp (30 mL) butter
- 2 cups (500 mL) milk

DRY THE POTATOES well and thinly slice. In a bowl, toss together the potatoes, flour, salt and pepper; layer half in a greased deep 8-cup (2 L) casserole. Sprinkle with half of the onion; dot with half of the butter. Repeat layers. Pour in the milk.

Cover and bake in a 350°F (180°C) oven for 30 minutes. Uncover and bake for another 30 to 35 minutes, until golden and bubbly.

Parmesan Oven-Fried Potato Slices

MAKES 4 SERVINGS

Crisp and delicious, these oven-baked potato slices rival potato chips, but they are cooked with little fat and are much less bother than deep-frying. If you wish, omit the

POTATOES

....

I find almost no other food as satisfying as a potato. It's such a simple vegetable, but brings great comfort—whether it's baked to steamy softness inside a crunchy skin and slathered with yogurt, perfectly mashed with milk and butter, deep-fried to a golden crispness, dressed in a tangy salad or made into a soothing, creamy soup.

There must be other Canadians who share my love of potatoes, since it is the country's most important vegetable crop, with the Maritimes leading the way in production since potatoes were first cultivated in Port Royal, Nova Scotia, in 1623.

My one big complaint about potatoes is that when we buy them here, we can't always tell what kind they are—not like apples that are either Empires, McIntoshes or so on. A few growers are now labelling potatoes like russet and Yukon Gold, and some companies are now labelling some potatoes as baking, which at least gives you an idea of what to do with them. As a general rule, without knowing any names for potatoes, you can discover their best use by looking at them. Round, smooth potatoes are best for boiling, as scalloped potatoes or in salads. Oblong potatoes with a faint crisscross kind of pattern on the skin usually have the floury texture that's best for baking, deep-frying and mashing.

lemon juice and Parmesan and sprinkle with salt instead.

SCRUB THE POTATOES well. Slice no thicker than ¼ inch (5 mm), dropping the slices into a bowl of cold water as you work. (Leave for at least 15 minutes, or up to 3 hours.)

Line a 15 × 10–inch (2 L) jelly-roll pan with foil for easier cleanup. Put the oil and butter in the pan; place in a 450°F (230°C) oven until the butter melts.

Drain the potatoes and pat dry. Add to the pan and toss to coat, spreading out as much as possible. Sprinkle with pepper to taste. Bake for 15 minutes.

With a spatula, turn the potatoes; sprinkle with the lemon juice and Parmesan cheese. Bake for 10 to 15 minutes, or until golden brown and crusty.

- 4 large potatoes (unpeeled)
- 2 Tbsp (30 mL) canola oil
- 2 Tbsp (30 mL butter)
- Pepper
- 1 Tbsp (15 mL) fresh lemon juice
- 2 Tbsp (30 mL) freshly grated Parmesan cheese

Cheese and Mushroom Potatoes

....

MAKES 4 SERVINGS

My friend Joan Mahaffey serves this yummy mixture as a dip for crackers, but it's fantastic on baked potatoes, too, for a fun supper you can prepare ahead. Accompany with a green salad.

PREHEAT THE OVEN to 425°F (220°C). Scrub the potatoes clean under cold, running water. Dry well, then prick 2 or 3 times with a fork or sharp knife. In a shallow pan just large enough to hold the potatoes, melt ¼ cup (60 mL)

- 4 large potatoes
- ¼ cup + 2 Tbsp (90 mL) butter, divided
- ½ tsp (2 mL) coarse salt
- 8 slices bacon, cut into ½-inch (1 cm) pieces
- 1 small onion, finely chopped
- 1 lb (500 g) mushrooms, sliced
- 2 Tbsp (30 mL) all-purpose flour
- 1 cup (250 mL) light sour cream
- 1 tsp (5 mL) fresh lemon juice
- Pinch cayenne pepper

butter over medium heat. Place the potatoes in the pan, rolling to coat them with the butter. Sprinkle with the coarse salt. Bake, uncovered and turning once, until tender, about 1 hour or more, depending on the size and variety of the potato.

While the potatoes are baking, cook the bacon until almost crisp in a large skillet; with a slotted spoon, transfer to a 9-inch (23 cm) pie plate. Discard any drippings from the skillet.

In the same skillet, melt the remaining butter over medium heat; cook the onion until softened but not browned, about 3 minutes. Add the mushrooms and cook, stirring often, until golden brown, about 3 minutes longer. Stir in the flour; cook over low heat, stirring constantly, for 3 minutes.

Stir in the sour cream, lemon juice and cayenne. Spoon into the pie plate and sprinkle evenly with the cheese. (The mixture can be prepared to this point, covered and refrigerated for up to 4 hours.)

Bake, uncovered, in a 350°F (180°C) oven for 20 to 30 minutes or until bubbly and heated through. Cut an "X" in each potato, gently squeeze to loosen the pulp slightly and spoon the topping on top.

- 2 cups (500 mL) shredded old Cheddar cheese (about ½ lb/250 g)

Sweet Potato Party Flan

....

MAKES 8 TO 10 SERVINGS

A smooth, flavourful purée is garnished with slices of the vegetable itself to resemble the crust on a flan.

SCRUB THE POTATOES. In a large saucepan of boiling salted water, cover and cook the sweet potatoes for about 25 minutes or until tender but not mushy.

- 3½ lb (1.75 kg) sweet potatoes (unpeeled)
- ¼ cup (60 mL) whipping cream
- 2 Tbsp (30 mL) butter, divided
- 2 Tbsp (30 mL) liquid honey
- ½ tsp (2 mL) nutmeg
- Salt and pepper

Drain, peel and thinly slice. Set aside enough slices to overlap in a ring around the rim of a deep 9-inch (23 cm) pie plate or baking dish.

In a food processor or blender, purée the remaining sweet potatoes, cream, half of the butter, the honey, nutmeg and salt and pepper to taste until smooth and fluffy. Taste and adjust seasoning.

Spoon into the greased dish; arrange the slices, overlapping slightly, around the inside of the rim. Dot with the remaining butter. (The recipe can be prepared to this point, covered with foil and refrigerated for up to 2 days.)

Bake, covered, in a 325°F (160°C) oven for about 30 minutes or until heated through.

Sautéed Rosemary Parsnips

MAKES 4 SERVINGS

Although parsnips are especially sweet if allowed to stay in the garden over the winter, I can never wait that long to enjoy this beautiful vegetable. This version is especially good with roast lamb.

- 1 lb (500 g) parsnips (about 4)
- ¼ cup (60 mL) all-purpose flour
- ½ tsp (2 mL) crushed dried rosemary
- ½ tsp (2 mL) salt
- ¼ tsp (1 mL) pepper
- 2 Tbsp (30 mL) butter (approx.)

PEEL THE PARSNIPS; cut into pieces about 2 inches (5 cm) long and 1 inch (2.5 cm) wide. In a saucepan of boiling salted water, cover and cook the parsnips for about 5 minutes, or until almost tender. Drain well.

In a small shallow bowl, stir together the flour, rosemary, salt and pepper; add the parsnips and roll to coat each piece.

In a large heavy skillet, melt the butter over medium heat; cook the parsnips until golden brown on all sides, about 3 minutes, adding a bit more butter if necessary and turning often.

Maple-Glazed Onions

MAKES 6 TO 8 SERVINGS

Maple syrup adds a wonderful depth of flavour to little pearl onions in this simple side dish, which would make a delicious accompaniment to roast pork or poultry.

- Two 10-oz (284 g) pkg pearl onions
- ⅓ cup (75 mL) maple syrup
- ¼ cup (60 mL) butter
- Salt and pepper

IN A POT OF boiling water, blanch the onions for 3 minutes; drain and refresh under cold running water. Drain well and peel them; cut an "X" in the bottom of each onion. Place in a greased shallow baking dish just big enough to hold them in a single layer.

In a small saucepan, boil the maple syrup until reduced by one-quarter; stir in the butter until melted. Pour over the onions; sprinkle with salt and pepper to taste and stir to coat. Bake, uncovered and basting occasionally, in a 350°F (180°C) oven for about 45 minutes or until tender and browned.

Brussels Sprouts Tossed in Orange Butter

MAKES 6 SERVINGS

These tiny, elegant members of the cabbage family will remain mild and retain their colour if not overcooked and served immediately. I serve them often for company and at holiday meals.

- 1½ lb (750 g) Brussels sprouts
- 2 Tbsp (30 mL) butter
- 1½ tsp (7 mL) grated orange zest
- ¼ cup (60 mL) fresh orange juice
- Salt and pepper

TRIM THE SPROUTS and, if large, cut an "X" in each bottom. Steam for 6 to 10 minutes or until barely tender when pierced with a knife. (Alternately, you can boil, uncovered, in a large pot of salted water for 4 to 8 minutes, or microwave with a small amount of water for 8 to 10 minutes.) Drain and halve lengthwise.

In a large skillet, melt the butter; toss in the sprouts and heat through. Toss with the orange zest and juice; season with salt and pepper to taste.

Gingered Squash and Pear Purée

MAKES 8 SERVINGS

Take advantage of the wonderful array of sweet winter squashes available in fall markets for this smooth purée with its intriguing ginger-pear flavour.

- 2¼ lb (1.12 kg) winter squash
- ¼ cup (60 mL) butter, divided
- 2 pears, peeled and cut into 1-inch (2.5 cm) chunks
- 2 Tbsp (30 mL) chopped candied ginger
- 1 Tbsp (15 mL) fresh lemon juice
- ½ tsp (2 mL) salt
- ¼ tsp (1 mL) pepper
- ¼ tsp (1 mL) ground ginger
- Pinch ground cardamom

CUT THE SQUASH in half and remove the seeds; cover and bake in a 350°F (180°C) oven for 40 to 60 minutes or until tender. (Or, cover with vented plastic wrap and microwave on high for 8 to 10 minutes, or until tender. Drain off any excess moisture.)

Meanwhile, in a skillet, melt 2 Tbsp (30 mL) of the butter over medium-low heat; cook the pears for about 15 minutes or until tender, stirring occasionally. Transfer to a food processor or blender.

Scoop out the pulp from the squash and add to the food processor with the remaining butter, candied ginger, lemon juice, salt, pepper, ground ginger and cardamom; process until very smooth. (Purée can be cooled, covered and refrigerated for up to 8 hours. Reheat for about 20 minutes in the top of a double boiler over boiling water.) Taste and adjust seasoning.

Braised Red Cabbage with Cranberries

MAKES 8 SERVINGS

Both red cabbage and cranberries add a beautiful splash of colour to any plate. Here, they team up in a delicious side dish that goes well with goose or duck.

CORE THE CABBAGE and thinly shred into a large glass bowl; toss with the vinegar and set aside.

In a large stainless steel saucepan, heat the oil over medium heat; chop one of the onions and cook until softened. Stir in the apples, sugar and orange juice.

Push the cloves into the remaining onion; add to the pan along with the cinnamon stick. Stir in the cabbage mixture and bring to a boil. Reduce heat to low and simmer, partially covered and stirring occasionally, until the cabbage is tender, about 15 minutes.

Increase heat to medium-high and add the cranberries; cook, uncovered and stirring often, until the berries begin to pop, about 5 minutes. Discard the whole onion and cinnamon stick.

(The cabbage can be served warm or cooled, spooned into a serving bowl, covered and refrigerated for up to 1 day. Bring to room temperature to serve.) Garnish with orange zest.

- 1 red cabbage (about 1½ lb/750 g)
- ¼ cup (60 mL) red wine vinegar
- 2 Tbsp (30 mL) canola oil
- 2 small onions, divided
- 2 apples, peeled and chopped
- 1¼ cups (300 mL) granulated sugar
- ¼ cup (60 mL) fresh orange juice
- 4 whole cloves
- One 3-inch (8 cm) cinnamon stick, broken in half
- 4 cups (1 L) cranberries
- Orange zest

Make-Ahead Baked Rutabaga Carrot Purée

MAKES 8 TO 10 SERVINGS

No traditional Christmas table would be complete without rutabaga (a vegetable we used to call yellow turnip), but don't wait for a holiday to make this creamy do-ahead casserole. The sweetness of carrots adds a certain mellowness to the rutabaga in an ideal accompaniment to turkey, roast chicken, pork or beef.

PEEL THE RUTABAGA and carrots and cut into ½-inch (1.25 cm) chunks.

In a saucepan, combine the rutabaga, carrots, onion, stock, three-quarters of the butter, the sugar and nutmeg; bring to a boil. Reduce heat and cook, partially covered, for about 45 minutes or until the vegetables are very tender, stirring occasionally.

With a slotted spoon, transfer the vegetables to a food processor or blender. Set the pan over high heat and boil the remaining liquid for 2 to 3 minutes or until reduced to about 1 Tbsp (15 mL). Add to the vegetable mixture along with the cream and purée until smooth. Taste and season with salt and pepper. Transfer to a greased 6-cup (1.5 L) casserole or soufflé dish.

Melt the remaining butter; stir together with the nuts. Sprinkle evenly around edge of the casserole to make a border. Let cool, cover and refrigerate for up to 24 hours. Remove from the refrigerator 30 minutes before reheating.

Bake, covered, in a 350°F (180°C) oven for about 30 minutes or until heated through, removing the lid for the last 10 minutes.

- 1 small rutabaga
- 4 carrots
- ½ onion, coarsely chopped
- 1½ cups (375 mL) chicken stock
- ¼ cup (60 mL) butter, divided
- 1 tsp (5 mL) packed brown sugar
- Pinch nutmeg
- ¼ cup (60 mL) whipping cream or light sour cream
- Salt and pepper
- 2 Tbsp (30 mL) finely chopped pecans or walnuts

Simple Garlic-Sautéed Green Beans

MAKES 8 SERVINGS

This is my favourite treatment of green beans when I have a dinner party. The beans can be cooked early in the day, wrapped in a tea towel and just sautéed briefly at the last minute.

- 2 lb (1 kg) green beans, trimmed
- 3 Tbsp (45 mL) olive oil
- 2 cloves garlic, cut in half
- Salt and pepper
- 2 tsp (10 mL) fresh lemon juice

IN A LARGE saucepan, bring a large quantity of salted water to a boil; gradually add the beans and cook over medium-high heat, uncovered, for about 5 minutes or until cooked but still firm. Drain in a colander and refresh under cold running water. (The beans can be prepared to this point, wrapped in a tea towel and refrigerated for up to 8 hours.)

In a large skillet, heat the oil over medium heat and cook the garlic until browned. Discard the garlic. Add the beans and shake the pan to coat them. Season with salt and pepper to taste. Cover and cook over low heat for about 2 minutes or until heated through. Toss with the lemon juice.

Special-Occasion Carrots Glazed with Honey and Mint

MAKES ABOUT 4 SERVINGS

This quick-and-easy side dish goes particularly well with grilled or roast lamb. If you want a wonderful accompaniment to roast chicken, substitute sage for the mint, cutting the amount in half.

- 15 thin carrots (about 1¼ lb/625 g)
- 2 Tbsp (30 mL) butter
- ½ tsp (2 mL) granulated sugar
- ¼ tsp (1 mL) salt
- ¼ tsp (1 mL) pepper
- ⅓ cup (75 mL) water
- 2 Tbsp (30 mL) liquid honey
- ¼ cup (60 mL) whipping cream
- 1 Tbsp (15 mL) finely chopped fresh mint

CUT THE CARROTS into 1-inch (2.5 cm) pieces and set aside.

In a large skillet, melt the butter over medium heat; cook the carrots, sugar, salt and pepper for 3 minutes, stirring occasionally. Add the water and reduce heat; cover and simmer for 5 minutes or just until tender-crisp.

Uncover and increase heat to medium-high; cook for 2 to 4 minutes or until the liquid has evaporated. Add the honey and stir for 1 minute to coat the carrots. Pour in the cream; boil until thick enough to coat a spoon, about 2 minutes. Taste and adjust seasoning if necessary. Sprinkle with the mint.

ANNE LINDSAY'S COUSCOUS WITH LEMON AND FRESH BASIL

Creamed Skillet Corn

When corn is in season, this easy side dish has all the good flavour of corn on the cob and is elegant enough for company.

IN A LARGE skillet, melt the butter over medium-high heat; cook the corn, shallots and sugar, stirring, for 3 minutes.

Add the water and cover; reduce heat to low and cook for 5 to 7 minutes, or until the corn is tender.

Gradually stir in the cream; increase heat to medium and cook, uncovered, for 3 to 5 minutes or until the cream is reduced and coats the kernels. Season with the salt, pepper and nutmeg.

- 3 Tbsp (45 mL) butter
- 2 cups (500 mL) uncooked corn kernels (about 2 ears)
- 2¼ cup (60 mL) minced shallots or mild onion
- Pinch granulated sugar
- 2 Tbsp (30 mL) water
- ½ cup (125 mL) whipping cream
- Pinch salt
- Pinch pepper
- Pinch nutmeg

Anne Lindsay's Couscous with Lemon and Fresh Basil

MAKES 8 SERVINGS

My good friend Anne Lindsay shared with me one of her favourite recipes for couscous from her cookbook, Lighthearted Everyday Cooking. Couscous is made from semolina wheat and looks like a grain. Because it's so fast and easy to prepare, having a package on hand is a good idea when you need "instant" side dishes for things like chicken or fish. Almost all couscous sold in this country is the quick-cooking type,

- 2 cups (500 mL) chicken stock
- 1 Tbsp (15 mL) olive oil
- 1½ cups (375 mL) couscous
- 2 Tbsp (30 mL) fresh lemon juice
- ½ cup (125 mL) lightly packed chopped fresh basil
- Pepper

but follow the package directions in terms of the amount of liquid needed because it might vary.

IN A SAUCEPAN, bring the chicken stock to a boil; add the oil and couscous. Remove from heat; cover and let stand for 5 minutes or until the grains are tender and the liquid is absorbed.

Fluff the couscous with a fork; add the lemon juice and basil. Season with pepper to taste.

Wild Rice Lemon Pilaf

MAKES 8 SERVINGS

Wild rice is special to serve at dinner parties and celebrations. Here, I've extended this treat by combining it with some white rice in a wonderful full-flavoured accompaniment to roast poultry or pork.

IN A LARGE saucepan, combine the stock, wild rice, 1 Tbsp (15 mL) of the butter, half of the lemon zest and all of the lemon juice; bring to a boil. Cover and reduce heat to medium-low; simmer for 35 minutes.

- 4 cups (1 L) chicken stock
- 1 cup (250 mL) wild rice, rinsed
- ¼ cup (60 mL) butter, divided
- 1 Tbsp (15 mL) grated lemon zest, divided
- 2 Tbsp (30 mL) fresh lemon juice
- 2 onions, chopped
- 1½ cups (375 mL) long-grain white rice
- 1 cup (250 mL) chopped pecans, lightly toasted
- ½ cup (125 mL) chopped fresh parsley

Meanwhile, in a skillet, melt the remaining butter over medium heat; cook the onions until softened, about 8 minutes. Add the white rice and stir to coat; stir into the wild rice mixture. Bring to a boil, reduce heat, cover and cook over medium-low heat until the liquid is absorbed, 15 to 20 minutes. Remove from heat; let stand, covered, for 5 minutes.

Stir in the remaining zest, the pecans and the parsley. (The pilaf may be cooled, covered and refrigerated in a casserole dish for up to 2 days. Microwave, covered, on high for 6 to 8 minutes or bake, covered, in a 350°F/180°C oven, stirring occasionally, for about 20 minutes or until heated through.)

Carrot Pilaf

················

Your food processor can make short work of chopping the carrots and parsley for this pretty rice dish that makes a perfect accompaniment to Quick Lamb Chop Curry (see p. 84).

- 2 Tbsp (30 mL) butter
- 3 carrots, chopped
- 1 cup (250 mL) long-grain rice
- 1 tsp (5 mL) ground cumin
- 2½ cups (625 mL) chicken stock
- ¼ cup (60 mL) chopped fresh parsley
- Salt and pepper

IN A LARGE saucepan, melt the butter over medium heat; cook the carrots for 2 minutes. Stir in the rice and cumin; cook for 1 minute.

Stir in the stock and bring to a boil; reduce heat, cover and simmer for about 15 minutes or until the rice is tender and the stock is absorbed.

Stir in the parsley; season with salt and pepper to taste.

Fiddleheads Sautéed with Morels

···································

MAKES 6 SERVINGS

When some people move to a new area, they seek out a new dentist, doctor or hairdresser. We try to find the local fern patch. The summer show of big majestic fronds from the ostrich fern (no other should be eaten) indicates where we should start looking for the tight, furled fronds or fiddleheads, just peeking up from the midst of last year's old, dead ferns, in mid-April.

- ½ lb (250 g) fresh fiddleheads, cleaned (or a 10-oz/284 g pkg frozen)
- ¼ cup (60 mL) butter
- 1 lb (500 g) morels or small mushrooms
- 2 Tbsp (30 mL) fresh lemon juice
- 1 tsp (5 mL) finely chopped fresh tarragon (or ¼ tsp/1 mL dried)
- Salt and pepper

I'm not telling you where our patch is, but if you find your own (they can be anywhere in Canada), leave about half the fiddleheads in each clump to ensure a continued crop.

To clean, pull out each curl and shake off the husk, then wash in several changes of water and trim any dark ends.

They're wonderful cooked simply: uncovered, in a large amount of boiling, salted water, for 5 to 7 minutes, then seasoned with butter, lemon juice and salt and pepper. Or, try this quick sauté.

If morels (wild honeycombed mushrooms) are unavailable, substitute with regular mushrooms.

IN A SAUCEPAN of boiling salted water, blanch the fiddleheads for 1 minute. (If using frozen, thaw just to separate.) Drain well.

In a large, heavy skillet, melt the butter over medium heat; cook the fiddleheads and morels, stirring often, for about 8 minutes or until tender.

Stir in the lemon juice, tarragon and salt and pepper to taste.

Glistening Maple Rutabaga Slices

···

MAKES ABOUT 4 SERVINGS

Mashed rutabaga (also called yellow turnip or Swede) is a popular side dish to serve with roast poultry, beef or pork. Sometimes, however, I like to serve slices glazed with butter and honey or maple syrup, so that I can enjoy the somewhat substantial texture of the vegetable.

- 2 lb (1 kg) rutabaga (1 small)
- 1 Tbsp (15 mL) butter
- ¼ cup (60 mL) maple syrup
- ¼ tsp (1 mL) dried thyme
- Pinch ginger
- Salt and pepper

PEEL THE RUTABAGA and cut into ½-inch (1.25 cm) thick slices; quarter the slices. In a saucepan of boiling, salted water, cook the rutabaga for 15 minutes or just until tender; drain.

Immediately stir in the butter and toss to coat. Stir

in the maple syrup, thyme and ginger; cook, stirring, for 1 minute. Season with salt and pepper to taste.

Rum-Glazed Squash Slices

....

MAKES 8 SERVINGS

Rum gives winter squash a very interesting flavour, but if you wish, substitute maple syrup for the rum and sugar. Although the long striped sweet potato squash yields uniform slices, you can use any winter squash available.

- 2 large sweet potato squash
- ¼ cup (60 mL) dark rum
- 2 Tbsp (30 mL) butter
- 1 Tbsp (15 mL) diced candied ginger
- 1 Tbsp (15 mL) granulated sugar
- ¼ tsp (1 mL) pepper
- 1 Tbsp (15 mL) chopped fresh parsley

HALVE THE SQUASH lengthwise and scoop out the seeds and stringy membrane; cut into ½-inch (1.25 cm) thick slices without peeling. (The slices will stay together better if not peeled.)

In a large skillet with a small amount of boiling salted water, cook the squash for 7 to 10 minutes or until almost tender; drain off the water. Add the rum, butter, ginger, sugar and pepper. (The recipe can be prepared to this point and set aside at room temperature for up to 2 hours.)

Cook the squash over medium heat, uncovered, basting often and turning the slices, for 5 to 10 minutes or until tender and richly glazed. Sprinkle with parsley to serve.

SPECIAL SALADS

···

THERE'S GREAT VARIETY in salads. They can be as simple as a bowl of lettuce tossed with a light vinaigrette, or, when used as a main course, they can be a composed arrangement of any number of vegetables, meats, fish, grains or pastas. The dressings are limitless, and the end result can be served chilled, at room temperature or even warm.

Choosing different greens will add interesting shapes, colours and tastes. Look for peppery arugula, delicate oak leaf, purplish red and crisp radicchio, lemony sorrel, Belgian endive and chewy mâche (corn salad or lamb's lettuce), along with the more-regularly found romaine, escarole, watercress and cabbage.

And don't be shy about combining fruits and vegetables or adding cheese or grains. They'll diversify not only the flavour but also the texture and appearance of a salad.

In this chapter you'll find updated favourites and some new combinations, all with light and fresh dressings.

Sparkling Beet and Orange Salad

MAKES ABOUT 4 SERVINGS

There's something homey about the distinctive aroma that pervades your kitchen when beets are cooking, and I love their earthy flavour so much that I often serve beets to guests. The cooking time given is for small garden-fresh beets; larger storage beets (available later in the year) will take longer, maybe even an hour.

- 7 small beets (about 1 lb/500 g)
- ⅓ cup (75 mL) olive oil
- 2 Tbsp (30 mL) fresh lemon juice
- 1 tsp (5 mL) Dijon mustard
- Pinch cayenne pepper
- Salt and pepper
- 2 oranges
- 2 heads Belgian endive

IN A SAUCEPAN of boiling salted water, cook the beets, covered, for 10 to 20 minutes or until tender. Drain and cool under cold running water. Peel and slice thinly; place in a bowl.

In a small bowl, whisk together the olive oil, lemon juice, mustard, cayenne and salt and pepper to taste; pour over the beets and toss to coat.

Peel the oranges using a sharp knife to remove the outer membrane. Cut the oranges into slices ¼ inch (5 mm) thick. (The recipe can be prepared to this point, covered and refrigerated for up to 8 hours.)

Separate the endive leaves; arrange around the edge of a large round platter. With a slotted spoon, remove the beets and arrange overlapping slices in a circle inside the endive. Mound the orange slices in the centre of the plate, sprinkling with any remaining dressing.

Watercress and Pear Salad with Stilton Vinaigrette

MAKES 4 TO 6 SERVINGS

This is one of my preferred simple green salads. If you wish, use two bunches of watercress and omit the radicchio. If walnut oil is unavailable, substitute with additional canola oil.

- 2 Tbsp (30 mL) red wine vinegar
- 2 tsp (10 mL) Dijon mustard
- ½ tsp (2 mL) coarsely ground pepper (approx.)
- Pinch salt
- ¼ cup (60 mL) walnut oil
- 2 Tbsp (30 mL) canola oil
- 1 large bunch watercress
- 1 small head radicchio
- 2 large pears, peeled and sliced
- ½ cup (125 mL) crumbled Stilton or other blue cheese
- ½ cup (125 mL) toasted walnut halves or pieces

IN A MEDIUM bowl, whisk together the vinegar, mustard, pepper and salt; gradually whisk in the walnut and canola oils. (The dressing can be refrigerated for up to 3 hours.)

Remove any large stems from the watercress and tear the radicchio into bite-size pieces. Arrange in a shallow salad bowl or on individual plates. Arrange pear slices on top.

Whisk the dressing and stir in the cheese; pour over the salad. Sprinkle with walnut halves and more pepper if desired.

Intriguing Grilled Asparagus, Mango and Red Pepper Salad

MAKES 4 SERVINGS

Barbecued asparagus has great flavour. Here it's combined with fruit and bits of red pepper for an interesting and colourful salad that everyone will love.

- ¾ lb (375 g) asparagus
- 2 Tbsp (30 mL) white wine vinegar
- 1 Tbsp (15 mL) Dijon mustard
- 2 tsp (10 mL) chopped fresh tarragon (or ½ tsp/ 2 mL dried)
- ½ tsp (2 mL) salt
- ¼ tsp (1 mL) pepper
- ⅓ cup (75 mL) olive oil
- 1 ripe mango, peeled and sliced
- ½ sweet red pepper, diced

TRIM THE ASPARAGUS and place in a sturdy plastic bag. In a small bowl, whisk together the vinegar, mustard, tarragon, salt and pepper; whisk in the oil. Pour into the bag, over the

WATERCRESS AND PEAR SALAD WITH STILTON VINAIGRETTE

asparagus, turning it to coat; let stand for 30 minutes at room temperature.

Reserving the marinade in the bag, place the asparagus on a greased medium high–temperature grill, or 4 inches (10 cm) from medium-hot coals; grill for about 4 minutes or until still bright green and tender-crisp, turning often with tongs.

Meanwhile, add the mango and red pepper to the marinade, squeezing the bag gently to coat them.

Let the asparagus cool slightly; cut each stalk into 3 diagonal pieces. Add to the mango mixture to coat with dressing. (The recipe can be refrigerated for up to 2 hours.) Transfer to a serving bowl.

Baked German Potato Salad

MAKES 4 TO 6 SERVINGS

Set this robust hot salad down beside a farmer's sausage, Quick Pickled Beets (see p. 133) and perhaps even a casserole of Maple Baked Beans (see p. 96) for a hearty but easy supper—perfect for an après-ski meal.

- 16 small red potatoes (unpeeled)
- ¼ lb (125 g) side bacon, diced (about 1 cup/250 mL)
- 2 stalks celery, sliced
- 1 onion, chopped
- 2 Tbsp (30 mL) all-purpose flour
- ½ tsp (2 mL) dry mustard
- ½ tsp (2 mL) salt
- ¼ tsp (1 mL) pepper
- ½ cup (125 mL) cider vinegar
- ⅓ cup (75 mL) granulated sugar
- 1 cup (250 mL) water
- ¼ cup (60 mL) chopped fresh parsley

SCRUB THE POTATOES. In a saucepan of boiling salted water, cook the potatoes until barely tender when pierced with the tip of a knife. Do not overcook. Drain and peel; cut into ¼-inch (5 mm) thick slices and arrange in a greased shallow 8-cup (2 L) casserole.

In a large skillet over medium heat, fry the bacon until crisp. Remove with a slotted spoon and set aside on paper towels.

Add the celery and onion to the drippings in the pan; cook over medium heat for 3 minutes. Stir in the flour, mustard, salt and pepper; cook for 2 minutes, stirring.

Stir in the vinegar, sugar, then water all at once, stirring constantly. Bring to a boil and cook for 1 minute. Stir in the parsley and cooked bacon; pour over the potatoes and toss gently to coat. (The potatoes can be prepared to this point, covered and refrigerated for up to 6 hours. Remove from the refrigerator 30 minutes before baking.)

Bake, uncovered, in a 375°F (190°C) oven for 45 minutes or until bubbly. Serve hot or warm.

Cranberry Waldorf

MAKES 8 TO 10 SERVINGS

This unusual salad is absolutely delicious with roast chicken or turkey. The juice drained from the cranberries would make a good base for a punch or refreshing cranberry spritzer with soda water. If you use frozen cranberries, do not thaw first.

- 4 cups (1 L) raw cranberries
- 1½ cups (375 mL) packed brown sugar
- 4 large pears, peeled and sliced
- 2 Tbsp (30 mL) fresh lemon juice
- 2 stalks celery, sliced
- 1 cup (250 mL) toasted walnut halves
- ⅓ cup (75 mL) light mayonnaise
- ⅓ cup (75 mL) light sour cream
- Watercress or celery leaves

IN A FOOD PROCESSOR or by hand, coarsely chop the cranberries. In a large bowl, gently stir together the cranberries, brown sugar, pears and lemon juice; cover and let stand in the refrigerator overnight.

About 30 minutes before serving, drain the cranberry mixture in a large sieve set over a large bowl. Set aside the juice for another use.

Just before serving, return the drained cranberry mixture to the bowl; gently fold in the celery and walnuts.

Stir together the mayonnaise and sour cream; blend into the cranberry mixture. Serve in a large shallow glass bowl lined with watercress or celery leaves.

CRANBERRIES

....

The bouncy little cranberry has a lot going for it. People fall in love with its beautiful rich colour—the "ruby of the bogs" at harvest time. Early settlers used strings of cranberries to add a bright red sparkle to their Christmas trees.

The native berry, long considered a valuable crop to Indigenous peoples in its wild form grown in bogs across the country, was commercially cultivated for the first time around 1870 in Nova Scotia. Commercial cultivation in the present remains specific to North America, and is carried on in British Columbia, Ontario, the Maritimes and Quebec. Although the methods of harvest vary from producer to producer, harvest time is usually in October for most of the country.

Harvesting at this time of year means that fresh cranberries are available to enjoy not only during Thanksgiving, but at Christmas as well. Their hard, outer skin allows cranberries to adapt well to baking and storing, and if the dry method of harvesting is used, they will keep for weeks without freezing. This long storage will not deplete their high nutritive content since they contain benzoic acid, a natural preservative.

It's this acid that also allows cranberries to stay fresh, whole and not clump together when frozen. This last characteristic, discovered by Indigenous peoples in a cold climate, allows you to treat the frozen fruit exactly as you would fresh berries. When cranberries are in season, therefore, remember to stock up since they will keep in your freezer for ten months—just before the annual harvest across the country. To freeze, just pop them into the freezer in the bag you bought them in; don't thaw to use.

With a good supply on hand, cranberries can function as more than just a sauce to accompany poultry. Try them wherever you would use other berries (especially blueberries) in a whole range of sweet and savoury dishes.

Carrot Fruit Salad

MAKES 4 TO 6 SERVINGS

When you think there's nothing in the house for an interesting salad, you probably do have the ingredients for this delicious combination—sure to become a favourite with all age groups. Rachel Van Nostrand, who was a wonderful cook in Ontario's Niagara Peninsula, gave me the idea.

- 1 cup (250 mL) raisins
- 2 Tbsp (30 mL) fresh lemon juice
- 4 carrots, finely grated
- 2 bananas, sliced
- 2 Tbsp (30 mL) grated shallots or onion
- ½ cup (125 mL) light sour cream or plain yogurt
- 2 Tbsp (30 mL) light mayonnaise
- ½ tsp (2 mL) salt
- White or black pepper
- ¼ cup (60 mL) chopped fresh parsley

IN A LARGE bowl, soak the raisins in the lemon juice for 30 minutes. Stir in the carrots, bananas and shallots.

Stir together the sour cream, mayonnaise, salt and pepper to taste; stir into the carrot mixture until well mixed. Sprinkle with the parsley.

New-Way Old-Fashioned Potato Salad

MAKES 8 SERVINGS

Nothing is more appealing with tangy-sweet ribs (like Barbecued Spare Ribs with Apple-Sage Glaze, see p. 62) than old-fashioned creamy potato salad. I've cut down on the fat in this one, without sacrificing any of its traditional flavour, by substituting plain yogurt for most of the salad dressing.

- 4 lb (2 kg) potatoes (about 12), unpeeled
- ⅓ cup (75 mL) canola oil, divided
- 2 onions, chopped
- ¾ cup (175 mL) chopped dill pickles
- 2 Tbsp (30 mL) cider vinegar
- 1 tsp (5 mL) dry mustard
- 1 tsp (5 mL) granulated sugar
- Salt and pepper
- ¾ cup (175 mL) plain yogurt
- ¼ cup (60 mL) Microwaveable Old-Fashioned Salad Dressing (see p. 180)
- ¼ cup (60 mL) chopped fresh parsley
- 2 tsp (10 mL) Dijon mustard
- 4 hard-cooked eggs, peeled and chopped
- Paprika

SCRUB THE POTATOES. In a saucepan of boiling salted water, cook the potatoes until just tender. Peel and dice.

Meanwhile, in a small skillet, heat 2 Tbsp (30 mL) of the oil over medium heat and cook the onions for 3 minutes. Transfer to a large bowl; add the warm potatoes and pickles.

Whisk together the remaining oil, the vinegar, dry mustard, sugar and salt and pepper to taste; pour over the potato mixture and toss to coat well. Cover and refrigerate for several hours or overnight.

Stir together the yogurt, salad dressing, parsley, Dijon mustard and eggs; toss with the potato mixture. Taste and adjust seasoning. Refrigerate for at least 1 hour, or up to 3 hours. Sprinkle with paprika to serve.

Brown Rice and Green Bean Salad with Lemon-Mustard Dressing

MAKES ABOUT 4 SERVINGS

The nutty flavour of brown rice and toasted pine nuts perfectly complements the good taste of fresh green beans. Little else is needed if you serve this salad for a family supper. It also makes a great salad for a party buffet—just double the recipe for a crowd.

- 1 cup (250 mL) whole grain or brown rice
- 1 tsp (5 mL) salt, divided
- ¼ cup (60 mL) fresh lemon juice
- 2 tsp (10 mL) Dijon mustard
- ¼ tsp (1 mL) pepper
- ½ cup (125 mL) olive oil
- ¼ cup (60 mL) diced sweet red pepper
- 1 lb (500 g) green beans, trimmed
- ½ cup (125 mL) toasted pine nuts

IN A LARGE saucepan, combine the rice and half of the salt in a pot of boiling water (2½ cups/625 mL for whole grain rice, 3 cups/750 mL for brown). Bring back to a boil, cover and reduce heat to low; cook for 25 minutes for whole grain, 45 minutes for brown rice, or until tender and the water has been absorbed. Let stand for 5 minutes; fluff with a fork.

In a large bowl, whisk together the lemon juice, mustard, pepper and remaining salt; gradually whisk in the oil. Add the warm rice and red pepper; toss. (The salad can be prepared to this point, covered and refrigerated for up to 12 hours.)

In a large saucepan of boiling water, cook the green beans, uncovered, for 4 to 5 minutes or just until tender; drain and refresh under cold running water. Cut crosswise into ¾-inch (2 cm) pieces. Stir into the rice mixture along with the pine nuts. Taste and adjust seasoning if necessary.

Black Bean and Red Pepper Salad

MAKES ABOUT 6 SERVINGS

Perfect for a buffet or potluck supper, this easy salad will keep for several days in the refrigerator. If you wish to make it even easier, you could use a can of rinsed and drained black beans. I discovered that although cooking the dried beans in a microwave oven isn't faster than on top of the stove, the beans do have a better texture.

- 1 cup (250 mL) dried black beans
- ¼ cup (60 mL) olive oil
- 2 Tbsp (30 mL) red wine vinegar
- 1 tsp (5 mL) salt
- ½ tsp (2 mL) pepper
- ½ tsp (2 mL) granulated sugar
- ½ tsp (2 mL) ground cumin
- 1 clove garlic, crushed
- 1 sweet red pepper, diced
- 1 cup (250 mL) diced Spanish onion
- 3 stalks celery, sliced
- 1 jalapeño pepper, diced
- ⅓ cup (75 mL) coarsely chopped fresh coriander (cilantro)

SORT AND RINSE the beans. In a saucepan, cover the beans with 3 times their volume of cold water; let soak overnight in the refrigerator.

Drain the beans and place in a 16-cup (4 L) microwaveable casserole; cover with 3½ cups (875 mL) cold water. Cover and microwave on high for 45 minutes or until tender. (Or, in a large saucepan, cover the beans with 3 times their volume of cold water and bring to a boil on the stove. Reduce heat and cook, uncovered, for 45 to 60 minutes, or until tender.) Drain well.

Whisk together the oil, vinegar, salt, pepper, sugar, cumin and garlic; pour over the beans and toss to coat.

In a large bowl, toss together the red pepper, onion, celery and jalapeño pepper; add the beans and toss to mix. Gently stir in the fresh coriander. Cover and refrigerate for at least 2 hours for the flavours to mingle, or up to 3 days.

Cucumbers in a Sweet-and-Sour Cream Dressing

MAKES ABOUT 4 SERVINGS

My friend and former assistant, Mary Lou Ruby Jonas, generously shared with me one of her best-loved family recipes. This sweet and tangy old-fashioned salad will soon become one of your favourites, too. If the cucumber skins are tender, leave them on.

- 2 cucumbers
- ½ cup (125 mL) whipping cream
- 3 Tbsp (45 mL) white vinegar
- 3 Tbsp (45 mL) granulated sugar
- ¼ tsp (1 mL) salt
- Tomato wedges

THINLY SLICE THE cucumbers. Transfer to a bowl of ice water and let stand for 30 minutes. Drain and pat dry. Transfer to a shallow dish.

Meanwhile, in a blender or food processor, blend the cream, vinegar, sugar and salt until very thick. Cover and refrigerate if making ahead. Pour over the cucumbers and mix. Garnish with tomato wedges.

Quick Pickled Beets

MAKES 6 TO 8 SERVINGS

When I used to line my cold cellar with preserves, pickled beets were always there and ready to round out lots of winter menus. Now I no longer have time to do much preserving, but when I get hungry for the old-fashioned pickle, I throw some beets in the oven and finish them off this way.

WASH THE BEETS and remove all but 1 inch (2.5 cm) of the stems and tails. Place in a shallow pan with ¼ inch (5 mm) water. Cover with foil and bake in a 375°F (190°C) oven for about 35 minutes or until tender when pierced with a knife. (The time depends very much on the age and size of the beets.) Drain and let cool; slip off the skins and slice into ¼-inch (5 mm) thick rounds. Place in a bowl.

In a measuring cup, whisk together the vinegar, mustard, salt, sugar, cinnamon, allspice and pepper; gradually whisk in the oil. Pour over the beets and toss gently to coat. (The beets can be covered and refrigerated for up to 5 days.)

- 12 small beets
- ¼ cup (60 mL) red wine vinegar
- 1 tsp (5 mL) Dijon mustard
- Pinch salt
- Pinch granulated sugar
- Pinch cinnamon
- Pinch allspice
- Pinch pepper
- ¼ cup (60 mL) olive oil

Romaine, Radicchio and Walnut Salad

MAKES 8 SERVINGS

Make this simple salad with the freshest greens you can find. The greens, dressing and walnuts can be prepared ahead. Anchovy paste is available in tubes from most supermarkets.

ON A BAKING sheet, toast the walnuts in a 350°F (180°C) oven for 5 minutes; let cool. Tear the romaine, radicchio and Boston lettuce into bite-size pieces. In a large salad bowl, combine the lettuces and the walnuts.

In a small bowl, whisk together the vinegar, anchovy

- 1 cup (250 mL) coarsely chopped walnuts
- ½ head romaine lettuce
- ½ head radicchio
- ½ head Boston lettuce
- 2 Tbsp (30 mL) red wine vinegar
- ½ tsp (2 mL) anchovy paste
- ¼ tsp (1 mL) salt
- ¼ tsp (1 mL) pepper
- ¼ tsp (1 mL) dry mustard
- ⅓ cup (75 mL) olive oil (preferably extra-virgin)

paste, salt, pepper and mustard; gradually whisk in the oil. Pour over the salad and toss to coat well.

VARIATION   *Warm Chèvre Salad on Mixed Greens*
This tangy hot salad makes an inviting opening to a special meal, or a refreshing course between the main course and dessert. Increase the olive oil to ½ cup (125 mL). Cut 1 lb (500 g) unripened cream-style goat cheese into 8 rounds and marinate (refrigerated) overnight in the oil, anchovy paste and mustard. Cut 8 circles of whole wheat bread just slightly bigger than the rounds of cheese.

Bring the marinated cheese to room temperature. Drain the oil mixture from the cheese, stir in the vinegar, salt and pepper; use as the dressing, proceeding with the salad as above. Just before serving, arrange the salad on 8 individual plates. Set the bread rounds on a baking sheet and toast lightly under the broiler. Set the cheese on the toast rounds and broil until the cheese is bubbling and brown, 5 to 6 minutes. Transfer each round to the centre of each salad and serve immediately.

Hot Tricolour Salad of Grilled Peppers

MAKES 6 TO 8 SERVINGS

Grilled peppers are one of the delights of the harvest season. Often I grill them until they're charred all over, then peel them before dressing with a vinaigrette. In this recipe, I grill them a short time so that the salad is crispy.

IN A SMALL bowl, whisk together the vinegar, parsley, garlic, oregano, cumin, salt, pepper and hot pepper sauce; gradually whisk in ¼ cup (60 mL) olive oil. Set aside.

Cut the peppers into

- 4 tsp (20 mL) white wine vinegar
- 1 Tbsp (15 mL) chopped fresh parsley
- 2 cloves garlic, minced
- 1 tsp (5 mL) finely chopped fresh oregano (or ¼ tsp/1 mL dried)
- ½ tsp (2 mL) ground cumin
- ¼ tsp (1 mL) salt
- ¼ tsp (1 mL) pepper
- Dash hot pepper sauce
- ¼ cup (60 mL) olive oil (approx.)
- 2 sweet yellow peppers
- 2 sweet red peppers
- 2 sweet green peppers

ROMAINE, RADICCHIO AND WALNUT SALAD

2-inch (5 cm) squares; brush all over with more olive oil. Place on a medium high–temperature grill, or 4 inches (10 cm) from medium-hot coals; cook for 3 minutes. Turn carefully so the pieces do not slip through the grill; cook for 3 minutes longer or just until lightly browned and still crisp. Place in a heatproof bowl; toss with the dressing. Serve immediately.

Hot Broccoli and Red Pepper Salad

....

MAKES 8 SERVINGS

This easy, colourful salad is a nice companion to a smooth vegetable purée on the same menu. If the broccoli is all ready to steam and the dressing made ahead, the salad takes only seconds to finish.

- 2 Tbsp (30 mL) fresh lemon juice
- ¼ cup (60 mL) minced shallots
- ½ tsp (2 mL) dry mustard
- ½ tsp (2 mL) salt
- ¼ tsp (1 mL) pepper
- ¼ tsp (1 mL) hot pepper sauce
- ¼ cup (60 mL) olive oil
- 2 bunches broccoli (1½ lb/750 g total)
- 1 sweet red pepper, slivered

IN A SMALL bowl, whisk together the lemon juice, shallots, mustard, salt, pepper and hot pepper sauce; gradually whisk in the oil. Let stand at room temperature for at least 1 hour, or up to 6 hours. Whisk again to recombine.

Cut the florets from the broccoli; peel the stalks and cut into ¼-inch (5 mm) thick slices. Steam for 4 to 5 minutes or until just tender but still bright green. Do not overcook.

In a salad bowl, toss the hot broccoli with the shallot dressing and red pepper; serve immediately.

Three-Ingredient Creamy Coleslaw

....

MAKES 6 SERVINGS

This easy, pretty salad would be perfect to carry out to a potluck supper, or to serve with Maple Baked Beans (see p. 96) at home.

IN A LARGE bowl, toss together the cabbage, red onion and cucumber.

In a small bowl, whisk together the mayonnaise, vinegar, sugar, salt and paprika until smooth. Pour over the cabbage mixture and toss to coat; cover and refrigerate for at least 1 hour, or up to 4 hours.

- 6 cups (1.5 L) finely shredded green cabbage
- ½ cup (125 mL) diced red onion
- ½ cup (125 mL) English cucumber (unpeeled)
- ⅔ cup (150 mL) light mayonnaise
- 2 Tbsp (30 mL) cider vinegar
- 4 tsp (20 mL) granulated sugar
- ½ tsp (2 mL) salt
- Pinch paprika

Warm Dandelion Salad with Bacon and Poached Eggs

....

MAKES 2 SERVINGS

When we first moved to Cambridge, Ontario, I remember our dear friend Edna Staebler arriving at our house one spring with two huge shopping bags full of dandelions. She proceeded to show my son, Allen, how to make her delicious dandelion salad that appears in her best-selling cookbook, Food That Really Schmecks. "In Waterloo County," she explained, "we say that dandelion greens purify the blood, grown sluggish and thick through the winter." Where did Edna get these voluminous leaves? "From my lawn, of course. If you have enough of them, you don't have to go anywhere. You just sit on the lawn and pick!"

If you have no source for wild unsprayed dandelion leaves, you can still make this delightful salad with those grown under sawdust or straw for markets. This isn't Edna's salad, but

- ¾ lb (375 g) dandelion leaves (about 4 cups/ 1 L, packed)
- 4 slices side bacon, diced
- ¼ cup (60 mL) olive oil, divided
- 2 Tbsp (30 mL) minced shallots
- Salt and pepper
- 3 Tbsp (45 mL) white wine vinegar
- 2 eggs
- ¼ cup (60 mL) white vinegar

I'm sure she would have enjoyed it. Serve as a special spring brunch for two with slices of crusty French bread.

REMOVE THE WHITE base from the dandelion stalks; thoroughly wash the leaves and dry well. Break each stalk into 2-inch (5 cm) pieces and place in a large heat-proof bowl.

In a large skillet, cook the bacon over medium-low heat until crisp and golden brown. Transfer to paper towels.

Discard the fat and wipe out the skillet. Heat 2 Tbsp (30 mL) of the oil over medium heat; cook the shallots, stirring often, for 5 minutes. Sprinkle with salt and pepper to taste. With a slotted spoon, add to the dandelion greens. Add the wine vinegar to the pan and bring to a boil; pour over the greens. Toss with the remaining oil and the bacon; set aside.

In a large amount of water and the white vinegar, poach the eggs, uncovered, for about 2½ minutes, bringing the whites up over the yolks with a spoon. With a slotted spoon, lift out the eggs and place on paper towels; trim any uneven edges.

Meanwhile, return the dandelion mixture to the skillet; toss over medium heat for 1 minute or until the greens are wilted. Divide between 2 small plates. Carefully set an egg in the centre of each salad and serve immediately.

Spinach and Mushroom Salad with Creamy Buttermilk Dressing

MAKES 6 TO 8 SERVINGS

Low on calories but high on flavour, this crunchy salad is delicious with grilled beef or Oven-Fried Golden Crisp Chicken Legs (see p. 58). If possible, use nice fresh loose spinach instead of the cellophane-packaged kind.

- 1 cup (250 mL) well-shaken buttermilk
- ½ cup (125 mL) light mayonnaise
- 2 cloves garlic, crushed
- 2 tsp (10 mL) Dijon mustard
- Salt and pepper

WHISK TOGETHER THE buttermilk, mayonnaise, garlic, mustard and salt and pepper to taste until frothy. (The dressing can be covered and refrigerated for up to 8 hours.)

Wash and dry the spinach well; discard any thick stems and tear the spinach into bite-size pieces. Toss in a large salad bowl with the mushrooms and bean sprouts. (The salad can be covered and refrigerated without the dressing for up to 3 hours.)

Just before serving, toss the spinach mixture gently with the dressing to coat. Sprinkle with the bacon.

- One 10-oz (284 g) pkg spinach
- ½ lb (250 g) mushrooms, sliced
- ¼ lb (125 g) bean sprouts (about 2 cups/500 mL)
- 5 slices crisply cooked bacon, crumbled

Fresh Peach and Roquefort Salad with Walnut Dressing

MAKES 4 SERVINGS

An assertive blue cheese, tangy greens and a nut dressing are happy companions to juicy bright peach slices in this quick salad.

IN A MEDIUM bowl, whisk together the lime juice, oil, vinegar, mustard and salt and pepper to taste. Peel, pit and slice the peaches ¼ inch (5 mm) thick; add to the dressing and toss to coat. Let stand for 30 minutes to marinate.

Arrange the watercress on a large platter or individual plates. Arrange the peach slices on top, drizzling with the dressing. Crumble the cheese over the peaches and sprinkle with the walnuts. Serve immediately.

- ⅓ cup (75 mL) fresh lime juice
- ¼ cup (60 mL) walnut or olive oil
- 2 tsp (10 mL) white wine vinegar
- ½ tsp (2 mL) Dijon mustard
- Salt and pepper
- 3 peaches
- Bunch watercress or arugula
- 3 oz (90 g) Roquefort cheese (or other blue cheese)
- ¼ cup (60 mL) toasted coarsely chopped walnuts

Grilled Vegetable Salad with Garlic-Herb Dressing

MAKES 4 SERVINGS

Use whatever vegetables you have on hand, and if you like the peppers crunchy, seed them, cut them into big pieces and grill for only 5 to 6 minutes, without charring or peeling.

DRESSING Whisk together the garlic, vinegar, olive oil, parsley, thyme, oregano and salt and pepper to taste; set aside for at least 30 minutes, or cover and refrigerate for up to 24 hours.

VEGETABLE SALAD Cut the eggplants in half lengthwise; place in a sieve and sprinkle cut sides with salt. Set aside for 30 minutes.

Place the peppers on a greased medium high–temperature grill, or 4 inches (10 cm) from medium-hot coals; grill, turning often, until charred all over, about 20 minutes. Pop into a paper bag for 10 minutes; peel, seed and cut lengthwise into 8 strips. Transfer to a large bowl.

Meanwhile, remove the outer skin from the onion, leaving the root and stem ends intact; cut in half crosswise. Brush with some of the canola oil and grill for 15 to 20 minutes or until lightly charred, turning once. Remove the charred skin and cut each half into quarters. Add to the bowl.

DRESSING
- 3 cloves garlic, minced
- 2 Tbsp (30 mL) red wine vinegar
- 2 Tbsp (30 mL) olive oil
- 1 Tbsp (15 mL) chopped fresh parsley
- 2 tsp (10 mL) chopped fresh thyme (or ½ tsp/ 2 mL dried)
- 2 tsp (10 mL) chopped fresh oregano (or ½ tsp/ 2 mL dried)
- Salt and pepper

VEGETABLE SALAD
- 2 small eggplants
- Salt
- 3 sweet peppers (red, orange, yellow)
- 1 red onion
- ¼ cup (60 mL) canola oil, divided
- 8 fat spears asparagus or 2 small zucchini, quartered lengthwise
- 4 large mushrooms
- Leaf lettuce

Rinse the eggplant under cold running water; dry well and brush with canola oil. Grill for about 5 minutes or until golden brown but not charred, turning once. Add to the bowl.

Brush the asparagus (or zucchini) and mushrooms with the remaining canola oil; grill for 5 minutes, turning the asparagus and mushrooms often (just turn the zucchini once). Add to the bowl, quartering the mushrooms.

Whisk any remaining canola oil into the dressing; pour over the vegetables and very gently toss to coat. Line a platter with lettuce; arrange the grilled vegetables on top.

EXQUISITE ENDINGS

....

THE FINAL COURSE of a meal should be like the punchline of a joke—simple and to the point, but with a lasting impact that will leave your audience remembering your wit and good taste.

Since most families tend not to have dessert at every meal (or if they do, it might be something like fresh fruit, ice cream or sherbet), I've included only a handful of family desserts in this chapter.

The majority of the recipes here are for entertaining . . . all simple, but with the lasting impression that you have served your guests something special indeed.

When you have a dinner party, these desserts are great fun because they are all make-ahead, look spectacular and taste great, but many of them are also made in a flash . . . the kind of thing your guests will think you've slaved over for hours, but on which, in fact, you have spent very little time.

Desserts

Maple Crème Brulées

Easy elegance personified, this creamy dessert gains a whole new dimension of flavour when finely grated maple sugar is caramelized on top. Serve the little custards with crisp cookies like the Pecan Lace Cookies (see p. 160). If you can't find maple sugar, grate or finely chop the sugar candy maple leaves found in gift shops and farmers' markets.

- 1½ cups (375 mL) whipping cream
- ¼ cup (60 mL) maple syrup
- 4 egg yolks
- ⅓ cup (75 mL) finely grated maple sugar

IN A SMALL heavy saucepan, heat the cream and maple syrup together until bubbles just start to form around the outside. Remove from heat. In a bowl, whisk the egg yolks slightly without allowing them to foam. Very gradually pour the hot cream into the yolks, stirring constantly.

Strain the custard through a fine sieve into a pitcher or measuring cup. Pour into six ½-cup (125 mL) heat-proof ramekins. Place in a baking pan just big enough to hold them; pour hot water into the pan to come two-thirds up the sides of the ramekins.

Cover with foil; bake in a 325°F (160°C) oven for about 25 minutes or until the custards are just set but still slightly jiggly in the centres. Remove the ramekins to cool on a rack; refrigerate until very cold. (The custards can be prepared a day ahead.)

Just before serving, sprinkle the custards with maple sugar; broil on a rack nearest the heat for about 3½ minutes, watching carefully, or until the sugar caramelizes to a golden brown. (Or, you can use a small kitchen blowtorch to caramelize the sugar.) Serve immediately.

Pavlova with Fresh Seasonal Fruit

Although it takes a while sitting in the oven, pavlova is one of the easiest desserts you'll ever make. Both Australia and New Zealand claim it as a national dessert, and this recipe comes from a friend who lived in that part of the world for a time. I made it for a special birthday party during a visit to New Zealand, topping it with fresh passion fruit and kiwi slices. Use whatever fresh fruit is in season—sliced strawberries, raspberries, peaches . . .

- 8 egg whites (about 1 cup/250 mL)
- 1½ cups (375 mL) granulated sugar
- 4 tsp (20 mL) white vinegar
- 4 tsp (20 mL) cornstarch
- 4 tsp (20 mL) vanilla
- Sweetened whipped cream
- Fresh seasonal fruit

LINE A BAKING sheet with parchment paper; draw an 11-inch (28 cm) circle on it. (Or grease an 11-inch/28-cm quiche dish.)

In a large bowl, beat the egg whites until soft peaks form; gradually beat in the sugar until stiff shiny peaks form. Stir together the vinegar, cornstarch and vanilla; carefully fold into the whites.

Spread onto the circle in the prepared pan, swirling and building up the sides to form a well in the middle. Bake in a 300°F (150°C) oven for 30 minutes. Reduce heat to 200°F (95°C); bake for 1½ hours longer. Turn off the oven but leave the pavlova in until cooled.

Just before serving, pile whipped cream into the well of the cooled meringue; arrange fruit attractively on top.

Strawberries with Almond Cream Sauce

When I was growing up on a farm at Duntroon, near Collingwood, Ontario, there was always fruit to pick—from the first pink stalks of rhubarb in the spring to the last crisp apple in late fall. But there was something special about getting out in the warm June sun to find perfectly ripe red strawberries hidden under protective green leaves. I like to present good fresh berries simply—mounded in a dish to enjoy with cream and sugar, or to eat out-of-hand with some sour cream and a bit of brown sugar for dipping.

This recipe is a simple celebration of the rich flavour of ripe fruit, yet the cream sauce adds a touch of elegance that makes it suitable for the finale of a special dinner party.

HULL THE STRAWBERRIES; slice if large. In a sieve set in a large bowl, sprinkle the strawberries with the sugar; refrigerate, covered, for 1 hour.

Divide the berries among 6 serving dishes. Whisk the sour cream and liqueur into the berry juice until smooth; pour over the berries and serve immediately.

- 5 cups (1.25 L) ripe strawberries
- ¼ cup (60 mL) instant dissolving (berry) sugar (or granulated sugar processed in a blender)
- 1 cup (250 mL) sour cream
- 2 Tbsp (30 mL) almond liqueur

Tropical Mango Ice with Kiwi Coulis

MAKES 4 SERVINGS

Tasty mangoes are better known than apples in more than half the world, but to us they're still exotic and wonderful. Let the ice stand for a few minutes at room temperature to soften slightly before serving.

TROPICAL MANGO ICE In a saucepan, bring the water and sugar to a boil over high heat; boil rapidly, uncovered, for about 5 minutes or until reduced to ⅔ cup (150 mL). Let cool and chill.

TROPICAL MANGO ICE
- 1 cup (250 mL) water
- ½ cup (125 mL) granulated sugar
- 2 cups (500 mL) cubed peeled ripe mangoes
- ¾ cup (175 mL) fresh orange juice
- ¼ cup (60 mL) fresh lime juice

KIWI COULIS
- 3 kiwifruit, peeled and coarsely chopped
- 2 Tbsp (30 mL) Cointreau
- 2 tsp (10 mL) granulated sugar

In a food processor or blender, purée the mangoes, orange juice, lime juice and the chilled syrup. Transfer to an ice-cream maker and freeze according to the manufacturer's directions.

KIWI COULIS In a food processor or blender, purée the kiwifruit; blend in the Cointreau and sugar. Spread on 4 dessert plates and top with scoops of mango ice.

Easy Rice Pudding

MAKES 4 TO 6 SERVINGS

Leftover rice takes on a total disguise in this old-fashioned classic, a baked rice custard. Make dessert for your family in a flash; stir it together right in the baking dish.

IN A DEEP 8-INCH (2 L) baking dish, combine the rice, sugar and eggs; stir well to blend. Stir in the milk, raisins, lemon zest, vanilla and salt; sprinkle with nutmeg to taste.

- 1 cup (250 mL) cooked rice
- ½ cup (125 mL) packed brown sugar
- 2 eggs, beaten
- 2 cups (500 mL) milk
- ½ cup (125 mL) raisins
- 1 tsp (5 mL) grated lemon zest
- ½ tsp (2 mL) vanilla
- ¼ tsp (1 mL) salt
- Grated nutmeg
- Milk (optional)

Place in a pan of hot water; bake in a 325°F (160°C) oven for about 1 hour or until almost set. Serve warm or cold with a small amount of milk poured overtop if desired.

Resplendent Raspberry Summer Pudding

MAKES 6 TO 8 SERVINGS

Growing up on our farm the fruit season began with a few strawberries, currants of two colours, gooseberries, a line of sour cherry trees, a couple of peach trees, pears, plums and then apples later on. But it was raspberries on which we really concentrated. The patch was huge, and the berries bigger than I've ever seen since.

I often think of all the wonderful fruit that used to grow on our farm, and the memories inspire me to search my local market for all I can find of summer's bounty. Then I make the following glorious pudding. Pass a pitcher of pouring custard with it, or accompany it with sweetened whipped cream or vanilla ice cream if you prefer.

- 6 to 8 slices homemade-style bread, crusts removed, divided
- 4 cups (1 L) red raspberries
- 2 cups (500 mL) pitted black sweet cherries
- 1½ cups (375 mL) stemmed red currants
- ½ cups (375 mL) black raspberries (see note)
- ¾ cup (175 mL) granulated sugar (approx.)
- 4 tsp (20 mL) cornstarch
- 2 Tbsp (30 mL) cold water
- 4 tsp (20 mL) quick-cooking tapioca
- 1 Tbsp (15 mL) amaretto (or other almond liqueur) or kirsch

LINE THE BOTTOM and sides of a 6-cup (1.5 L) bowl or mould with as much bread as needed to cover it completely, trimming where necessary. Reserve the remaining pieces for the top.

In a large heavy saucepan, sprinkle the red raspberries, cherries, currants and black raspberries with the sugar. Bring to a boil over medium-low heat and cook, stirring, for about 3 minutes or until the sugar has melted. Remove from heat; transfer 2 Tbsp (30 mL) of the juice to a small container and refrigerate.

In a small bowl, stir the cornstarch into the water; stir in the tapioca and immediately mix into the fruit mixture. Cook over low heat, stirring frequently, until slightly thickened, about 3 minutes. Remove from heat; stir in the amaretto or kirsch. Taste and add more sugar if too tart.

Spoon the fruit mixture into the bread-lined mould; cover the surface completely with a layer of the remaining bread. Put a plate that fits just inside the dish on top of the pudding; weigh down with a heavy object. Refrigerate overnight.

To serve, remove the weight and plate. Invert onto a serving plate and brush with the reserved juice.

NOTE Although black raspberries make the dessert extra special, you can increase the amount of red raspberries to 5½ cups (1.4 L) if black ones are not available. I have also used thimbleberries instead of black raspberries.

Peaches Catherine

MAKES 12 SERVINGS

Catherine Betts, a friend in the Maritimes, brought this delightful recipe home with her from New Zealand. It's one of those recipes that takes very little work to put together and everyone loves. Since it can be made only during peach season, I always plan a big party just around this dessert. Invariably I find a guest out in the kitchen after dinner scraping the empty dish clean with a spoon.

- 15 ripe peaches
- 2 Tbsp (30 mL) fresh lemon juice
- 2 cups (500 mL) whipping cream
- ¾ cup (175 mL) packed brown sugar

PEEL, SLICE AND arrange the peaches in a 12-cup (3 L) shallow gratin dish or other attractive baking dish, sprinkling with lemon juice as you work.

Whip the cream; spread all over the peaches. Sprinkle with the brown sugar by putting it through a fine sieve. Cover with plastic wrap and refrigerate overnight. (This is necessary.)

Just before serving, broil the peaches about 4 inches (10 cm) from the heat for about 2 minutes, or until crispy golden on top.

Wonderfully Satisfying Apple Crisp

MAKES 4 TO 6 SERVINGS

I remember occasionally relishing a cold dish of my mother's apple crisp when I returned home from public school at the end of the day. But this family favourite is best served warm with Cheddar cheese, vanilla ice cream or sweetened whipped cream.

- 8 tart apples (about 2 lb/1 kg)
- ½ cup (125 mL) water
- ¼ cup (60 mL) granulated sugar
- 1 tsp (5 mL) cinnamon, divided
- ½ tsp (2 mL) vanilla
- Pinch salt
- ¾ cup (175 mL) packed brown sugar

PEEL, CORE AND thinly slice the apples. Place in a greased 8-inch (2 L) square baking dish. Stir in the water, granulated sugar, ½ tsp (2 mL) of the cinnamon, vanilla and salt.

- ¾ cup (175 mL) all-purpose flour
- ¼ tsp (1 mL) nutmeg
- ⅓ cup (75 mL) butter

In a small bowl, stir together the brown sugar, flour, remaining cinnamon and nutmeg. With a pastry blender or 2 knives, cut in the butter until the mixture is crumbly.

Sprinkle over the apple mixture; bake, uncovered, in a 375°F (190°C) oven for about 45 minutes or until the apples are very tender.

Frozen Strawberry Yogurt

MAKES 3 CUPS (750 ML)

When you crave a rich, creamy ice cream, try this smooth low-cal cousin with its fresh, intense strawberry flavour. It's quick to make and superior to commercial frozen yogurts, which often contain enough sweeteners and artificial flavours to equal ice cream in calories.

For best results, use plain low-fat yogurt (with about 1% milk fat) and have it at room temperature to prevent lumping. The frozen yogurt is best when first made, but it can be stored in a covered container in the freezer for up to one week. You will have to leave it out of the freezer for a few minutes to soften enough to scoop.

- 2 cups (500 mL) strawberries, hulled
- ½ cup (125 mL) instant dissolving (berry) sugar (or granulated sugar processed in a blender)
- 1 Tbsp (15 mL) fresh lemon juice
- ½ tsp (2 mL) grated orange zest
- 1 envelope unflavoured gelatin
- 3 Tbsp (45 mL) cold water
- 1½ cups (375 mL) low-fat plain yogurt, at room temperature

IN A FOOD processor or blender, purée the strawberries, sugar, lemon juice and orange zest.

In a small saucepan, sprinkle the gelatin over the

cold water; let stand for 5 minutes to soften. Stir over medium-low heat until the gelatin is dissolved, about 5 minutes. (Or, in a microwaveable bowl, soften the gelatin in the water, then microwave on high for 30 seconds and stir.) Stir into the fruit purée.

Stir in the yogurt; transfer to an ice cream maker and freeze according to the manufacturer's instructions.

Oven-Caramelized Pears

MAKES 4 SERVINGS

This wonderful fruit dessert takes only a few minutes to prepare and can cook while you enjoy your main course. It's best served warm with a crisp cookie on the side. Use pears that are ripe but firm.

- 6 pears
- ⅓ cup (75 mL) granulated sugar
- ¼ cup (60 mL) butter, in bits
- ½ cup (125 mL) whipping cream
- Pinch nutmeg
- Pinch ground ginger

PEEL, CORE AND slice the pears; arrange in a well-greased 9-inch (2.5 L) square baking dish. Sprinkle with the sugar and dot with the butter.

Bake, uncovered, in a 500°F (260°C) oven for 30 minutes or until the sugar is golden, gently stirring once.

Stir together the cream, nutmeg and ginger; pour over the pears. Bake for about 5 minutes or until a light brown syrup has formed.

Cider-Baked Applesauce

MAKES ABOUT 2 CUPS (500 ML)

I often make this simple, apple-intense sauce when I have a pork roast or chicken in the oven to serve alongside. It's also good as a dessert, or with yogurt and granola for breakfast. Use Empire or McIntosh apples or, if you're lucky enough to find them at an August farmers' market, Yellow Transparents.

PEEL, CORE AND cut the apples into eighths; place

in an 8-inch (2 L) square baking dish. Toss with the lemon juice and sprinkle with the brown sugar, cinnamon and nutmeg. Drizzle with the cider; stir gently until the sugar dissolves.

Cover and bake in a 350°F (180°C) oven for 35 to 45 minutes, or until the apples are soft. Mash with a potato masher.

- 5 apples
- 1 Tbsp (15 mL) fresh lemon juice
- ¼ cup (60 mL) packed brown sugar
- Pinch cinnamon
- Pinch nutmeg
- ¼ cup (60 mL) apple cider or apple juice

Spicy Raisin-Filled Baked Apples

MAKES 6 SERVINGS

When I was growing up on the farm, fragrant baked apples were a standard fall and winter dessert. Like many good-tasting ideas, this one came from the farm kitchen of Mary Lou Ruby Jonas. Cutting the apples in half enables more of their surface to be cloaked in the spicy syrup. Choose an apple that holds its shape when cooked, something like a Northern Spy. Serve warm with unsweetened, lightly whipped cream.

- 1 cup (250 mL) water
- ⅓ cup (75 mL) granulated sugar
- ⅓ cup (75 mL) packed brown sugar
- 1 Tbsp (15 mL) butter
- 1 Tbsp (15 mL) fresh lemon juice
- ½ tsp (2 mL) cinnamon
- ¼ tsp (1 mL) ground cloves
- 3 large apples
- ⅔ cup (150 mL) raisins

IN A SMALL saucepan, combine the water, both sugars, butter, lemon juice, cinnamon and cloves; bring to a boil. Reduce heat to a brisk simmer and cook, uncovered, for 10 minutes.

Meanwhile, cut the apples in half crosswise and remove the cores; arrange cut side up in a shallow baking dish just large enough to hold them. Fill the hollow centres with raisins and pour the sugar mixture overtop. Bake, uncovered and basting often with the

syrup, in a 375°F (190°C) oven for 30 to 45 minutes or until the apples are tender.

Fresh Pineapple with Hot Rum Sauce

MAKES 4 SERVINGS

Here's a quick, light dessert for a taste of the tropics.

IN A BOWL, pour the rum over the pineapple slices; sprinkle with 1 tsp (5 mL) sugar. Cover and marinate at room temperature for several hours or overnight, stirring occasionally.

Drain completely, reserving the marinade and placing the pineapple slices on 4 dessert plates.

- ¼ cup (60 mL) light rum
- 4 slices fresh pineapple (at least ½ inch/1 cm thick)
- 1 tsp (5 mL) granulated sugar
- ¼ cup (60 mL) unsalted butter
- ¼ cup (60 mL) granulated sugar
- 3 egg yolks, beaten
- ¼ cup (60 mL) coarsely grated coconut (preferably fresh)

In the top of a double boiler or heatproof bowl over simmering water, combine the butter and sugar until melted but not cooked. Stir in ¼ cup (60 mL) of the marinade and the egg yolks; whisk over simmering water until thickened, about 4 minutes.

Pour over the pineapple; sprinkle with the coconut. Serve immediately.

Silky Ginger Ice Cream with Dark Chocolate Sauce

MAKES 4 CUPS (1 L)

This creamy golden ice cream with its quick-and-easy chocolate sauce reminds me of the candied ginger at our local candy shop—spicy-sweet and enveloped in cool dark chocolate.

SILKY GINGER ICE CREAM In a small saucepan, stir together the water, honey and fresh ginger; bring to a boil. Reduce heat and simmer, uncovered and stirring occasionally, for 5 minutes.

Scald the 10% or 18% cream with the crystallized ginger; add the fresh ginger syrup. Cover and steep for 20 minutes.

In a large bowl, beat the yolks with the granulated sugar and zest until pale yellow; transfer to a heavy saucepan. Gradually whisk in the cream-ginger mixture, then the whipping cream. Cook, stirring constantly, over medium-low heat until slightly thickened, about 8 minutes. Do not boil.

Strain through a fine sieve into a cool large clean bowl. When the mixture stops steaming, press plastic wrap onto the surface; refrigerate until very cold, several hours or overnight.

Freeze in an ice cream maker according to the manufacturer's directions.

DARK CHOCOLATE SAUCE In a small heavy saucepan, bring the cream to a boil; remove from heat. Add the chocolate and stir until melted. Stir in the butter; let cool slightly before using. (The sauce can be cooled, covered and refrigerated for up to 1 week. Reheat over low heat until warm to serve.)

Serve ice cream topped with warm Dark Chocolate Sauce.

SILKY GINGER ICE CREAM

- ½ cup (125 mL) water
- ⅓ cup (75 mL) mild-flavoured liquid honey
- ⅓ cup (75 mL) minced peeled fresh ginger
- ¾ cup (175 mL) cream (10% or 18%)
- 1 Tbsp (15 mL) finely chopped crystallized ginger
- 6 egg yolks
- ¼ cup (60 mL) granulated sugar
- ¼ tsp (1 mL) grated lemon zest
- 1½ cups (375 mL) whipping cream

DARK CHOCOLATE SAUCE

- ¾ cup (175 mL) whipping cream
- 5 oz (150 g) bittersweet or semisweet chocolate, broken up
- 1 Tbsp (15 mL) butter

Dessert Crêpes

MAKES 18 TO 24 CRÊPES

Crêpes, popular a couple of decades ago, are in fashion again, judging from all the crêperies popping up around town.

IN A BLENDER or food processor, place the milk, liqueur, eggs, salt, sugar and flour (in that order). Cover and blend at top speed for 1 minute in a blender, or 20 seconds in a food processor, scraping down the sides once. Cover and refrigerate for at least 2 hours, or overnight.

Place an 8-inch (20 cm) crêpe or omelette pan over medium-high heat and brush with melted butter; heat until drops of water bounce and sputter when sprinkled on the pan.

Stir the soda water into the batter. Lift the pan and pour in about 3 Tbsp (45 mL) batter; swirl to coat the pan and quickly pour any excess batter back into the blender.

With a spatula, lift up the edge of the crêpe when set; cook just until the bottom is lightly browned. Turn the crêpe over and cook for 2 to 3 seconds longer, or until the edges are lightly browned. Remove to a plate and let cool. Repeat with the remaining batter, brushing the pan with butter when necessary. Don't stack the crêpes until cool. (The crêpes can be covered and refrigerated overnight, or frozen in an airtight container for up to 3 weeks.)

- ¾ cup (175 mL) milk
- 3 Tbsp (45 mL) pear or apple liqueur
- 3 eggs
- Pinch salt
- 2 Tbsp (30 mL) granulated sugar
- 1 cup (250 mL) all-purpose flour
- Unsalted butter, melted
- ¾ cup (175 mL) soda water

Fresh Winter Fruit Crêpes with Hot Maple Syrup

MAKES 6 SERVINGS

The mellow sweetness of maple syrup complements tart apples and pears in this easy but elegant dessert. Serve with a pitcher of additional maple syrup and more whipped cream if desired. If you wish, serve with maple whipped cream made by adding ¼ cup (60 mL) maple syrup to 1 cup (250 mL) whipping cream just as you finish beating it.

- 1 tsp (5 mL) grated lemon zest
- ¼ cup (60 mL) fresh lemon juice
- 2 tart apples (Ida Red or Spy if available)
- 2 pears
- ¼ cup (60 mL) unsalted butter
- ½ cup (125 mL) packed brown sugar or maple sugar
- ¼ tsp (1 mL) nutmeg
- 1 Tbsp (15 mL) pear or apple liqueur
- 12 Dessert Crêpes (see p. 147)
- Whipped cream
- Mint sprigs
- Maple syrup

DIVIDE THE LEMON zest and juice between 2 small bowls. Peel and thinly slice the apples and pears, placing apples in one bowl and pear slices in the other as you work. Toss the slices to coat well.

In a large skillet, melt the butter with the sugar over medium heat. Add the apple mixture and nutmeg; cook, stirring often, for 4 minutes. Add the pear mixture; cook for 3 or 4 minutes or until the fruit is tender but not mushy. Stir in the liqueur.

Spread each crêpe with about 2 Tbsp (30 mL) filling; fold in quarters and arrange on a platter. Garnish with rosettes of whipped cream and mint sprigs. In a small saucepan, warm maple syrup over low heat or in a pitcher in the microwave. Drizzle over the crêpes.

Brandied Peach Clafoutis

MAKES 8 SERVINGS

A cake-like custard or thick fruit pancake from Limousin, France, clafoutis was originally made with black cherries, but I think it's more wonderful with peaches. It's one of those quick, simple, not-too-sweet desserts that's just right for family or company, and it's great for brunch. If you wish, serve with a dollop of whipped cream.

- 3½ cups (875 mL) sliced peeled peaches (6 to 8)
- 2 Tbsp (30 mL) brandy or cognac
- ⅓ cup (75 mL) granulated sugar, divided
- 2 cups (500 mL) cream (10% or 18%)
- 3 eggs
- ¼ cup (60 mL) all-purpose flour
- Pinch salt
- 1 tsp (5 mL) vanilla
- Icing sugar

IN A BOWL, toss the peaches with the brandy; set aside.

Grease an 8-cup (2 L) shallow baking dish; sprinkle with 2 Tbsp (30 mL) of the sugar.

Blend the cream, eggs, flour and salt for 2 minutes in a blender or 1 minute in a food processor. Add the remaining sugar and vanilla; blend for a few seconds.

Arrange the peaches and any juice in the prepared dish; pour the cream mixture overtop.

Bake in a 375°F (190°C) oven for 45 to 50 minutes, or until puffed and golden. Let cool until barely warm. (The clafoutis will naturally fall as it cools.) Sprinkle with icing sugar and serve.

Upside-Down Pear Gingerbread

MAKES 8 SERVINGS

Serve this old-fashioned soft gingerbread hot, with softly whipped cream flavoured with chopped candied ginger.

- 3 Tbsp (45 mL) butter, softened
- 2 Tbsp (30 mL) granulated sugar
- 2 large pears
- 1 cup (250 mL) butter, at room temperature
- ½ cup (125 mL) packed brown sugar
- 1 egg
- 1 cup (250 mL) molasses

SPREAD THE SOFT butter on the bottom of a 9-inch (2.5 L) square baking dish; sprinkle with the granulated sugar. Peel, core and slice the pears; arrange in the dish and set aside.

In a large bowl, cream the room-temperature butter with the brown sugar; beat in the egg until light and fluffy. Stir in the molasses.

Dissolve the baking soda in the boiling water. Sift or stir together the flour, ginger, cinnamon, salt and cloves; add to the creamed mixture alternately with the soda mixture, stirring just until blended. Pour over the pears. Bake in a 350°F (180°C) oven for 45 to 60 minutes or until a tester inserted in the centre comes out clean. Let cool for 15 minutes. Invert onto a serving plate. Serve warm and cut into squares.

- 2 tsp (10 mL) baking soda
- 1 cup (250 mL) boiling water
- 3 cups (750 mL) all-purpose flour
- 1 Tbsp (15 mL) ground ginger
- ½ tsp (2 mL) cinnamon
- ¼ tsp (1 mL) salt
- ¼ tsp (1 mL) ground cloves

Rhubarb Crisp

....

MAKES 6 SERVINGS

Fruit crisps are always popular with everyone, and this easy rhubarb version is particularly good with its crunchy topping of oats and toasted walnuts. Serve warm with whipped cream, vanilla ice cream or a custard sauce.

- ⅓ cup (75 mL) walnut pieces
- ½ cup (125 mL) all-purpose flour
- ½ cup (125 mL) rolled oats
- ½ cup (125 mL) packed brown sugar
- ¾ cup + 1 Tbsp (190 mL) granulated sugar, divided
- ¼ tsp (1 mL) cinnamon
- ¼ tsp (1 mL) nutmeg
- ¼ cup (60 mL) butter, softened
- 5 cups (1.25 L) coarsely chopped (1-inch/ 2.5 cm pieces) rhubarb

TOPPING Spread the walnuts on a baking sheet; toast in a 375°F (190°C) oven for 5 minutes. Let cool and chop finely.

In a bowl, combine the walnuts, flour, rolled oats, brown sugar, 1 Tbsp (15 mL) granulated sugar, cinnamon and nutmeg; work in the butter until crumbly. Set aside.

Toss the rhubarb with the ¾ cup (175 mL) granulated sugar; arrange in an even layer in a buttered 8-inch (2 L) glass baking dish. Sprinkle with the walnut mixture and bake, uncovered, in a 375°F (190°C) oven for 35 to 40 minutes or until the rhubarb is tender and the top golden brown.

Cakes

....

Chocolate-Marzipan Torte

MAKES 8 SERVINGS

When I'm pressed for time but want to make an elegant dessert, I always turn to this easy but absolutely delicious torte. The better the chocolate, the better the taste.

- ⅔ cup + 2 Tbsp (180 mL) granulated sugar, divided
- 4 eggs, separated
- ¾ cup (175 mL) unsalted butter
- 6 oz (175 g) bittersweet chocolate
- ¼ cup (60 mL) all-purpose flour
- 2 Tbsp (30 mL) ground blanched almonds
- Pinch cream of tartar
- Pinch salt
- ½ lb (250 g) marzipan
- ⅓ cup (75 mL) whipping cream
- 6 oz (175 g) sweet chocolate, coarsely chopped
- ⅓ cup (75 mL) sliced blanched almonds, lightly toasted

IN A LARGE bowl, beat together ⅔ cup (150 mL) sugar and the egg yolks until pale yellow. In the top of a double boiler or heatproof bowl, melt the butter with the bittersweet chocolate over simmering water, stirring until smooth. Remove from heat. Add the yolk mixture and blend well; thoroughly stir in the flour and almonds.

In a medium bowl, beat the egg whites until foamy. Add the cream of tartar and salt; beat until soft peaks form. Gradually beat in the remaining 2 Tbsp (30 mL) sugar until stiff peaks form. Stir one-quarter of the beaten whites into the chocolate mixture; fold in the remaining whites.

Turn the batter into a well-greased and floured 9 inch (2.5 L) springform pan, tapping the pan on a counter to smooth the top. Bake in a 375°F (190°C) oven until the edges are dry but the centre still moist, about 30 minutes. Do not overbake. Let cool completely on a rack before removing the pan.

Transfer to a large plate. Between 2 pieces of waxed paper, roll out the marzipan into a circle almost as big as the top of the cake. Place on the cake.

In a small saucepan, bring the cream to a boil over medium-low heat; add the chocolate and stir until melted and smooth. Let cool for a few minutes until spreadable.

Place strips of waxed paper under the edges of the cake to prevent icing from dripping onto the plate; spread the cake with the glaze. Sprinkle the almonds around the top of the cake to form a border about 1 inch (2.5 cm) from the edge. Refrigerate until chilled or for up to 2 days. Let stand at room temperature for about 20 minutes before serving.

Decadent Chocolate Fruitcake

MAKES 6 CAKES

For something quick, easy and delicious, this moist fruitcake gets a new twist with chocolate. Wrap it with brandy-moistened cheesecloth for a week or two to quickly ripen it. The strips I've suggested facilitate slicing and make convenient gifts if you wish to share this good cake with friends.

- 2 lb (1 kg) mixed candied pineapple and cherries (about 4½ cups/1.12 L)
- 2 cups (500 mL) coarsely chopped toasted pecans
- 4 oz (125 g) unsweetened chocolate, finely chopped
- 3 oz (90 g) semisweet chocolate, finely chopped
- 1 cup (250 mL) golden raisins
- 2 cups (500 mL) all-purpose flour, divided
- 2 tsp (10 mL) baking powder
- ½ tsp (2 mL) salt
- ¾ cup (175 mL) unsalted butter, at room temperature
- 1 cup (250 mL) granulated sugar
- 6 eggs
- ¾ cup (175 mL) brandy, divided
- 1 tsp (5 mL) vanilla

IN A LARGE bowl, toss together the pineapple and cherries, pecans, unsweetened and semisweet chocolate, raisins and half of the flour. In a separate bowl, stir together the remaining flour, baking powder and salt; set aside.

In another large bowl, cream the butter and beat in the sugar until light and fluffy. Add the eggs, one at a time, beating thoroughly. Beat in ¼ cup (60 mL) of the brandy and the vanilla. Gradually stir in the dry ingredients until well blended. Stir in the fruit mixture.

Turn into a greased 13 × 9–inch (3.5 L) metal baking pan. Tap on the counter several times to fill all the corners and prevent holes in the batter. Bake in a 300°F (150°C) oven for about 1½ hours or until a cake tester inserted in the centre comes out clean. Let cool on a wire rack.

Cut the cake crosswise into 6 strips. Heat the remaining brandy but do not boil. Make several holes through the cake with a skewer and pour in the brandy.

Moisten cheesecloth with additional brandy; wrap around the individual strips. Wrap in waxed paper, then foil; store in an airtight tin in the refrigerator or a cool place for at least 1 week, or up to 2 months. Occasionally check that the cake is not too dry and add more brandy, if necessary.

Lemon-Almond Pound Cake

MAKES 12 SLICES

This moist lemon pound cake was created by my good friend Elizabeth Baird, former Food Director of Canadian Living magazine. Elizabeth says that it freezes well for a head start on weekend company or a casual party.

- 1 cup (250 mL) butter, softened
- 1 cup (250 mL) granulated sugar
- 4 eggs
- 2¼ cups (550 mL) sifted cake-and-pastry flour
- 1 tsp (5 mL) baking powder
- ½ tsp (2 mL) salt
- 1¼ cups (300 mL) sliced almonds, divided
- 1 Tbsp (15 mL) coarsely grated lemon zest
- 3 Tbsp (45 mL) fresh lemon juice
- ½ cup (125 mL) icing sugar
- 2 Tbsp (30 mL) fresh lemon juice

IN A BOWL, cream the butter with the sugar until fluffy. Beat in the eggs, one at a time.

In a separate bowl, stir together the flour, baking powder and salt; mix in 1 cup (250 mL) of the almonds. Stir half of the flour mixture, the lemon zest and the juice into the butter mixture; stir in the remaining flour mixture. Spoon into a parchment or waxed paper–lined 9 × 5–inch (2 L) loaf pan, smoothing the top. Sprinkle with the remaining almonds.

Bake in a 350°F (180°C) oven for 40 to 45 minutes or until a tester inserted into the centre comes out clean.

Combine the icing sugar with the lemon juice. Pierce the cake all over with a cake tester and spoon the glaze evenly overtop of the hot cake. Let the cake cool on a rack before removing from the pan. Wrap and store at room temperature for 1 day before slicing.

Almond Torte with Raspberry Sauce

MAKES 12 SERVINGS

This close-textured cake is so delicious that you will never believe how easy it is to make.

ALMOND TORTE In a large bowl, beat together the granulated sugar, butter and almond paste; beat in the eggs, one at a time. Stir in the liqueur and almond extract. Add the flour and baking powder, stirring only until mixed; do not overbeat. (This can be done in a food processor, but be sure not to overprocess after adding the flour.)

Pour into a well-greased and floured 9-inch (2.5 L) springform pan. Bake in a 350°F (180°C) oven for about 40 minutes or until a tester inserted in the centre comes out clean. Let cool in the pan on a rack.

ALMOND TORTE
- ⅔ cup (150 mL) granulated sugar
- ½ cup (125 mL) unsalted butter, at room temperature
- ½ lb (250 g) almond paste, softened
- 3 eggs
- 1 Tbsp (15 mL) almond liqueur
- ¼ tsp (1 mL) almond extract
- ¼ cup (60 mL) all-purpose flour
- ½ tsp (2 mL) baking powder
- Icing sugar

RASPBERRY SAUCE
- One 12-oz (340 g) pkg frozen raspberries, thawed
- 2 Tbsp (30 mL) granulated sugar
- 1 Tbsp (15 mL) kirsch

RASPBERRY SAUCE In a food processor or blender, process the raspberries and sugar until puréed. Press

LEMON-ALMOND POUND CAKE

through a sieve to remove the seeds; stir in the kirsch.

To serve, remove the cake from the pan and place on a serving plate. Dust with icing sugar and accompany with the Raspberry Sauce.

Chocolate Meringue Torte with Grand Marnier Cream

MAKES 8 SERVINGS

This easy make-ahead dessert has such a delightful flavour and texture that it's bound to be a real hit at any dinner party.

COVER 2 BAKING sheets with parchment or brown paper. On the paper, draw three 9-inch (23 cm) circles.

In a large bowl, beat the egg whites until frothy. Beat in the cream of tartar, salt and vanilla until soft peaks form. Very gradually beat in the sugar until stiff peaks form.

Spoon the mixture onto the circles, smoothing their tops with a spatula. Bake in a 250°F (120°C) oven for 1 hour; turn off the oven but leave the meringues to cool inside the oven for at least 6 hours, or overnight. Using a metal spatula, carefully remove the meringues from the paper.

Melt the chocolate chips; using a metal spatula, spread over 2 meringue layers. Whip the cream and beat in the liqueur.

Place 1 chocolate-covered meringue on a serving plate; spread with one-third of the cream. Top with the plain meringue, then half of the remaining cream. Place the second chocolate-covered layer on top and spread

- 8 egg whites
- ¼ tsp (1 mL) cream of tartar
- Pinch salt
- 1 tsp (5 mL) vanilla
- 1½ cups (375 mL) instant dissolving (berry) sugar (or granulated sugar processed in a blender)
- 1 cup (250 mL) semi-sweet chocolate chips (6 oz/175 g)
- 2 cups (500 mL) whipping cream
- ¼ cup (60 mL) Grand Marnier or other orange liqueur
- Chocolate curls

with the remaining cream.

Garnish with chocolate curls. Cover loosely and chill for 24 hours before serving. (If there's any moisture on the plate at serving time, blot with a paper towel.)

Glazed Cranberry Cheesecake

MAKES ABOUT 12 SERVINGS

Lighter and less sweet than most, this delicious cheesecake would make an attractive finale to any meal with company.

CRUST In a bowl, stir together the flour, almonds and sugar; make a well in the middle. Place the butter, egg yolk and vanilla in the well; blend with a fork, then mix with your fingers just until the dough holds together yet is still fairly crumbly. Press evenly onto the bottom and sides of a lightly greased 9-inch (2.5 L) springform pan; bake in a 325°F (160°C) oven for 10 minutes.

FILLING In a food processor, or by hand, coarsely chop the cranberries; set aside.

In a food processor or a bowl with an electric mixer, break up the cream cheese slightly. Add the sugar, sour cream, eggs, flour, vanilla and almond extract; process just until smooth and blended, being careful not to let the mixture liquefy. Stir in the cranberries.

Pour the cream cheese

CRUST
- 1 cup (250 mL) all-purpose flour
- ¼ cup (60 mL) finely chopped almonds
- ¼ cup (60 mL) granulated sugar
- ⅓ cup (75 mL) butter, softened
- 1 egg yolk
- ½ tsp (2 mL) vanilla

FILLING
- 1½ cups (375 mL) cranberries
- 1 lb (500 g) cream cheese
- 1 cup (250 mL) granulated sugar
- 1 cup (250 mL) sour cream
- 5 eggs
- 2 Tbsp (30 mL) all-purpose flour
- 1 tsp (5 mL) vanilla
- ½ tsp (2 mL) almond extract

GLAZE
- 1 cup (250 mL) cranberry juice
- 1 Tbsp (15 mL) cornstarch

mixture into the partially baked crust. Bake for 1 hour and 15 minutes or until almost set and starting to crack around the outside while still wobbly in the centre. Remove from the oven and immediately run a sharp knife around the inside of the pan. Let cool to room temperature on a wire rack.

GLAZE In a small saucepan, stir together the cranberry juice and cornstarch. Cook over medium heat, stirring constantly, until clear and thickened, about 4 minutes. Let cool for 10 minutes. Spoon a thin layer over the top of the cheesecake; let stand for 5 to 10 minutes or until set. Spoon the remaining glaze overtop. Cover and refrigerate for at least 6 hours. Remove the sides of the pan and cut into wedges to serve.

Traditional Fresh Strawberry Shortcake

MAKES 6 SERVINGS

Throughout the decades, strawberry shortcake has been the focus of many festivals and summer suppers—a dessert everyone must have at least once in strawberry season. Use this old-fashioned shortcake base (which is best served slightly warm) for peach, blueberry or raspberry shortcakes throughout the summer. Just sweeten the fruit to taste.

IN A LARGE bowl, sift or stir together the flour, 2 Tbsp (30 mL) of the granulated sugar, the baking powder and salt; cut in the butter until it resembles fine crumbs. In a measuring cup, beat together the 10% or 18% cream and the egg; quickly stir all at once into the

- 2 cups (500 mL) all-purpose flour
- 3 Tbsp (45 mL) granulated sugar, divided
- 1 Tbsp (15 mL) baking powder
- ½ tsp (2 mL) salt
- ½ cup (125 mL) butter
- ⅔ cup (150 mL) cream (10% or 18%)
- 1 egg
- 1 cup (250 mL) whipping cream, divided
- 4 cups (1 L) strawberries, hulled
- ⅓ cup (75 mL) icing sugar, divided
- 1 tsp (5 mL) vanilla
- Butter, softened

dry ingredients to moisten.

Form into a ball; pat into an ungreased 8-inch (2 L) square cake pan. Brush with 2 tsp (10 mL) of the whipping cream and sprinkle with the remaining granulated sugar. Bake in a 450°F (230°C) oven for 12 to 15 minutes or until golden brown on top. Place on a rack and let cool for about 30 minutes.

Meanwhile, set aside 6 whole strawberries for garnish. Slice or chop the remaining berries and place in a bowl; sprinkle with all but 1 Tbsp (15 mL) of the icing sugar. Set aside for at least 30 minutes.

In a chilled bowl, beat the remaining whipping cream with the remaining icing sugar and the vanilla. Cut the shortcake into 6 pieces then slice each horizontally in half. Set the bottom halves on individual serving plates, cut side up. Butter both cut sides and spoon on the sliced berries and their juices; top with remaining shortcake halves. Spread whipped cream overtop and garnish each with a whole berry.

Black Forest Cupcakes

MAKES 24 CUPCAKES

Even as a young child my daughter, Anne, did the bulk of the family baking. These dense chocolate cakes with their cherry-cheese topping baked right on were one of her best-loved recipes. They were certainly much easier to make than the traditional Black Forest cake my son, Allen, sometimes requested for his birthday.

TOPPING Drain the cherries; coarsely chop and set aside. In a bowl, cream the cream cheese. Beat in the egg until fluffy. Stir in the

TOPPING
- One 14-oz (398 mL) can pitted sour red cherries
- ¼ lb (125 g) light cream cheese
- 1 egg
- ½ cup (125 mL) chocolate chips

CUPCAKES
- ½ cup (125 mL) butter, softened
- 1½ cups (375 mL) packed brown sugar
- 1 egg
- 1½ cups (375 mL) all-purpose flour

chocolate chips and cherries and set aside.

CUPCAKES Line twenty-four 2½-inch (6 cm) muffin cups with paper liners.

In a large bowl, cream the butter and beat in the sugar. Beat in the egg. In a medium bowl, sift or stir together the flour, cocoa, baking powder and salt. In a measuring cup, stir the baking soda into the sour cream. Stir the dry ingredients into the butter mixture alternately with the sour cream just until mixed, making 3 dry and 2 sour cream additions.

Spoon into the prepared cups, filling three-quarters full. Place a heaping spoonful of topping on each and bake in a 350°F (180°C) oven for about 20 minutes, or until a tester inserted in the cake part comes out clean.

- ½ cup (125 mL) unsweetened cocoa powder
- ½ tsp (2 mL) baking powder
- Pinch salt
- 1 tsp (5 mL) baking soda
- 1 cup (250 mL) sour cream

Cookies, Bars and Squares

....

CLAIRE'S FAMOUS CHOCOLATE CHIP COOKIES (FORMERLY ANNE'S FAMOUS CHOCOLATE CHIP COOKIES)

No-Bake Peanut Butter Cookies

Even young children can help make these super-fast cookies, which contain one of the flavours that kids love the best.

- ½ cup (125 mL) lightly packed brown sugar
- ½ cup (125 mL) chunky peanut butter
- ½ cup (125 mL) corn syrup
- 2 cups (500 mL) cornflakes

IN A SAUCEPAN, combine the brown sugar, peanut butter and corn syrup; warm over medium heat, stirring constantly, just until the sugar has dissolved. Remove from heat and stir in the cornflakes.

Using 2 teaspoons, drop the mixture in mounds onto waxed paper, working quickly so the mixture doesn't harden. (If it does, reheat gently just until soft enough to spoon.) Let cool and set at room temperature before packing into an airtight container.

Claire's Famous Chocolate Chip Cookies (formerly Anne's Famous Chocolate Chip Cookies)

MAKES ABOUT 4 DOZEN

My daughter started making these cookies as soon as she could see over the kitchen counter. They became famous because everyone knew how good they were and that she could make them in a flash. I have no idea where she got the recipe, but her copy was printed in a child's hand with bad spelling, big chocolate chips drawn on the border, a message at the top "very good (Yum)" and a big note on the bottom: "Check in oven before turning on." (The latter

- ½ cup (125 mL) butter, softened
- ½ cup (125 mL) packed brown sugar
- ¼ cup (60 mL) granulated sugar
- 1 egg
- 1 tsp (5 mL) vanilla
- 1 cup (250 mL) all-purpose flour
- ½ tsp (2 mL) baking soda
- ½ tsp (2 mL) salt
- One 6-oz (175 g) pkg chocolate chips (1 cup/250 mL)
- ½ cup (125 mL) coarsely chopped walnuts or pecans

because of my habit of drying my pans in a warm oven.) I've renamed them because my granddaughter Claire has taken over their production—even demonstrating them on Kitchener's CTV Noon News and making them for our 50th anniversary party.

IN A LARGE bowl, cream the butter; add the brown and granulated sugars and beat well. Beat in the egg, then the vanilla. Stir in the flour, baking soda and salt. Blend in the chocolate chips and nuts.

Using 2 teaspoons, drop by spoonfuls, 2 inches (5 cm) apart, onto ungreased baking sheets. Bake in a 375°F (190°C) oven for 8 to 10 minutes or until golden brown. Remove to a rack and let cool.

Cranberry Filbert Cookies

MAKES 3½ DOZEN

These soft cookies not only taste delicious, but they look pretty and are very easy to make. Don't thaw the cranberries if they're frozen.

- 1 cup (250 mL) softened butter
- 1 cup (250 mL) packed brown sugar
- 1 egg
- 1 Tbsp (15 mL) water
- 2 cups (500 mL) all-purpose flour
- ½ tsp (2 mL) baking soda
- Pinch salt
- 1 cup (250 mL) ground hazelnuts (filberts)
- 1 cup (250 mL) flaked, unsweetened coconut
- 1 cup (250 mL) whole cranberries (fresh or frozen), coarsely chopped

IN A LARGE bowl, cream together the butter and sugar. Beat in the egg and water. Sift or stir together the flour, baking soda and salt; stir into the creamed mixture. Stir in the hazelnuts, coconut and cranberries.

Form into 1-inch (2.5 cm) balls; place about 2 inches (5 cm) apart on lightly greased baking sheets. Flatten with the tines of a fork or the bottom of a glass. Bake in a 350°F (180°C) oven for 10 to 12 minutes or until golden brown. Remove to racks and let cool.

Mocha-Glazed Coffee Drops

MAKES ABOUT 4 DOZEN

These easy-to-make drop cookies are lightly flavoured with coffee.

COFFEE DROPS In a large bowl, cream the butter; beat in the sugar until light and fluffy. Beat in the egg and vanilla. Sift or stir together the flour, baking powder, baking soda and salt; add alternately with the hot coffee to the creamed mixture, stirring just until mixed. Stir in the nuts.

Using 2 teaspoons, drop the dough by heaping spoonfuls 2 inches (5 cm) apart onto lightly greased baking sheets. Bake in a 375°F (190°C) oven for 8 to 10 minutes or until lightly browned. Remove to wire racks and let cool.

MOCHA GLAZE In a small bowl, alternately add the icing sugar and cold coffee to the butter, stirring until smooth. Stir in the cocoa. Spread the glaze liberally on the cooled cookies. Let stand at room temperature to air dry for 3 to 4 hours or until the glaze hardens and sets. Store in an airtight container.

COFFEE DROPS
- ½ cup (125 mL) butter, softened
- ¾ cup (175 mL) packed brown sugar
- 1 egg, beaten
- 1 tsp (5 mL) vanilla
- 1½ cups (375 mL) all-purpose flour
- ½ tsp (2 mL) baking powder
- ½ tsp (2 mL) baking soda
- ¼ tsp (1 mL) salt
- ⅓ cup (75 mL) hot strong coffee
- ½ cup (125 mL) chopped pecans or walnuts

MOCHA GLAZE
- 1½ cups (375 mL) icing sugar
- 3 Tbsp (45 mL) cold strong coffee
- ¼ cup (60 mL) butter, softened
- 1 Tbsp (15 mL) unsweetened cocoa powder

Pecan Lace Cookies

MAKES 5 DOZEN

Crisp and lacy, these delicate cookies are extremely quick to make and go wonderfully well with sorbets.

When I need to make elegant cookies in a hurry, I always turn to these winners. Many years ago I had the privilege of serving them to the famous chef Jacques Pépin, who declared them exquisite.

IN A HEAVY saucepan, combine the butter, brown sugar and corn syrup; bring to a boil over medium heat, stirring just until the sugar is dissolved. Remove from heat; stir in the flour, vanilla and nuts.

Drop the dough in scant teaspoonfuls, placing each ball of dough 4 inches (10 cm) apart on greased baking sheets. Bake in a 325°F (160°C) oven for 8 to 10 minutes or until set and lightly browned.

Remove from the oven and let cool on the pans for 2 minutes. Remove to let cool perfectly flat on finely meshed racks or waxed paper. Store in an airtight container with waxed paper between the layers.

- ½ cup (125 mL) unsalted butter
- ½ cup (125 mL) packed brown sugar
- ½ cup (125 mL) corn syrup
- 1 cup (250 mL) all-purpose flour
- ½ tsp (2 mL) vanilla
- ¾ cup (175 mL) finely chopped pecans

Grandma's Chewy Double Ginger Cookies

MAKES ABOUT 6 DOZEN

Do you remember your grandmother's kitchen smelling wonderful while old-fashioned cookies like these baked? Old-fashioned maybe, but they're a snap to make and they store well.

IN A LARGE bowl, cream together the butter and sugar until light and fluffy. Beat in the eggs, one at a time, then beat in the molasses.

- ½ cup (125 mL) butter or lard, at room temperature
- 1 cup (250 mL) granulated sugar
- 2 eggs
- 1 cup (250 mL) molasses
- 3½ cups (875 mL) all-purpose flour
- 1 Tbsp (15 mL) ground ginger
- 1¼ tsp (6 mL) baking soda
- 1 tsp (5 mL) ground cloves
- ½ tsp (2 mL) cinnamon

TOASTING NUTS

In most of my recipes calling for nuts or coconut, I suggest that they be toasted first. Toasting brings out the oils that highlight their flavour. It also helps bring back to life any nuts that are slightly stale. By the way, always taste any nuts, especially walnuts and Brazils, before incorporating them into a recipe, because rancid ones can render a whole dish less than palatable.

To toast nuts, spread out on a baking sheet and bake in a 350°F (180°C) oven until golden brown and fragrant, 5 to 12 minutes depending on the size and kind of nut.

Just one word of warning about toasting any variety of nut: watch them carefully! There's a little demon inside my oven (very much like the one in the dryer that demolishes one sock of any given pair) that will seize any opportunity to make a whole pan of sliced almonds totally black one second after they're toasted.

Sift or stir together the flour, ground ginger, baking soda, cloves and cinnamon; stir into the creamed mixture in 3 parts. Mix in the crystallized ginger until smooth.

Remove the dough from the bowl and wrap in floured waxed paper; refrigerate for at least 2 hours, or overnight. (The dough will be quite soft.)

With floured hands, form the dough into 1-inch (2.5 cm) balls and gently roll in granulated sugar. Place about 2 inches (5 cm) apart on greased baking sheets. Bake in a 350°F (180°C) oven for 10 to 12 minutes or just until set but not overbaked. Remove to wire racks to let cool.

- ½ cup (125 mL) finely chopped crystallized ginger
- Granulated sugar

Sensational Turtle Brownies

....

MAKES 16

This is a very easy brownie batter that is lightly baked and covered with pecans, chocolate chips and a quick caramel sauce for a decadent treat no one will be able to resist. For a sundae, use as a base with chocolate, coffee or vanilla ice cream and chocolate sauce (see p. 176).

BROWNIES In the top of a double boiler or a heat-proof bowl over simmering water, melt the butter with the chocolate. Stir in the sugar until well combined. Stir in the eggs and vanilla. Gradually add the flour and salt, stirring well after each addition.

Pour into a greased

BROWNIES
- 1 cup (250 mL) butter, in pieces
- 4 oz (125 g) unsweetened chocolate, coarsely chopped
- 1¾ cups (425 mL) granulated sugar
- 4 eggs, well beaten
- 1 tsp (5 mL) vanilla
- 1¼ cups (300 mL) all-purpose flour
- ½ tsp (2 mL) salt

TOPPING
- ½ cup (125 mL) whipping cream
- ½ cup (125 mL) packed brown sugar
- ¼ cup (60 mL) butter
- 1½ cups (375 mL) pecan halves

13 × 9–inch (3.5 L) baking pan; bake in a 400°F (200°C) oven for 10 minutes. (The batter will not be totally cooked but will be set enough to add the topping.)

TOPPING Meanwhile, in a small saucepan, combine the cream, brown sugar and butter; bring to a boil and boil for 2 minutes.

Sprinkle the partially baked base with the pecans and drizzle evenly with the caramel syrup. Bake for 8 to 10 minutes or until golden but not browned.

Remove from the oven and sprinkle with the chocolate chips. Let melt slightly for 1 to 2 minutes; swirl with a knife so that some caramel and nuts show through. Let cool on a rack. Cut into squares.

- 1 cup (250 mL) chocolate chips

Quick-and-Easy Raspberry Oatmeal Squares

....

MAKES ABOUT 3 DOZEN

These delicious squares can be made in a flash with whatever is on hand. If you have no raspberry jam, try apricot, grape or cherry, puréeing it slightly if the fruit is in large pieces.

IN A LARGE bowl, stir together the flour, sugar, lemon zest, baking soda and salt. With 2 knives or a pastry blender, cut in the butter until the mixture is crumbly. Stir in the rolled oats.

Press two-thirds of the mixture evenly into a greased 9-inch (2.5 L) square baking pan. Stir the almonds into the remaining oat mixture; set aside.

- 1 cup (250 mL) all-purpose flour
- ½ cup (125 mL) packed brown sugar
- 2 tsp (10 mL) grated lemon zest
- ¼ tsp (1 mL) baking soda
- ¼ tsp (1 mL) salt
- ¾ cup (175 mL) butter
- 1½ cups (375 mL) rolled oats
- ⅓ cup (75 mL) finely chopped almonds
- 1 cup (250 mL) raspberry jam
- 1 Tbsp (15 mL) fresh lemon juice

Stir together the jam and lemon juice; spread evenly over the base. Gently sprinkle with the remaining oat mixture; pat lightly down into the jam. Bake in a 350°F (180°C) oven for 30 minutes or until golden brown. Cut into squares while warm and let them cool on a rack before serving.

Norman Plum Square

MAKES ABOUT 6 SERVINGS

This simple elegant dessert is often made with apples in Normandy, France. Plums make a delightful varia-tion. They also make for a wonderful lattice-top or open-faced pie using ordi-nary pie pastry.

- 3 lb (1.5 kg) Italian prune plums (about 30)
- One 14-oz (397 g) pkg frozen puff pastry, thawed
- ½ cup (125 mL) granulated sugar
- 2 Tbsp (30 mL) fresh lemon juice
- Whipped cream or crème fraîche (see p. 28)

(see p. 28)

HALVE AND PIT the plums; cut lengthwise into quar-ters. Set aside.

On a lightly floured surface, roll out the pastry to a 12-inch (30 cm) square. Place on a greased baking sheet, crimping up the edges slightly. Arrange the plums over the pastry in slightly overlapping rows. Sprinkle with the sugar and lemon juice.

Bake in a 450°F (230°C) oven for 20 minutes or until the pastry is golden and the plums are tender. Serve warm with whipped cream.

Cherry Nanaimo Bars

MAKES ABOUT 4 DOZEN

Popular Nanaimo bars satisfy even the sweetest sweet tooth.

BASE In a bowl, stir together the crumbs, coconut and pecans. In a small saucepan,

BASE
- 2 cups (500 mL) graham cracker crumbs
- 1 cup (250 mL) flaked unsweetened coconut
- ½ cup (125 mL) toasted chopped pecans

gently heat together the butter, cocoa and sugar until the butter melts. Remove from heat and whisk in the egg; blend into the crumb mixture. Press into a greased 9-inch (2.5 L) square cake pan; bake in a 350°F (180°C) oven for 10 minutes. Let cool on a rack.

CHERRY LAYER Pat the cher-ries dry. In a bowl, blend half of the icing sugar with the butter; mix in the cherry liquid, almond extract, remaining icing sugar, orange zest and cherries. Spread over the base.

CHOCOLATE TOPPING Melt the chocolate and stir in the butter. Spread evenly over the cherry layer; let cool. Cut into bars; garnish each with a small piece of maraschino cherry. (The bars can be covered and refrigerated for up to 2 weeks, or frozen for up to 2 months. Let the bars soften slightly at room tempera-ture before slicing.)

- ⅔ cup (150 mL) butter
- ⅓ cup (75 mL) sifted unsweetened cocoa powder
- ¼ cup (60 mL) gran-ulated sugar
- 1 egg, beaten

CHERRY LAYER
- ½ cup (125 mL) quartered maraschino cherries
- 2 cups (500 mL) icing sugar
- ¼ cup (60 mL) butter, softened
- 2 Tbsp (30 mL) mara-schino cherry liquid
- Dash almond extract
- 2 tsp (10 mL) grated orange zest

CHOCOLATE TOPPING
- ¼ lb (125 g) semi-sweet chocolate
- 1 Tbsp (15 mL) butter
- Maraschino cher-ries, chopped

Triple Decker Squares

MAKES 5 DOZEN

No matter what else appears at a potluck supper, everyone raves over these simply made, delightful and rich morsels that my friend Mary Lou Ruby Jonas makes.

- 2 cups (500 mL) all-purpose flour
- ¼ cup (60 mL) granulated sugar
- 2 cups (500 mL) butter, divided

PLUM GOOD FRUIT

....

When I was growing up, I remember the most marvellous plum tree beside our house. Its trunk was very dark and gnarled, its branches erratic and the fruit big, dark purple and deliciously warm and sweet.

I have no idea what kind of plums grew on our tree, nor had I thought much about plums at all until I started to notice endless rows of baskets at our local farmers' markets during the late summer and fall of every year.

Except for knowing that almost every farm harbours at least one old knotted tree, I didn't realize until I started doing extensive research for a magazine article that the plum is one of the world's most widely distributed fruits, growing on almost every continent and encompassing more than 2,000 varieties. The fruit itself, with its flat seed, can be elliptical, heart-shaped, oblong, ovate or round, making a ripe appearance in a rainbow of colours—purple, blue, scarlet, yellow or green.

There are about eighteen plum species that are horticulturally important. These include two main types—the Japanese varieties and the European varieties. The former, medium to large and famous for their juiciness, are usually more for eating out of hand. A variety of shapes, they are not usually blue or purple or freestone. European varieties (of which there are more in markets) include the most common prune, and are always blue or purple. Usually smaller, they are oval or roundish with a milder flavour and firmer texture than Japanese plums.

Plums are always a winner eaten out of hand, but few people realize how delicious they are in so many other ways.

Enjoy them in pies, tarts, cakes, sauces, jams, salads, chutneys, soups, sorbets, shortcakes, crisps or sautéed with meat or poultry. Reine Claude (Greengage), Valor, Burbank (for canning) and the prune varieties are all good for cooking.

To freeze plums when they're in season, merely wash, halve lengthwise and pit. Pack in airtight heavy plastic bags with ¾ cup (175 mL) granulated sugar to 4 cups (1 L) fruit. To use, thaw only enough to separate the amount you need, and adjust the amount of sugar called for in the recipe to compensate for the sugar in the plums.

IN A LARGE bowl, stir together the flour and granulated sugar; cut in 1 cup (250 mL) of the butter until the mixture is crumbly. Press evenly into a greased 13 × 9–inch (3.5 L) baking pan. Bake in a 350°F (180°C) oven for about 25 minutes or until lightly coloured.

- 1 cup (250 mL) packed brown sugar
- ¼ cup (60 mL) corn syrup
- 1 can (300 mL) sweetened condensed milk
- 1 tsp (5 mL) vanilla
- 2 cups (500 mL) semi-sweet chocolate chips

Meanwhile, in a saucepan, combine the remaining butter, brown sugar, corn syrup and condensed milk; stir over low heat until the sugar is dissolved. Bring to a boil over medium heat, stirring constantly; boil gently for 5 minutes, stirring to prevent sticking.

Remove from heat; add the vanilla and beat well. Pour over the warm base and spread evenly. Let cool on a rack.

Melt the chocolate chips and spread over the cooled filling. Let the chocolate set before cutting into squares.

Almond Shortbread Bars

....

MAKES 2 DOZEN

Simple to make and easy to pack, these delightful bars are perfect for lunch boxes or potluck suppers.

IN A LARGE bowl, cream together ½ cup (125 mL) of the butter and the icing sugar. Stir together the flour and salt, then gradually mix into the creamed mixture.

With floured hands, pat mixture into an ungreased 9-inch (2.5 L) square pan. Bake in a 350°F (180°C) oven for 12 to 15 minutes or

- ¾ cup (175 mL) butter, at room temperature, divided
- ½ cup (125 mL) icing sugar
- 1 cup (250 mL) all-purpose flour
- Pinch salt
- ½ cup (125 mL) packed brown sugar
- 1 Tbsp (15 mL) water
- 1 tsp (5 mL) fresh lemon juice
- ¾ cup (175 mL) sliced almonds
- ½ tsp (2 mL) almond extract

until lightly coloured.

Meanwhile, in a small saucepan, melt the remaining ¼ cup (60 mL) butter. Stir in the brown sugar, water and lemon juice; bring to a boil, stirring constantly. Remove from heat; stir in the almonds and almond extract.

Spread over the base; bake for 12 to 15 minutes longer, or until golden brown. Cut into bars while still warm but not hot.

Pies

Food Processor Pastry

Mary Lou Ruby Jonas, who was my assistant for a time, is of Mennonite background and one of the most accomplished pie-makers I know. This is her pastry and along with it goes the advice to work quickly and not over-handle the pastry.

- 1½ cups (375 mL) all-purpose flour
- Pinch salt
- ½ cup (125 mL) cold lard, in bits
- ¼ cup (60 mL) ice water
- 1 tsp (5 mL) vinegar or fresh lemon juice

IN A FOOD processor, blend the flour and salt; cut in the lard, pulsing until crumbly.

In a measuring cup, stir together the water and vinegar (or lemon juice). With the machine running, gradually pour in the water mixture, using just enough to form the dough into a ball. Do not overprocess.

Turn out onto a lightly floured surface; knead a few times to form a soft ball. Roll out and line a pie plate. Refrigerate for at least 30 minutes before filling.

Irresistible Almond Streusel Cherry Pie

MAKES 8 SERVINGS

Fruit pies are always irresistible, and no one will be able to pass up this juicy cherry pie with its attractive almond topping. By the way, it travels well if you need something for that family picnic or potluck supper.

- 1¼ cups (300 mL) granulated sugar, divided
- ½ cup (125 mL) all-purpose flour
- ¼ cup (60 mL) ground almonds
- ½ cup (125 mL) cold butter
- 5 cups (1.25 L) pitted fresh or frozen sour cherries (see note)
- 3 Tbsp (45 mL) quick-cooking tapioca
- 3 Tbsp (45 mL) fresh lemon juice

IN A SMALL bowl or a food processor, stir together ½ cup (125 mL) of the sugar, the flour and the almonds; cut in the butter until the mixture resembles coarse crumbs. Set aside.

In a large bowl, stir together the cherries, remaining sugar, tapioca, lemon juice and almond extract. Arrange the cherry mixture in the pie shell; sprinkle with the flour mixture.

- ¼ tsp (1 mL) almond extract
- One 10-inch (25 cm) unbaked pie shell (see above)

Bake in a 425°F (220°C) oven for 10 minutes. Reduce heat to 375°F (190°C); bake for about 40 minutes longer, or until the topping and pastry are golden brown.

NOTE If using frozen, don't thaw. (You may have to bake the pie slightly longer.) If the cherries have been frozen with sugar, adjust the amount of sugar in the cherry mixture accordingly.

Caramel Apple Pie

MAKES 8 TO 10 SERVINGS

Nothing emits a more pleasant aroma of fall than a kitchen when an apple pie is baking in the oven. This open-faced pie is special indeed with its caramel coating. For an interesting pie, try a mixture of apples.

- 6 tart apples (2 lb/1 kg)
- 2 Tbsp (30 mL) fresh lemon juice
- 1¼ cups (300 mL) granulated sugar, divided
- 2 Tbsp (30 mL) all-purpose flour
- 1 tsp (5 mL) cinnamon
- ¼ tsp (1 mL) salt
- ¼ tsp (1 mL) nutmeg
- One 9-inch (23 cm) unbaked pie shell (see above)
- ¼ cup (60 mL) butter, cut into bits
- ½ cup (125 mL) whipping cream
- ½ cup (125 mL) toasted coarsely chopped walnuts

PEEL, CORE AND slice the apples; place in a large bowl and toss with the lemon juice. Combine ¼ cup (60 mL) of the sugar, the flour, cinnamon, salt and nutmeg; toss with the apples.

Spread the apple mixture in the pie shell and cover with a circle of parchment or waxed paper. Bake in a 425°F (220°C) oven for

HARVEST PIES

....

I can remember those noon meals when a crowd of men would come in from the fields to gather around our big round kitchen table. There would be a choice of apple, squash, plum and maybe even an old-fashioned butterscotch pie with meringue topping. Before my family bought a modern combine, harvest time meant a threshing machine travelled from farm to farm and everyone helped their neighbour. Each farmer's wife would take her turn at providing meals for the hungry threshers.

There was always pie for dessert—with much expert assessment among the men as to who made the best elderberry or peach I'm sure.

The variety was infinite—raisin, pear, lemon meringue, grape, custard, maple syrup, even green tomato—but it always depended on what was in season and what was at hand; abundant choices, indeed, at harvest time. Although it may seem extraordinary to many young cooks, a pie was just about the easiest thing a busy farm wife could make. It was also an economical method of making a few ingredients go a long way around a table of hungry diners. Early cooks had already discovered that round pans could help them literally cut corners and stretch ingredients. The other advantage was that a pie didn't have to be eaten immediately. Farm men came in for dinner when their work was finished, not when dinner was ready.

Appetites have changed, and my own family hasn't seen as many pies as I remember from my well-fed childhood, but no matter what other sophisticated desserts I serve, a good old-fashioned pie is still a treat—especially during harvest season.

PIE POINTERS

- Measure ingredients exactly—dry ingredients in dry measures and liquids in liquid.
- Work quickly and do not overwork the dough.
- Keep your work surface, equipment and hands cool and use chilled shortening, lard or butter and ice water.
- If the dough has a chance to rest in the refrigerator before baking, it will be more tender and will not shrink as much.
- Use as little flour as possible when rolling out the dough. A stockinet covering for your rolling pin will help.
- Invest in a good pie plate or two. Avoid foil plates or plates that are too shallow.
- Bake pies in the bottom third of your oven following the exact temperatures given.

RHUBARB

....

Every spring I recall the long row of vigorous green leaves that marked the rhubarb patch running along the garden's edge on our farm. And I never think of rhubarb without remembering a teaching colleague of mine who loved it with such a passion that she nibbled on long stalks right from the patch.

Although not everyone may love it to this extent, this tart, refreshing "fruit" is generally regarded as a "spring tonic," the harbinger of other good seasonal fruit to come.

Actually, this "fruit" is botanically a "vegetable," but don't let that deter you from using its celery-like stalks in a wonderful array of welcome desserts and sweets. Its tart flavour is good on its own or teamed with other fruits in sauces, jams, chutneys, cakes, crisps, sorbets, soufflés, drinks and, of course, pies—that confection from which rhubarb gets its nickname: "pie plant."

Because rhubarb freezes so well, you don't have to restrict your "taste of spring" to one season. Simply prepare as you would for immediate use. Choose firm, crisp stalks; trim off the thick bottom end of every leaf (which are toxic, by the way). Wash and dry well; cut into 1-inch (2.5 cm) pieces. Either pack immediately into plastic freezer bags and freeze, or spread in a single layer on cookie sheets to freeze, then package, to keep the pieces separate.

If you wish to freeze with sugar, add 1 cup (250 mL) to 4 cups (1 L) chopped rhubarb and label clearly with the amount.

For most recipes like pies, stewed rhubarb and jam, do not thaw, but you may have to adjust the cooking time. For baked goods like muffins, thaw the rhubarb almost completely (leaving some ice crystals) and pat dry with paper towels, otherwise the extra moisture will make the muffins heavy.

20 minutes. Remove the paper and reduce heat to 375°F (190°C); bake for 30 to 35 minutes or until the crust is golden and the apples are tender, covering with foil if the apples or crust become too brown.

In a heavy saucepan, heat the remaining sugar over medium heat without stirring, but shaking the pan gently as the sugar begins to melt. When the sugar is a medium-brown caramel colour, gradually whisk in the butter. Just before the butter is all blended, carefully whisk in the cream (it will sputter); return to a boil. Remove from heat and stir well. Let cool for 5 minutes, then pour over the hot apples. Sprinkle with the walnuts. Let cool before serving.

Deep-Dish Pear Pie with Spiced Crust

....

MAKES 6 TO 8 SERVINGS

A true taste of fall, this spicy pear pie is a cinch to make since you just put the pastry on the top. Choose a dish that's square or round and roll the pastry 1 inch (2.5 cm) bigger than the top. This filling fits perfectly into a 9-inch (23 cm) round dish that's 2 inches (5 cm) deep.

To make the spiced crust, add cinnamon, nutmeg and ginger to the flour mixture of Food Processor Pastry (see p. 168) before cutting in the fat.

IN A LARGE bowl, toss the pears with the lemon juice. Stir together the brown and granulated sugars, tapioca, cardamom and salt; toss well with the pears. Arrange in a baking dish and dot with the butter.

- 8 cups (2 L) sliced peeled pears (about 8 large)
- 2 Tbsp (30 mL) fresh lemon juice
- ⅓ cup (75 mL) packed brown sugar
- ⅓ cup (75 mL) granulated sugar + extra for sprinkling
- 3 Tbsp (45 mL) quick-cooking tapioca
- 1 tsp (5 mL) ground cardamom
- Pinch salt
- 2 Tbsp (30 mL) butter, in bits
- One 9-inch (23 cm) pie crust (see p. 168)
- 1 tsp (5 mL) cinnamon
- ½ tsp (2 mL) nutmeg
- ½ tsp (2 mL) ground ginger
- Light cream or milk

Follow the instructions for the Food Processor Pastry on page 168, adding the cinnamon, nutmeg and ginger to the flour before cutting in the fat. Roll out the pastry 1 inch (2.5 cm) larger than the top of the baking dish; place over the pears and fold the edges under. Crimp the edges and cut steam vents. Cut out pear and leaf shapes from the scraps of pastry if desired. Brush the pastry with cream and arrange the pastry decoration on top; brush again and sprinkle with granulated sugar. Bake in a 425°F (220°C) oven for 25 minutes; reduce the temperature to 375°F (190°C) and bake for 20 to 25 minutes longer, or until thick syrup starts bubbling through the vents.

Rhubarb Custard Pie

....

MAKES 6 SERVINGS

If my family knew they could have only one pie all year, this is the one they'd choose. It was my mother's recipe and the very first thing I ever demonstrated on television over forty years ago.

PIE In a large bowl, stir together the rhubarb, sugar, flour and butter; stir in the egg yolks. Arrange in the pastry shell. Bake in a 425°F (220°C) oven for 10 minutes; reduce heat to 350°F (180°C) and bake another 30 minutes. Remove the pie and let cool until lukewarm.

MERINGUE Meanwhile, in a large bowl, beat the egg whites until foamy. Add the cream of tartar and beat until soft peaks form. Very gradually beat in the sugar. Add the

PIE
- 3 cups (750 mL) coarsely chopped (1-inch/2.5 cm pieces) rhubarb
- 1 cup (250 mL) granulated sugar
- 3 Tbsp (45 mL) all-purpose flour
- 2 Tbsp (30 mL) butter
- 2 egg yolks, beaten
- 1 unbaked 9-inch (23 cm) pastry shell (see p. 168)

MERINGUE
- 2 egg whites
- ¼ tsp (1 mL) cream of tartar
- ¼ cup (60 mL) granulated sugar
- 2 Tbsp (30 mL) water
- ½ tsp (2 mL) vanilla
- ¼ tsp (1 mL) salt

water, vanilla and salt; beat until stiff, shiny peaks form.

Spread the meringue over the lukewarm pie, sealing right to the pastry rim. Swirl into decorative peaks. Bake in a 375°F (190°C) oven for 12 to 15 minutes or until the tips of the meringue become golden. Let meringue cool slowly in a warm place.

Open-Faced Apple Tart

MAKES 6 TO 8 SERVINGS

This simple French-style tart highlights the fresh flavour of crisp, just-picked fall apples. Although very easy to make, the tart looks and tastes sensational, especially served slightly warm with softly whipped cream scented with a touch of cinnamon.

- 4 tart apples (about 1½ lb/750 g)
- Grated zest and juice of 1 lemon
- ¼ cup (60 mL) butter
- ½ cup (125 mL) granulated sugar
- 1 pkg (411 g) puff pastry, thawed (you will only need half the package)
- 1 Tbsp (15 mL) Calvados or apple liqueur

PEEL THE APPLES and cut in half lengthwise. Core and thinly slice each half cross-wise, dropping into a bowl and tossing with the lemon zest and juice as you work.

In a large skillet, melt the butter over medium heat; cook the apples and sugar, stirring often, for 4 minutes. Remove to the bowl with a slotted spoon.

Bring the butter mixture to a boil; boil for 5 minutes. Remove from heat and set aside.

On a lightly floured surface, roll out half of the contents of the puff pastry package to a 13 × 7–inch (33 × 18 cm) rectangle; transfer to an ungreased baking sheet. Straighten the edges and pinch up a fluted border all around, using your index finger and thumb.

Arrange the apples in overlapping rows crosswise over the pastry; sprinkle with Calvados, syrup from the skillet and any juice from the bowl. Bake in a 400°F (200°C) oven for about 25 minutes or until the apples are tender. Let cool slightly or come to room temperature, but do not refrigerate.

Classic "Runny" Butter Tarts

MAKES 18 TARTS

One of the few food special-ties that Canada can claim as its very own, butter tarts have had a wide and faithful following in this country for many years. I've seldom met anyone who didn't start to salivate at their mere

- 2 cups (500 mL) packed brown sugar
- 2 eggs
- 1 Tbsp (15 mL) butter
- 1 tsp (5 mL) vanilla
- 2 Tbsp (30 mL) hot water
- 18 unbaked tart shells

mention—especially the runny kind. The more set variety has its disciples, too, but the following wonderfully easy-to-make tarts will probably drip down your chin at the first bite. The recipe comes from the farm kitchen of my late aunt Lexie Armstrong in Orillia, Ontario. Feel free to add any of those ingredients Canadians have used over the years—walnuts, raisins, coconut or currants, remembering that you'll need more tart shells.

WHISK TOGETHER THE sugar, eggs, butter, vanilla and hot water. Pour into the tart shells, filling each about two-thirds full. Bake in a 450°F (230°C) oven for 10 to 12 minutes or until golden brown.

In the Kitchen with my grandchildren, Claire and Mitchell.

FINISHING TOUCHES

SOMETIMES SIMPLY COOKED meat, fish or poultry can take on great new dimensions with the addition of an easy sauce. In this chapter, there are just such embellishments. They are primarily for main courses, but a few will bring extra life to fruits or desserts.

Lemon-Apricot Butter

....

MAKES ¾ CUP (175 ML)

This butter is great on toast or Fresh Mint Quick Bread (see p. 39).

IN A SMALL bowl, cream the butter; beat in the lemon zest and juice. Blend in the apricots. (The butter can be covered and refrigerated for up to 5 days. Bring to room temperature before serving.)

- ½ cup (125 mL) butter, at room temperature
- 1 tsp (5 mL) finely grated lemon zest
- 2 tsp (10 mL) fresh lemon juice
- ¼ cup (60 mL) finely chopped dried apricots

Quick Chocolate Sauce

....

MAKES 1 CUP (250 ML)

For a special-company sauce, add 2 tsp (10 mL) brandy or liqueur after the butter.

IN A SMALL heavy saucepan, bring the cream to a boil; remove from heat. Whisk in the chocolate until melted. Whisk in the butter and brandy, if desired. Let cool slightly before using. (The sauce can be covered and refrigerated for up to 1 week. Reheat over low heat and serve warm.)

- ¾ cup (175 mL) whipping cream
- 5 oz (150 g) semisweet chocolate, broken up
- 1 Tbsp (15 mL) butter
- 2 tsp (10 mL) brandy or nut liqueur (optional)

Plum Chutney

....

MAKES ABOUT 8 CUPS (2 L)

Serve this dark purple, rich and spicy chutney with pork, poultry or cold cuts. It's also good spread over cream cheese on bagels. (See

- 4 lb (2 kg) purple prune plums
- 2 lb (1 kg) apples (about 8, any kind)

Preserving Pointers, next page.)

WASH AND PIT the plums; cut into eighths and place in a large non-aluminum heavy kettle. Peel, core and coarsely chop the apples; add to the plums along with the vinegar. Bring to a boil; reduce heat and simmer, uncovered, for 1 hour, stirring occasionally.

- 1½ cups (375 mL) white vinegar
- 4 cups (1 L) packed brown sugar
- 1 Tbsp (15 mL) pickling salt
- 1½ tsp (7 mL) ground allspice
- 1½ tsp (7 mL) ground ginger
- 1½ tsp (7 mL) ground cloves
- 1½ tsp (7 mL) ground cinnamon

Stir in the sugar, pickling salt, allspice, ginger, cloves and cinnamon; bring to a boil. Reduce heat and simmer, uncovered and stirring often, until thickened, about 1 hour. Ladle into hot sterilized jars leaving a ½-inch (1.25 cm) headspace; seal with prepared discs and rings. Boil in a boiling-water canner for 10 minutes. Remove the jars and let cool on a rack. Wipe the jars and store in a cool, dark, dry place.

Fresh Tomato-Cucumber Salsa

....

MAKES ABOUT 1 CUP (250 ML)

Instead of using heavy cream sauces or butters, serve this fresh, zesty salsa with Lime-Grilled Salmon (see p. 91) or grilled chicken.

IN A SMALL bowl, toss together the tomato, cucumber, onion, fresh coriander, jalapeño pepper, lime juice, sugar and salt and pepper to taste. Cover and refrigerate for up to 2 days.

- 1 tomato, seeded and finely chopped
- ½ cup (125 mL) finely chopped cucumber
- ¼ cup (60 mL) chopped red onion
- 1 Tbsp (15 mL) finely chopped fresh coriander (cilantro)
- 1 Tbsp (15 mL) minced jalapeño pepper
- 1 Tbsp (15 mL) fresh lime juice
- Pinch granulated sugar
- Salt and pepper

PRESERVING POINTERS

Use proper preserving jars, the ones available in supermarkets and hardware stores. Check that any jars you're reusing are chip and crack free. Each time you use a jar it will require a new disc (lid). Jar rings or bands, if not bent or rusted, can be reused. Before sealing the jars, warm the lids in a bowl of barely hot water.

To use a boiling water canner, heat the jars before filling them with preserves. Fill a boiling-water canner two-thirds full of hot water; add the clean, empty jars upside down on the rack in the canner. Cover and bring to a simmer, timing the process so that the jars are hot and ready to fill when the preserve is finished. With canning tongs, remove the jars, drain well and set them upright on a tray.

To fill the jars, use a funnel and small metal cup or ladle; fill up to the headspace level recommended in each recipe. Wipe the jar rim, if needed. Centre a disc on top of the jar and screw on a jar ring or band until you meet resistance, tightening without forcing (a.k.a. "fingertip tight").

Place the jars upright on the rack in the canner. Lower the rack and add more boiling water if needed, to come up 1 inch (2.5 cm) above the tops of the jars. Cover the canner; bring to a boil, timing the processing time from this point.

Turn off the heat, remove the lid from the canner and let the boiling subside, about 5 minutes. Remove the jars to cool on a rack or folded terry towels.

FRESH SALSA

....

Salsa means sauce in Spanish, but it is unlike most other sauces we know. There is nothing hidden in a salsa, which is a combination of finely diced fruit or vegetables with herbs, spices and flavourings like lime juice or rice vinegar. Salsas are fresh tasting, adding interest to the simplest of grilled fish or chicken, even plain tacos.

I like salsas because they're quick and easy. You don't even have to worry about measuring accurately, nor do you need any special cooking techniques—just chop and stir.

I also like their flavours and textures. They can be sharp and sweet or hot and cool, sometimes all at once. They're usually a little crunchy and a little smooth, too.

The other lovely appeal salsas have is their lightness and freshness—lots of flavour without using a mountain of butter or cream.

Citrus-Cranberry Salsa

MAKES 1½ CUPS (375 ML)

I love the refreshing tartness of raw cranberries. Enjoy this one with not only turkey, but also chicken, duck or goose. If using frozen cranberries, do not thaw before chopping.

- 1 large orange
- 1 cup (250 mL) finely chopped cranberries
- 2 Tbsp (30 mL) fresh lime juice
- ¼ cup (60 mL) packed brown sugar
- 4 green onions, finely chopped
- Pinch salt
- Pinch hot pepper flakes
- 2 Tbsp (30 mL) dried currants

GRATE 1 TSP (5 ML) zest from the orange; peel and finely chop the pulp, reserving the juice.

In a bowl, combine the orange pulp, juice and grated zest.

Stir in the cranberries, lime juice, brown sugar, green onions, salt and hot pepper flakes until the sugar is dissolved. Stir in the currants. Cover and refrigerate for up to 1 day.

Fresh Peach Salsa

MAKES ABOUT 1¾ CUPS (425 ML)

The only true peach is one ripened on the tree, and it's one yearning you just can't satisfy in winter, because those peaches grown in other countries, picked green and shipped here from miles away, have the texture of a sponge and absolutely no flavour or juice. But a true peach, ripened on the tree, has a sinfully smooth texture and juice that drips right down to your elbow—and a flavour worth the year's wait.

Serve this light, fresh sauce with grilled veal, pork, chicken or fish.

- 3 peaches
- 1 Tbsp (15 mL) white wine vinegar or lime juice
- ¼ cup (60 mL) diced red onion
- 1 Tbsp (15 mL) chopped fresh coriander (cilantro)
- 1 tsp (5 mL) minced jalapeño pepper
- Salt and pepper

PEEL AND FINELY dice the peaches to make 1½ cups (375 mL), placing them in a small bowl and sprinkling with the vinegar as you work.

Stir in the onion, fresh coriander and jalapeño pepper; season with salt and pepper to taste. Cover and refrigerate for up to 8 hours.

All-Purpose Cooked Tomato Sauce

MAKES 6 CUPS (1.5 L)

This versatile sauce can be the basis for many good meals. Try it as is over pasta, or add browned ground beef, mushrooms and Parmesan cheese for a hearty meat sauce to use on spaghetti or in lasagna. Use for home-made pizza or with chicken, veal or grilled fish. Store in small containers.

- 2 Tbsp (30 mL) olive oil
- Two 28-oz (796 mL) cans tomatoes (preferably plum), diced
- One 5½-oz (156 mL) can tomato paste
- ½ cup (125 mL) chopped fresh parsley
- 3 cloves garlic, minced
- 2 Tbsp (30 mL) freshly grated Parmesan cheese
- 1 Tbsp (15 mL) granulated sugar
- 2 tsp (10 mL) dried basil
- 1 tsp (5 mL) dried oregano
- ½ tsp (2 mL) salt
- ½ tsp (2 mL) pepper
- ¼ tsp (1 mL) hot pepper flakes

IN A LARGE stainless steel saucepan, heat the oil; add the tomatoes, tomato paste and a tomato paste can of water along with the parsley, garlic, cheese, sugar, basil, oregano, salt, pepper and hot pepper flakes. Bring to a boil.

Reduce heat to very low; simmer, uncovered, for about 1 hour or until thickened and fairly smooth. Taste and adjust the seasoning. (The sauce can be cooled and refrigerated in small containers for a few days or frozen for several months; taste and adjust the seasoning if frozen for more than 2 months.)

Zesty Homemade Barbecue Sauce

MAKES 1¾ CUPS (425 ML)

This spicy sauce will keep for several days in the refrigerator, or it can be frozen for longer storage. Use it for basting meat on a barbecue or in oven-barbecued chicken or spare ribs. For oven-baked chicken, pour over the pieces and bake, uncovered, in a 350°F (180°C) oven for 60 minutes, turning once. For ribs, roast, uncovered, in a 400°F (200°C) oven for 30 minutes; pour on the sauce, cover and roast at 350°F (180°C) for 1 hour. Makes enough for 4 lb (2 kg) spare ribs or 3 lb (1.5 kg) chicken.

- 1 Tbsp (15 mL) canola oil
- 1 large onion, finely chopped
- ¼ cup (60 mL) packed brown sugar
- ¾ cup (175 mL) ketchup
- ¼ cup (60 mL) fresh lemon juice
- 1 Tbsp (15 mL) Worcestershire sauce
- 1 Tbsp (15 mL) Dijon mustard
- 1 tsp (5 mL) chili powder
- Pinch cayenne pepper

IN A SMALL saucepan, heat the oil; cook the onion until softened but not browned. Stir in the sugar. Cook over low heat, stirring constantly, until the sugar has dissolved.

Remove from heat and stir in the ketchup, lemon juice, Worcestershire sauce, mustard, chili powder and cayenne.

Microwaveable Old-Fashioned Salad Dressing

MAKES 2¾ CUPS (675 ML)

One of my favourite uses for the microwave oven is to make sauces and creamy cooked dressings. If you made this old-fashioned salad dressing in a double boiler, it would take 10 minutes of constant stirring. The dressing is wonderful on shredded cabbage or cooked potatoes for those salads you remember from years ago.

IN AN 8-CUP (2 L) microwaveable measuring cup, combine the sugar, flour, mustard and salt; beat in the eggs. Stir in the milk, water and vinegar.

Microwave on medium-high (70 percent) for 6 minutes. Stir and microwave on high for 5 minutes or until bubbly and thickened, stirring halfway through.

Let cool at room temperature for a few minutes, stirring often.

(The dressing can be stored in a covered jar in the refrigerator for up to 2 weeks.)

- ½ cup (125 mL) granulated sugar
- 3 Tbsp (45 mL) all-purpose flour
- 1 Tbsp (15 mL) dry mustard
- 1 tsp (5 mL) salt
- 2 eggs
- 1 cup (250 mL) milk
- 1 cup (250 mL) water
- ¾ cup (175 mL) white vinegar

Muriel's Blue Cheese Dressing

MAKES 2⅔ CUPS (650 ML)

My sister, Muriel Barbour, was a great cook and specialized in crisp green salads. She called this tangy dressing her "House Dressing," and I think you'll probably want to keep a jar on hand, too. Although I normally wouldn't suggest using dried chives or dried onion, I do so in this recipe since the dressing will keep for days if you do, but it won't if you use raw onions.

- 1 cup (250 mL) light sour cream
- 1 cup (250 mL) light mayonnaise
- ¼ cup (60 mL) fresh lemon juice
- 2 Tbsp (30 mL) Worcestershire sauce
- 2 tsp (10 mL) dried onion or chive flakes (optional)
- 1 tsp (5 mL) dry mustard
- ½ tsp (2 mL) salt
- 6 oz (175 g) blue cheese, crumbled

IN A SMALL bowl, whisk together the sour cream, mayonnaise, lemon juice and Worcestershire sauce until smooth. Whisk in the dried onion (if using), mustard and salt. Mash the cheese with a fork and stir it in. Cover and refrigerate overnight before using or for up to 1 week.

STOCKING THE PANTRY
....

Besides the essentials like flour, sugar, eggs, butter and milk, most cooks have their personal lists of ingredients without which they would feel lost in the kitchen. My own list includes a hunk of real Parmesan cheese (which keeps for ages in the refrigerator, ready to be grated when I need it), a good-size chunk of fresh ginger, candied ginger, hot pepper sauce, fresh garlic, fresh lemons, Dijon mustard, Worcestershire sauce, soy sauce, cans or tetra packs of chicken and beef broth, bittersweet or semisweet chocolate, chocolate chips, canola oil, olive oil, rice and wine vinegars and a vast selection of herbs and spices.

The following is a list of handy ingredients that are easy to use and give lots of flavour to a dish. Many of them may also help out in the case of unexpected company.

Opened jars and bottles of ingredients like mustard or Tabasco keep better in the refrigerator.

CANS, JARS AND TUBES
- salmon, tuna and anchovy paste
- artichoke hearts
- beans of all kinds (kidney, white, chickpeas, etc.)
- several can sizes of tomatoes (whole, diced, crushed), tomato sauce and tomato paste (a tube is handy if you can find one)
- jams and jellies, such as red currant, apricot, peach and orange marmalade for glazes and sauces
- horseradish
- hot pepper sauce (Tabasco), soy sauce and Worcestershire sauce
- jalapeño peppers and olives
- regular prepared and Dijon mustard, dry mustard
- white and cider vinegar, rice and wine vinegars
- canned or tetra-packed chicken and beef broth (instant stock mixes for emergency tablespoonfuls only, since they tend to be very salty and often contain MSG)
- good-quality olive oil and canola oil
- honey, molasses and corn syrup

REFRIGERATOR AND FREEZER STAPLES
- Parmesan and Cheddar cheese
- lemons and oranges for zest and juices
- apples
- nuts and coconut in the freezer

Pickled Cherries

. . . .

MAKES 10 CUPS (2.5 L)

Set a little bowl of these easy-to-make cherries inside the Food Processor Gougère Ring (see p. 22) for an unusual and tantalizing treat. Or, serve them with a selection of cheeses. Make these when black cherries are in season so that you have a year-round supply.

- 8 cups (2 L) sweet black cherries (with stems)
- 2 cups (500 mL) water
- 1 cup (250 mL) cider vinegar
- ½ cup (125 mL) packed brown sugar
- 2 Tbsp (30 mL) pickling salt

WASH THE CHERRIES, but do not pit them; set out on paper towels to dry.

In a heavy non-aluminum saucepan, bring the water, vinegar, sugar and pickling salt to a boil, stirring until the sugar is dissolved.

Meanwhile, pack the cherries carefully into sterilized jars. Cool the syrup to the temperature of the jars, pour over the cherries and seal immediately. Cool and store in the refrigerator for about 6 weeks before eating.

Chocolate Cream Cheese Icing

. . . .

MAKES 1½ CUPS (375 ML)

This easy icing, which is not overly sweet, can be the crowning glory on white or chocolate cakes. Makes enough icing for an 8- or 9-inch (20 to 23 cm) cake or torte.

- ¼ lb (125 g) light cream cheese
- 3 Tbsp (45 mL) sour cream
- ½ cup (125 mL) icing sugar
- 2 Tbsp (30 mL) unsweetened cocoa powder

IN A BOWL or food processor, cream together the cheese and sour cream until fluffy. Sift together the sugar and cocoa; beat into the cheese mixture until thickened.

ACKNOWLEDGEMENTS

Thanks as always to my husband Kent for his constant support and his tireless proofreading. I also appreciate all those who happily shared their recipes, ideas and friendship—Julia Aitken, Elizabeth Baird, Anne Lindsay, Mary Lou Ruby Jonas, Joan Mahaffey and Monda Rosenberg. Thanks to Nick Rundall and Whitecap Books, particularly Patrick Geraghty and Andrew Bagatella, for keeping this favourite book alive. Thanks as well to the Light Imaging Production people including Leisa Mercer and Tara Ballantyne, for making the food in the book look like mine.

INDEX